Julia Augusti

Julia, the only daughter of Emperor Augustus, became a living example of the Augustan policy. By her marriage and motherhood she encapsulated the Augustan reforms of Rome and helped secure a dynasty.

An unidentified scandal, distorted or concealed in the ancient sources which led to her summary banishment, has discredited Julia, or at least clothed her in mystery. However, studying the abundant historical evidence available, this biography illustrates each stage of Julia's life in remarkable detail:

- her childhood – taken from her divorced mother to become part of a complex and unstable family structure
- her youth – set against the brilliant social and cultural life of the new Augustan Rome
- her marriages – as tools for Augustus' plans for succession
- Julia's defiance of her father's publicized moral regime and implicit exposure of his hypocrisy by claiming the same sexual liberty he had once enjoyed.

Reflecting new attitudes and casting fresh light on their social reality, this accessible but penetrating portrait from one of the foremost scholars of Augustan literature and history will delight, entertain and inform anyone interested in this engaging Classical figure.

Elaine Fantham taught for eighteen years at the University of Toronto and was Giger Professor of Latin at Princeton University until her retirement in 2000.

Women of the Ancient World
Series editors: Ronnie Ancona and Sarah Pomeroy

The books in this series offer compact and accessible introductions to the lives and historical times of women from the ancient world. Each book, written by a distinguished scholar in the field, introduces and explores the life of one woman or group of women from antiquity, from a biographical perspective.

The texts will be authoritative introductions by experts in the field. Each book will be of interest to students and scholars of antiquity as well as those with little or no prior knowledge of ancient history or literature, combining rigorous scholarship with reader-friendly prose. Each volume will contain a guide to further reading, a brief glossary, and timelines, maps, and images, as necessary.

Women of the Ancient World will provide an opportunity for specialists to present concise, authoritative accounts, uncovering and exploring important figures in need of historical study and advancing current scholarship on women of the past. Although there is a growing body of excellent scholarship on the lives and roles of women in the ancient world, much work remains. This series will be the first of its kind.

Olympias, Mother of Alexander the Great
Elizabeth Carney

Julia Augusti, The Emperor's Daughter
Elaine Fantham

Julia Domna, Syrian Empress
Barbara Levick

Julia Augusti
The Emperor's Daughter

Elaine Fantham

 Routledge
Taylor & Francis Group

LONDON AND NEW YORK

First published 2006
by Routledge
2 Park Square, Milton Park, Abingdon, Oxon OX14 4RN

Simultaneously published in the USA and Canada
by Routledge
711 Third Avenue, New York, NY 10017, USA

Routledge is an imprint of the Taylor & Francis Group, an informa business

Typeset in Sabon by
Keystroke, Jacaranda Lodge, Wolverhampton

British Library Cataloguing in Publication Data
A catalogue record for this book is available from the British Library

Library of Congress Cataloging in Publication Data
Fantham, Elaine.
    Julia Augusti/Elaine Fantham.
        p.   cm.
    Includes bibliographical references and index.
    1. Julia, daughter of Augustus, Emperor of Rome, 39 B.C.–14 A.D.
    2. Rome–Princes and princesses–Biography. 3. Augustus, Emperor of Rome,
    63 B.C.–14 A.D. – Family. 4. Rome–History–Augustus, 30 B.C.–14 A.D.
    5. Rome–Social life and customs. I. Title.
    DG291.7.J85F36 2006
    937′.07092—dc22   2006000404

ISBN10: 0–415–33145–5 (hbk)
ISBN10: 0–415–33146–3 (pbk)
ISBN10: 0–203–39242–6 (ebk)

ISBN13: 978–0–415–33145–6 (hbk)
ISBN13: 978–0–415–33146–3 (pbk)
ISBN13: 978–0–203–39242–3 (ebk)

This book is dedicated to my daughter Julia

Contents

Illustrations

Plates

Plates reproduced courtesy Deutsches Archaeologisches Institut.

Figures

Preface

It is a life-long hardship to be born a princess, as any student of modern constitutional monarchies can see. I grew up admiring the young British princesses, one of whom became Queen at twenty-five and has since devoted over fifty years to an exemplary life of constant public service and very restricted power or even social influence. Her younger sister, excluded from any real opportunity to be useful, and denied marriage to the man she loved, apparently led a life of pleasure and irresponsibility. We cannot know what she would have achieved if she had been a free agent. If we compare the position of Augustus' daughter Julia, we find similar elements.

Born the only child of a man who came to control the Mediterranean world and beyond, and born the wrong sex, she could only satisfy him by providing an heir, and each of her three marriages was dictated by his desire to mark his chosen successor for the immediate future and produce an heir descended from his own blood for the ensuing generation. Reports of Julia's witty retorts to her father show that this spirited woman wanted to make her own choices, at least in more day-to-day matters. But her all-powerful father appropriated her older sons through adoption, and then eliminated her from society, ruining both her life and her reputation with posterity. Male scholars have found it far easier to believe in her loose living than even the debauchery of Augustus' other propaganda victim, Mark Antony. Without any need for a formal damnation of her memory, the self-censorship of cities and provinces seems to have eliminated even the busts and statues that would have preserved her portrait for us, and only two busts have survived which may show us her features.

When I accepted the editors' invitation to write this book I was moved by the desire to compensate for these injustices. I cannot do this by proving Julia's political or sexual innocence or even by justifying her right to enjoy the same sexual licence that her father had indulged in, because her father has controlled the historical record. Even so Julia lived in what the Chinese call 'interesting times', and along with some idea of her adult life we can recover a picture of the newly sophisticated culture of art and poetry and architecture in the 'world-class' city where she grew up. I have aimed, accordingly, to narrate her life, with those of the five children she bore to

Agrippa, opening up the rich context of the expanding world around them to offset the grim realities of the dynastic struggles which ultimately destroyed them all.

Elaine Fantham
January 2006

Acknowledgements

I owe many debts to friends, fellow scholars and hospitable institutions. Let me start with the series editors Ronnie Ancona and Sarah Pomeroy, who read my text and advised me with experience and patience, and opportune suggestions. My intellectual debts to the published work of other friends such as Barbara Levick, Natalie Kampen and Susan Treggiari are, I hope, acknowledged throughout the text, but are far exceeded by what I have learned from them in person. Conversations with them, and with Dr Donna Hurley, a shrewd expert on Suetonius' Julio-Claudian lives, have drawn my attention to various historical problems. Natalie Kampen generously lent me the use of her apartment and specialist library, which compensated for the fact that the Metropolitan's wall paintings from Boscotrecase have been inaccessible for several years (as are the wall paintings in the Museo Nazionale in Naples). She and Bettina Bergmann and Ellie Leach have at different times helped me to understand what I do not, and we cannot, know about identifying owners of villas and changes of architectural style. But I am sometimes wilful, and none of these fine scholars should be blamed for any idiosyncrasies or errors in my text.

As a novice in obtaining illustrative material I benefited from the expertise of Dottoressa Luisa Veneziano at the Deutsches Archaeologisches Institut: all my illustrations except the three coins are published by permission of the institute. Susan Lusnia most helpfully sent me a copy of her photograph of what is probably Julia on the north wall of the Ara Pacis, and Terence Volk of the Cambridge Faculty of Classics most kindly took the handsome photographs of my own coins with portraits of Gaius and Lucius Caesar and helped me to obtain permission from the Museum of the Castello Sforzesco for the coin representing the princes flanking their mother Julia.

I shall always owe gratitude to my colleagues in my former department at Princeton, and to the university's wonderful library collection, but two other universities have welcomed and supported me in recent years: the Classics Faculty and library staff of Cambridge University have repeatedly offered me the best working environment I have ever experienced, while the University of Toronto, where I taught for eighteen years, has welcomed the prodigal daughter back from the fleshpots in my retirement, offering me their space and renewed friendship. I cannot adequately express how much this has meant to me, both intellectually and emotionally. To all these friends my deepest thanks.

Abbreviations

Note: References to works by classical authors follow the abbreviations of the *Oxford Classical Dictionary*.

AJA   *American Journal of Archeology*
AJP   *American Journal of Philology*
Ann. Epi. *Année Epigraphique*
ANRW *Aufstieg und Niedergang der Römischen Welt*, ed. W.Haase,
     H. Temporini, Berlin/New York
BICS   *Bulletin of the Institute of Classical Studies*, London
Bil.   *Billon*, a collection of inscriptions from Lesbos
Bull. Corr. Hell. *Bulletin de Correspondence Hellenique*
CAH X *Cambridge Ancient History Vol. X: The Augustan Empire*,
     44 BC–AD 70, ed. A. K. Bowman, E. Champlin, A. Lintott,
     Cambridge, 1996
CIL   *Corpus Inscriptionum Latinarum*
CP   *Classical Philology*
DAIR   *Deutsche Akademische Institut* (Romische Abteiling)
EMC   *Echos du Monde Classique*/Classical Views
FGH   *Fragmenta der Griechischen Historiker*
GRBS   *Greek, Roman and Byzantine Studies*
ICS   *Illinois Classical Studies*
IG   *Inscriptiones Graecae*, A. Kirchhoff et al., Berlin, 1875
IGR   *Inscriptiones Graecae ad Res Romanas Pertinentes*, R. Cagnat
     et al., Paris, 1901–27
ILS   *Inscriptiones Latinae Selectae*, 5 vols, H. Dessau, Berlin,
     1892–1916
JHS   *Journal of Hellenic Studies*
JRA   *Journal of Roman Archaeology*
JRS   *Journal of Roman Studies*
LTUR   *Lexicon Topographicum Urbis Romae*, ed. E. Steinby, Oxford,
     1993
MAR   *Mapping Augustan Rome, Journal of Roman Archaeology*
     Suppl. 50, L. Haselberger et al., 2002

MDAIR	*Mitteilungen des Deutschen Archaeologischen Instituts*, Rome
MEFRA	*Mémoires de l'École Française de Rome et Athènes*
OGIS	*Orientis Graecae Inscriptiones Selectae*, 4 vols, W. Dittenberger, 1903–5
PCPS	*Proceedings of the Cambridge Philological Society*
Phil.	*Philologus*
PIR	*Prosopographia Impereii Romani*
RE	*Paulys Real-Encyclopädie der Classischen Altertumswissenschaften*, ed. Kroll; Neue Bearbeitung, Stuttgart, 1917
Rh. M	*Rheinisches Museum*
RPC	*Roman Provincial Coinage*, Vol. I, eds A. Burnett, G. Amndry, P. Ripolle, London/Paris, 1998
RRC	*Roman Republican Coinage*, M.H. Crawford, London/Cambridge, 1974
SEG	*Sylloge Epigraphica Graeca*
TAPA	*Transactions of the American Philological Association*
ZPE	*Zeitschrift für Papyrologie und Epigraphie*

Family Trees

Women of the Julio-Claudian Dynasty

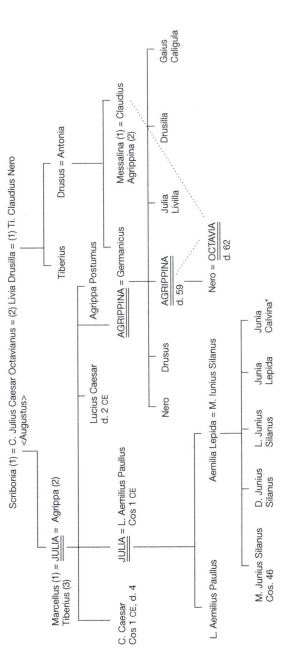

* Junia Calvina, great-great-great-granddaughter of Augustus and Scribonia, exiled for alleged incest with her brother, the betrothed of Octavia, lived on to 79 CE [Suet. Vesp. 23]

Julia's family and descendants

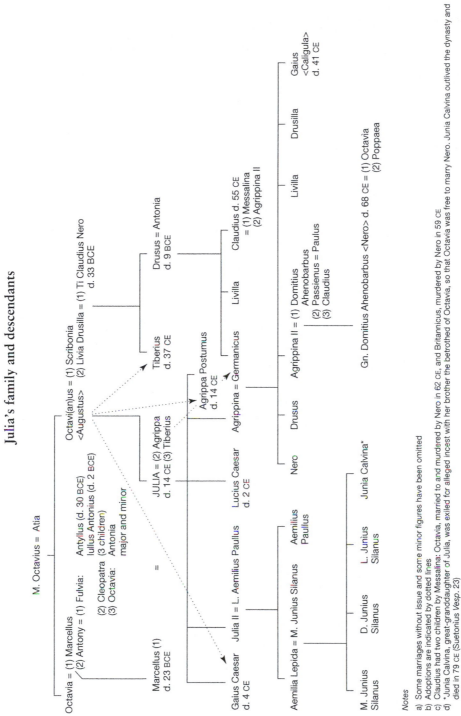

M. Octavius = Atia

Octavia = (1) Marcellus
         (2) Antony = (1) Fulvia: Antyllus (d. 30 BCE)
                      (2) Cleopatra   Iullus Antonius (d. 2 BCE)
                      (3) Octavia: (3 children)
                                         Antonia
                                         major and minor

Octavi(an)us = (1) Scribonia
<Augustus>   (2) Livia Drusilla = (1) Ti Claudius Nero
                                        d. 33 BCE

Marcellus (1)
d. 23 BCE

JULIA = (2) Agrippa
d. 14 CE (3) Tiberius

Julia II = L. Aemilius Paullus

Gaius Caesar
d. 4 CE

Lucius Caesar
d. 2 CE

Agrippa Postumus
d. 14 CE

Agrippina = Germanicus

Tiberius
d. 37 CE

Drusus = Antonia
d. 9 BCE

Livilla   Claudius d. 55 CE
               = (1) Messalina
                 (2) Agrippina II

Nero   Drusus   Agrippina II = (1) Domitius
                                     Ahenobarbus
                                 (2) Passienus = Paulus
                                 (3) Claudius

Gn. Domitius Ahenobarbus <Nero> d. 68 CE = (1) Octavia
                                           (2) Poppaea

Livilla   Drusilla   Gaius
                       <Caligula>
                       d. 41 CE

Aemilia Lepida = M. Junius Silanus

Aemilius
Paullus

M. Junius   D. Junius   L. Junius   Junia Calvina*
Silanus   Silanus   Silanus

Notes

a) Some marriages without issue and some minor figures have been omitted

b) Adoptions are indicated by dotted lines

c) Claudius had two children by Messalina: Octavia, married to and murdered by Nero in 62 CE, and Britannicus, murdered by Nero in 59 CE

d) *Junia Calvina, great-granddaughter of Julia, was exiled for alleged incest with her brother the betrothed of Octavia, so that Octavia was free to marry Nero. Junia Calvina outlived the dynasty and died in 79 CE (Suetonius *Vesp.* 23)

1 Introduction

Daughters and wives in Roman society in the late republic

The lives of elite Roman women were essentially determined by their marriages, and so the story of Julia, daughter of Augustus, was inevitably shaped by her marriages and their outcome. Despite the lapse of two millennia there are quite a number of ways in which Roman elite families behaved like the privileged families of modern North America or Europe, and had similar aspirations for their children. But they had far more control over the marital choice of their children of either sex than we have known in the past 100 years. We are best informed about families with both wealth and political standing, whose largely inherited money would follow both their sons and their daughters. But when a daughter became a wife, family wealth would pass through her dowry and other rights of inheritance into the family of her husband.

The pattern of age at marriage among the propertied classes tended to be different from those in Western urban societies either now or fifty years ago. Elite young men would usually marry in their mid-twenties, after a year or more of military service and some initial experience attending cases and even pleading in the criminal or civil courts, but their brides would be markedly younger women between fifteen and twenty.[1] This was in part because the family felt no need to retain the daughter at home in order to give her a full education, and partly from fear that once into the flush of adolescence the girl might throw away her virginity or lose the reputation for chastity which was a prerequisite for marriage. So betrothal tended to follow as soon as possible after puberty, even when the girl's physique suggested postponement of consummation in marriage, because she seemed insufficiently developed to carry a healthy pregnancy or survive the high risks of childbirth.

As the young man learned how to serve as an advocate in the forum by observing an elder, so the young wife would have learnt some of the complexities of running a large household by observing her mother, and her training would be supplemented by the slave staff of her new household. However, her immediate duty was not as chatelaine, but to ensure the continuation of the clan by producing the next generation.

We can imagine our young Roman couple anxiously awaiting their first-born, say in the year of Cicero's consulship, when Octavian was born as younger child of the senator M. Octavius and his wife Atia.[2] Naturally they would hope for a boy, and a handsome child, physically and mentally active. He could follow either of two respected career paths to lead him to distinction, one as an army officer, the other, now becoming more common, as an advocate and then politician. Success whether in the army or the courts, would normally lead the young man to election, first to one of the twenty junior offices held around age twenty-five, then to more competitive office. Young men from good families or with good personal reputations could stand for election as Aedile, an expensive office which earned popularity by spending private fortunes on public games and festivals,[3] or as tribune of the people, an office favoured by men with a talent for popular speaking, often but not always, radical in their political colour.[4] There were traditional ages at which it was legitimate to stand for the higher offices, but a man with a good record and influential friends could hope to be elected Praetor around the age of forty, to spend the year administering one of the standing tribunals at Rome, and if lucky a further year or two governing a Roman province. On his return, he would be eligible to stand for the highest regular office, as one of the two consuls. The consuls of each year were regularly awarded the position of governor in one of the more challenging provinces: within their province, particularly an overseas region like Spain or Africa or Asia Minor, they were effectively in total control as military commanders, as administrators and as civil and criminal judges. They received no salary, but could expect to return to Rome wealthy even without practising the usual level of corruption. Men reached this climax of the Roman career structure at or soon after forty-five, but the Roman pattern of life expectation even for privileged people meant that most Roman fathers would not live to see their sons approach high office: indeed a father would be quite likely to die around the age of fifty, when his son would be entering junior office. As for the son himself, he might not have long to live after his consulship: many ex-consuls would have only a few years as elder statesmen in the Senate.

Of course there was an even chance that our young parents would not produce a son from the first pregnancy, and would have to keep trying. There were also many miscarriages and stillbirths, so many that they went unreported by historians unless the mother died in childbirth, or as a consequence of a recent birth, like the daughters of Caesar and Cicero. Usually we can only guess at miscarriages from gaps between the birth-dates of siblings. It took Cicero and his wife another ten years after their first-born daughter to produce their son Marcus, and Julius Caesar, for all his sexual activity, seems to have had only the one child – a girl. But supposing the first-born child was in fact a girl. What would our elite parents hope for their daughter, and what could they hope from a daughter? Daughters were expensive, because their only role was marriage, and a good match required a proportionate dowry, one that would satisfy the groom's family and honour the bride's social standing. (This might be less than the portion parents expected to leave each son in their wills, but it had to keep her 'in the style to which she was accustomed', and the money or property must be handed over within little more than a year of marriage.) For fathers whose wealth consisted chiefly in land, it would be hard to provide cash or securities. After education in the home, perhaps sharing the elementary tuition of a brother in *grammatike* (reading and writing Greek and Latin) and accounting, the girl would not be likely to benefit from the next stage of education in rhetoric, which only began at or after puberty. As soon as she reached puberty and was eligible for betrothal and marriage, her parents would seek out a good match for her – the most promising son of the best family among their acquaintance – but this is exactly where the clash arose between parental ambition and personal concern for their daughter's happy adult life, which often played second fiddle. The more prominent her family, the less it was likely that the girl would have much choice in the age, appearance or character of her new husband. The original pattern of marriage gave the bride into her husband's control or *manus,* so that she owed him the obedience of a daughter to her father, and her actions were legally subject to his authority. Even when the self-interest of families led to fathers retaining power over their daughters and their property, and offering them in marriage *sine manu*, many brides were immature teenagers ten or more years younger than their husbands so that the initial relationship would tend to be paternal. But the new wife would learn to know her husband and, given goodwill on both sides, such marriages often led to a balanced relationship in which the bride would find private satisfaction in rearing their children and take vicarious pride in her husband's public successes.

If both partners came from the same background and the husband was outgoing as well as ambitious, one might hope for a real working partnership between the couple, eased by their possession of a slave household and enjoyment of more than one home. Among the elite it was normal to own both a townhouse in Rome and one or more villas in the Alban hills or in the inviting climate of Campania. For the typical political careerist and his wife, the chief hardship was separation for a year or more when the husband had to go on campaign or govern a province away from Rome.[5]

This is how the poet Propertius saw the life of Cornelia, the stepsister of the Julia who is our subject. Cornelia died in her thirties, before her children reached puberty, and Propertius' elegy presents her funeral eulogy in her own voice:

'I saw my brother twice occupy curule office, and I died when he was appointed consul. I lived long enough to win the matron's robe and was not taken from a childless family; you my sons Lepidus and Paullus were my consolations after death, and my eyes were closed by your hand in death. Daughter, you were born to be the model of your father's censorship; Copy me and live as wife of a single husband. This is the highest reward of a woman's triumph, when frank opinion praises how well she served her marriage'.

(Prop. 4.11.65–72)

Here we see through male eyes the aspirations of the dead noblewoman for both herself and her daughter.

But Cornelia was fortunate in that her father was unimportant – so unimportant that scholars still debate his identity. Julia, Cornelia's stepsister, had the misfortune to be born child of C. Iulius Caesar Octavianus, the future Augustus, and the fact that she was his child, and his only child, dogged her through a troubled life. So far we have played down the other half of the equation, that is, what (apart from grandsons) parents wanted *from* (not *for*) their daughters. Essentially, the ambitious father would hope to use his daughter's marriage to gain for himself powerful allies – the right son-in-law might bring him a consulship – or, if he had sons, to bring the same influence to help her brothers' career. And this can be best illustrated by fully documented examples.

We should start with the marital record of the republic's two greatest generals, Gnaeus Pompeius Magnus (Pompey), born in 106 BCE and Gaius Julius Caesar, born six years later. Plutarch's life of Pompey records five marriages, of which two ended with the deaths of his wives. Although Pompey's father had been both consul and general when he died in 87, his unpopularity left his son an outsider, who had to make his own way. Thus the young man's first marriage came about as a result of his prosecution for possession of state property (booty appropriated by his father) in his twentieth year: he was acquitted by the presiding judge P. Antistius, whose daughter he then married. But three years later, when Cornelius Sulla returned wealthy and victorious from his Asian command against Mithridates and his Greek allies, Pompey won such great successes as commander, first of his own local militia, then of forces fighting for Sulla, that Sulla began to see the young man's military glory as a dangerous threat to his own power. He realized he needed to bind Pompey to him and did so by a marriage alliance. Sulla had no daughter, but persuaded Pompey to divorce Antistia, so that he could marry Aemilia, Sulla's stepdaughter by his noble wife Metella. Plutarch reports that Antistius had died in poverty and Antistia's mother had killed herself, leaving her an orphan. No matter, let Pompey become Sulla's son-in-law by marrying Aemilia. But Aemilia herself was already married (her husband is unknown) and in advanced pregnancy. Plutarch reports that her stepfather now engineered the pregnant woman's divorce and remarriage, but she had scarcely entered Pompey's home, when she died of complications in childbirth.[6] It was typical that Romans resolved on a political marriage would not wait for the woman to give birth in the house of her child's father: it was enough that his paternity was established. Plutarch, the honest bourgeois from a small Greek town, is rightly shocked, and calls this behaviour tyrannical (*Pompey* 9) but it is a pattern that will be repeated.

We do not know when Pompey made his third marriage to Mucia, a kinswoman of the same family, the Metelli. The marriage has to be dated by inference from the ages of the three children she bore him, Gnaeus Pompeius (old enough to fight at Pharsalus in 48 BCE, so born at the latest in the early 60s) his younger brother Sextus (so young he was kept out of mainland Greece during the campaigns) and Pompeia, old enough for marriage in the mid 50s. We do know that Pompey himself was away campaigning in Spain from 78–72 BCE, and in the eastern Aegean and the hinterland of Asia Minor for four or five years from 67 BCE. Indeed Plutarch reports that when Pompey was offered the eastern Aegean command, he complained that he was not being allowed to stay in Italy and enjoy the company of his wife, but then Pompey was known for pretending reluctance to accept commands or high office. But it is perhaps not surprising that on his return to Italy in December 62 BCE, Pompey divorced Mucia, alleging adultery (Plut. *Pompey* 42). Writing to Atticus in January 61, Cicero claims that Pompey's action met with general approval.[7]

We have reached the point where both the political biography of Pompey and his personal life converge with the career of Julius Caesar, the great-uncle who restored the prominence of his family and gave his name to Julia's father, Octavius. In 61, Caesar had held the praetorship but was still to be elected as Consul, but Pompey, as the newly returned victor over Mithridates, was the most important and powerful individual in Rome. Even so, Pompey needed political allies to ensure the official ratification of his eastern settlement and the allocation of land in Italy for the demobilization of his soldiers. Pompey was open to aligning himself with the main body of senatorial conservatives, if they would only authorize his recommendations and meet his needs, but he was also open to offers of alliance from more radical quarters. Let us leave him between his third and fourth marriages while we retrace the early marital history of Caesar.

Caesar, like Pompey, was an outsider, but from a decayed patrician family: although a member of his clan had held the consulship as recently as 91 BCE, his own father had not held high office. The biggest asset to his political future had been the marriage of a kinswoman – his aunt Julia, to the 'new man' Gaius Marius, the great commander and reiterated Consul of 107, 104–100 and, finally, 86 BCE. Both ancient biographies of Caesar, by Plutarch and by Suetonius, have lost their opening chapters, but Suetonius reports that Caesar had divorced Cossutia, daughter of a wealthy but non-senatorial family, to marry Cornelia, the daughter of Cornelius Cinna (who had seized power in Rome and was re-elected Consul from 87–84 BCE). This marriage may have been connected with his proposed appointment as *Flamen Dialis*, a position which he ultimately rejected. This peculiar patrician religious office was no secular priesthood like the pontificate he would hold from 73 BCE. Uniquely, it required a patrician wife like Cornelia, but the nomination may have been contrived in the first place to save his life and satisfy his enemies by excluding him from a political career.[8] What matters to our understanding of Caesar's marital history is that when Sulla returned with his army from Asia and demanded that Caesar divorce Cornelia, he refused, and remained married to her until her death in 68 BCE. Cornelia was the mother of Caesar's only known child, Julia, born some time before 74 BCE, and he honoured his wife on her death by claiming the right to give her a public funeral oration (Suet. *D.J.* 6.1). Shortly after this, he married Pompeia, the daughter of the late Consul Pompeius Rufus and granddaughter of Sulla (Suet. *D.J.* 6.2: this woman was not related to Gnaeus Pompey).

Caesar himself held office at Rome as Aedile (65) and Praetor (62), and his mother Aurelia lived in his city house along with his wife and, presumably, his young daughter. It was there that a public scandal arose when, in December 62, young Publius Clodius disguised himself as a flute girl in order to spy on the women's festival of the Good Goddess (which no man might attend) and allegedly to have intimacy with Pompeia. There is no doubt that he had smuggled himself into the house, but the charge of adultery (or even attempted adultery) lacks plausibility on this crowded occasion, and Caesar himself, presiding as Pontifex Maximus[9] over the religious investigation, refused to believe the story. This was, however, the notorious situation in which he declared that Caesar's wife had to be above suspicion, and Cicero reports his divorce of Pompeia in a letter of February 61, only a month after the news of Pompey's divorce. Caesar left Rome almost immediately to serve as proconsular governor of Further Spain for 61 and most of 60 BCE.

Now, indeed, the scene was set for marital and political realignments. Pompey and his political intentions still dominated Roman political gossip, which was intensified when he began negotiations for a remarriage. Plutarch's *Pompey* (47) reports two contrasting overtures by Pompey. In the first, he approached Rome's leading conservative statesman M. Porcius Cato, asking for a double marriage alliance in which he himself would marry one of Cato's nieces, while his son Gnaeus would marry the other. Despite some enthusiasm on the part of Cato's womenfolk, he strongly rejected the offer, and would point in 59 to the disgrace they would have felt if they had been associated with Pompey's hostile treatment of the Senate. Plutarch quotes Cato as claiming that 'it was intolerable to have supreme power prostituted by marriage alliances and to see men helping one another to power and armies by means of women' (*Pompey* 47). But we shall see shortly that Cato himself had an equally repugnant and materialistic approach to the question of marriage. When Pompey's proposals were rejected by Cato, as reported by both Plutarch (*Pompey* 47, *Caesar* 14) and Suetonius, he turned towards Caesar and accepted Caesar's offer of marriage to his own young daughter Julia. From the time of this marriage in spring of 59, Caesar as Consul treated Pompey as *princeps senatus*, senior statesman and first speaker in all senatorial debates. There can be no doubt that this union took Roman society by surprise. It seems also to have provoked some (feigned?) moral indignation, not because of the gap in age, which never seems to have deterred scheming Roman families, but (according to Suetonius *D.J.* 50.1) because conservative gossips found it outrageous that Pompey should marry the daughter of the very man whom he accused of seducing his wife and the mother of his three children. Whatever the truth of the remark, it does reflect the value that Romans put on wives – that is, on mothers. In the language of these gossips, it was as mother that Mucia had earned indulgence for her infidelity by bearing Pompey his two sons and his daughter.

Caesar himself now married Calpurnia, the daughter of L. Calpurnius Piso Caesoninus, and backed her father for the consulship of 58. Piso became Consul, and later censor. Calpurnia and Caesar were childless, but would remain married until his death.

It is worth taking some time to consider what is known about Caesar's daughter Julia, not least because she is thrown into the limelight by the glamour and importance of Caesar for his contemporaries and subsequent Roman history, as the later Julia would be by her father, Julius Caesar's heir Octavian. The actual blood relationship between the two Julias was remote, deriving only from Caesar's parents, who were grandparents of the older Julia and great-great-grandparents of the younger, but the two women were only a generation apart. Although we know more about the marriage of Caesar's daughter Julia to Pompey than about most of her contemporaries, this is relatively little. For historians like Velleius and poets like Lucan, she was simply a guarantee of harmony or cooperation (*pignus concordiae*) between the great generals. We know that Pompey was older than Julia's father, and in his forty-seventh year when he married her, but Julia's age has to be argued from probability: Caesar had married her mother Cornelia before Sulla's domination of Rome, but since Julia had only recently been betrothed and this was her first marriage, she can hardly have been more than sixteen or seventeen – born, therefore, in 77 or 76 (see Syme 1984). Her mother had died when she was a child, and she had shared her father's home with her stepmother Pompeia until the divorce of 61. During her father's absence in Spain, Julia's family life will have been governed by her live-in grandmother, Caesar's mother Aurelia.

The marriage of Julia and Pompey is exceptional among politically motivated unions in its happiness. According to Plutarch, she loved Pompey because he was a loyal and devoted husband. Indeed, he was reproached for spending his time with her visiting the resorts of Campania instead of taking a more active part in political life. But these reproaches may reveal more about the problems of Roman public life, to which Pompey proved ill suited, that about Roman attitudes to marriage. Caesar himself may not have seen his daughter alive after he left for Gaul in early 58. In his absence Pompey was alienated from the conservatives in the Senate and threatened with rumours of planned assassination. Afraid to participate in day-to-day political conflict, he was elected Consul for 55 BCE by intimidation and awarded a five-year command in Spain, which he seems to have been afraid to take up. There was constant political violence, and on one occasion

Pompey was covered with blood while presiding over an election. When attendants brought his bloodstained toga home to exchange it for a clean one, the shock and fear for her husband caused Julia a miscarriage. It must have been only a year later when she died in childbirth in 54. Was the child a boy or a girl?[10] It did not matter: the baby lived only a few days. Pompey wanted to bury her in the privacy of his villa at Alba, but the people rioted and seized the body 'in spite of the tribunes'. They took it to a place of public honour on the Campus Martius, where she was given a grand official burial.[11] As for Caesar, he promised gladiatorial games and a feast in his daughter's memory, but was not able to provide them until 46 BCE. Suetonius calls this public vow unprecedented, but what was unprecedented was not memorial games, rather to offer games in memory of a mere woman.

Caesar's daughter Julia can only have been twenty-one or twenty-two years old, and was clearly a far simpler person than the jealous fury which Lucan conjures up, assimilating her in part to Virgil's abandoned Dido and in part to his own image of her demonic father, but then Lucan's Julia appears only as imagined in the nightmare experienced by Pompey as he leaves Italy never to return, and in the self-reproaches of Cornelia, her successor as Pompey's wife.[12]

Historians saw the death of Caesar's daughter as breaking the bonds between her father and husband, bonds which were finally dissolved in 53 by the defeat and death at Carrhae in Mesopotamia of Crassus, the third member of their political compact. Without Crassus as third party, Pompey was again torn between his agreement with Caesar (away since 58 conquering Gaul) and the attraction he felt towards the conservatives. His choice was signalled by his last marriage, to Cornelia, the daughter of a rather mediocre nobleman, Q. Metellus Scipio, born in the family of the Scipios but adopted by the childless Metellus Pius (Consul in 81). The new marriage, which earned Metellus Scipio a consulship as Pompey's colleague for the second half of the year 52 brought Pompey himself personal happiness. Cornelia herself had only recently been widowed by the death in battle of young Publius Crassus, serving as a junior commander in his father's disastrous campaign against the Parthians. She was still (relatively) young, and both gentle and well educated, and Pompey returned her devotion. She followed Pompey to the East in 49, where he insisted on her staying in relative safety at Mytilene in Lesbos. After his defeat at Pharsalus, he paused in his flight to gather Cornelia and his younger son from Mytilene, and they were present as helpless onlookers at his treacherous murder by the agents of Ptolemy XIII of Egypt.

Were these marital careers exceptional? Exceptional, perhaps, only in the degree to which these two men controlled such power that it made them a magnet for other men's ambitions. There were other ways in which Romans had a very pragmatic and unsentimental outlook on marriage. Let us turn back to the leading conservative, M. Porcius Cato and the strange story of how he used marriage in his own material interest. Plutarch (*Cato minor*

25 and 52) is not our only source for the story that Cato's older friend, the orator Hortensius, now widowed, approached him to request the hand of Cato's daughter Porcia in marriage. We are told that Hortensius was hoping to have children by a new wife of guaranteed fertility, no doubt because his grown son was proving such a wastrel. Porcia, as it happens, was already married to Bibulus and mother of two sons, and Cato, to his credit, was not willing to disturb her marriage. Instead he offered Hortensius his own second wife, Marcia, although she was pregnant at the time, and actually obtained the consent of Marcia's father before he himself took on the father's role and gave his own wife away to his friend. This must have occurred during the 50s, when Cato was most prominent, and when Hortensius died after a few years, in 50 BCE, Marcia returned to Cato with a generous legacy, and our sources report that they remarried.[13] We do not know whether Marcia objected to this arrangement (if she had not returned to Cato we might have wondered whether she seized the opportunity to escape him) but Cato was seen as acting on principle, as part of his obligation to help a friend, and a woman, or at least the wife he had married, was simply the instrument of fulfilling this obligation. (We might add that there is no evidence that she was in Cato's *manus* or legal control, as is clear from the need for her father's consent to this arrangement.)[14] Three different factors seem to have operated in these negotiations: the need for heirs (Cato already had two sons and a daughter by his previous wife, although Hortensius had a son – and a rather capable daughter – he was dissatisfied with the young man); the need to bind allies by marriage (Cato could be sure of the elderly Hortensius' goodwill, but may have felt he needed to keep that of Bibulus), and the considerable material benefits from Hortensius' wealth, played down by Cato but given prominence by his enemies.

These, then, are some aspects of matchmaking and parental direction of their sons' and daughters' lives in the last generation of the Roman republic, when Octavius, the future Augustus, was adopted as his great-uncle Julius' heir and assumed a premature manhood. He too had been married twice before he met the wife, Livia, who would stay with him until his death (and be adopted as his heiress beyond it). But that is another story.

Good and bad marriages

In a sense, the lives of all women in antiquity were defined around their expectation and achievement of marriage: first as young girls, then as wives and, if all went well, as mothers. In their later years, it was statistically probable that they would survive their husbands and live as widows. From day to day, and on a larger scale, their obligations and opportunities depended on the man or men to whom they were married. Since this book will be following the career of a woman whose experiences were uniquely shaped by the series of marriages imposed upon her, we need to explore more fully the evolution of Roman attitudes to marriage as an equal or unequal partnership and the ways in which these unions were not only made, but dissolved. We have seen that Roman elite marriages (and most marriages between less privileged families) were arranged by the parents of the couple, and predominantly by the fathers, to satisfy social or political aims. It is natural but misguided for modern Western readers, used to marrying from personal choice, to think that such an arranged union between a young man and a girl who did not already know and like each other might be awkward and unrewarding. But given average physical attractiveness and sufficient goodwill, the couple would usually recognize that it was up to them to learn to understand each other's needs and make the best of their partnership. If the Romans, like most societies until quite recently, thought that a wife should accept her husband's authority without question, this obedience would come more easily, given the age differential of anything up to fifteen years, which was common in upper-class urban marriages in both the Greek and Roman world.[15] As a relatively young and inexperienced girl, the wife would probably admire her husband for his maturity and sophistication, while he would make allowances for her lack of experience. On the other hand, we should not think of all Roman marriages in terms of nuclear couples. Apart from the contingency of divorce, the frequency with which young women died in childbirth meant that a large proportion of new brides would be brought into a home with stepchildren, and the grown son's obligation to assume responsibility for a widowed mother meant that quite a few new brides entered a household already under the control of a resident mother-in-law. The new couple's problem might be finding time to be alone together, rather than learning to live with a stranger. Add to this the ubiquitous slaves of the household with their own established hierarchy, and the poor bride would not have anyone to accept what little authority she could muster.

No one outside a marriage can know exactly what kind of compromises have to be made by either or both partners, but despite the reticence of our Roman sources about their family life, we know plenty of affectionate husbands who treated their wives with sympathy and respect – for example the elder Tiberius Gracchus and Cornelia, Atticus and his wife Pilia, Varro and Fundania, Pompey and his last two wives, even Cicero and Terentia for over twenty years until they were driven apart by Cicero's exile and near bankruptcy, political eclipse, enforced tour of duty in Cilicia and prolonged separation during the campaign of Pharsalus and beyond.

Our evidence for the previous century is more polarized. Cato the censor is quoted or improved on by Livy as declaring that if Roman husbands failed to control their wives, and prevent them from public demonstrations, the wives would usurp authority. More dramatically, he claimed that a husband who divorced his wife was acting as her judge, like the public censor, and might exercise whatever *imperium* over her he thought fit. If she had been drinking wine she should be fined, and if she actually committed a shameful act with another man, she should be condemned (to death?), adding 'if you caught your wife in the act of adultery, you could kill her without a trial and go unpunished, but if she found you committing adultery or being offered adultery she would not dare to lift a finger against you, nor does she have any such right' (Gellius 11.10.23). But the stern utterances of a man like Cato reflect, rather, the way he thought authority should be wielded in the family than the way families actually behaved. Even in his own day, the elder Cato probably represented an outdated tradition. His comments are best seen as a reaction to the influx of economic and social change when Rome emerged from Hannibal's occupation of Italy to become itself the occupier, bringing back both luxuries and surplus wealth from its Eastern conquests. The very fact that this comment on husband and wife comes from a speech entitled 'About Dowries' shows that Roman society had already moved from any kind of absolute marital control to something like a protocol for balancing the property rights of husband and wife.[16] The problems in most marriages were probably routine disagreements over everyday activities and separation or changes of location from town to country house: nothing as dramatic as adultery, but it was the sexual escapades that stimulated gossip and were the food of comedy. In about the same generation as Cato's prime, the comic writer Plautus gives an old woman slave a protest against the lack of reciprocity in sexual liberties allowed to husbands:

> Upon my word women live on harsh terms, poor things, much more unfair than their husbands do. For if a man hires a tart without his wife's knowledge, and the wife finds out, the man gets away with it. But if a wife goes out without her husband knowing, he has grounds for divorce and she is driven from the marriage. If only there was the same law for man and wife! For a good wife is content with her one husband; how come a man is not content with one wife? I'll wager that if men were punished for hiring a tart unknown to their wives, just as guilty women are thrown out, there would be more men unmarried than there now are women.
>
> (Plautus, *The Merchant*, 817–29)

It is perhaps representative of social prejudices that in comedy lust does not succeed. The husband accused here is actually innocent of the misbehaviour which the old woman suspects, while his lecherous old friend who has bought himself the pretty girl slave is not allowed by the playwright to enjoy her, but is caught and humiliated. Extramarital affairs must always have been something of a luxury, more often imagined by gossip than achieved. But what evidence there is for the years of the republic represents accusations of sexual or other misconduct within marriage as a private family affair, to be judged by family councils (*consilia,* probably limited to older adult males), if judgement were needed. Since such family discussions were private, there is simply insufficient evidence to establish whether women were invited to take part, or whether consideration of marital problems did or did not include representatives of both the wife's and husband's families.

But although troubled relations between husband and wife were largely a matter to be judged by their families, the institution of dowry meant that for at least the last two centuries of the republic, money and property disputed at the end of a marriage became a matter of civil law. The Romans themselves reconstructed a kind of fictional moral history to explain the evolution of marital customs. Thus, the Augustan Greek writer Dionysius of Halicarnassus, and Plutarch, writing around 100 CE, both attributed to Rome's first king, Romulus, an austere code governing marriages. Dionysius offers an extreme version, but is useful in evoking what was the norm in classical Rome by his list of legal actions not yet available. Thus, under the code attributed to Romulus as reported by Dionysius, the husband did not have an action against his wife for adultery or for leaving the house without due cause; she could not bring an action against him for ill-usage (*kakosis*) or desertion, and there were not yet any laws for the recovery of dowry. Instead, Romulus made it law that a woman joined to her husband in sacred marriage should share all his properties and rites. If she was virtuous and obedient to her husband, she was as much mistress of the house as he was its master and heir to his property after his death like a daughter, sharing equally with any children he had. But if she did anything wrong, her husband was her judge and determined her punishment. If she either committed adultery or drank wine, she could be punished with death. The milder version of this antiquarian reconstruction reported by Plutarch (*Romulus* 22.3) claims that Romulus forbade a wife to leave her husband but permitted him to put her aside (not condemn her to death) if she used drugs or poisons, deceived him by smuggling in a child or committed adultery. However, if he discarded her without such cause, he should forfeit half his property to her and the other half to the goddess Ceres. Both authors aim to contrast an early model of marriage that admitted divorce only for major violations with a more recent recognition of morally neutral divorce.[17] And this model of marriage was certainly the older form, which committed the wife into her husband's *manus* (control) admitting her into his descent clan but put her in the position of his daughter, subject to the same level of obedience she had formerly owed her father. It is hardly surprising that this was felt to be a union that could not, or should not, be dissolved.

The piecemeal anecdotal record seems to show that as late as the end of the fourth century, a senator was demoted by the censors for divorcing the wife who had come to him as a virgin without arguing his case for discarding her before a family council, but references to this and other public penalties for marital or sexual offences during this period are sparse and seem at times random. When wives were fined by aediles for extramarital intercourse (*stuprum*) we can hardly imagine that they were one-time offenders; it is far more likely that these women were charged with receiving money or rewards for something nearer to prostitution and brought to the magistrate's notice either by personal enemies or public scandal.

L. Annius was penalized by the public censors in 307 (Valerius Maximus 2.9.2) for divorcing an innocent wife without justifying his action to a family council, but seventy years later Spurius Carvilius Ruga, Consul in 231 BCE, formally divorced his wife simply because he was required by the censors to declare he had a wife for the sake of producing children (the Roman marriage formula attested in scenes of betrothal) and felt that her infertility would make this declaration perjury. He gave this as his reason for divorcing a woman who had not committed any marital offence. The case was seen as a landmark and is cited by several authors as the beginning of what we might call a purely civil divorce, after which it became apparent that there must be a legal process to determine how and when the dowry which came to the marriage with a wife would be returned if the marriage ended in divorce. Such divorces might of course be consensual and suit both partners, but it is not clear how soon the right of husbands to unilateral divorce was extended to wives. This, too, seems to be implied as legally possible by a Plautine comedy, the *Amphitryo*, in which Alcumena, disgusted by her husband's accusation of infidelity, renounces their common property and declares that she is leaving him (*Amphitryo* 928–9).[18] Certainly, the republican jurists evolve a formula by which the husband must give back his wife's dowry, with stated deductions: one-sixth for each child of the marriage, one-sixth (and only one-sixth!) if she is guilty of adultery, or one-eighth if she is deemed guilty of lesser forms of bad behaviour.

But, given an unhappy marriage, there were many complications that would deter either husband or wife from action. First, we must take into account the change that occurred between the second century and the end of the republic from a marriage that put the wife into her husband's *manus* to the modified marriage *sine manu* (without legal control). The woman married *sine manu* remained legally her father's dependent daughter (*filiafamilias*), inheriting within her own family and owing obedience to her father as long as he lived. Let us suppose that she found her husband arbitrary and inflexible; or that they quarrelled continually, like Cicero's brother Quintus and his wife Pomponia. If her husband wanted a divorce, he had only to utter or send her a formal dismissal, but he would also need to raise the funds to cover the return of her dowry, and he would probably be well advised to persuade her family of his reasons. Even if she were actually unfaithful, it might be socially advantageous to avoid recriminations by offering a more neutral excuse of incompatibility. But if she wanted a divorce while her father lived, she would have to persuade her father that this was the right course, not so much because his permission was required by law – this is disputed by experts – but because she would have to leave her marital home and return to her father's house and live among her old family. He could effectively make it too unpleasant for her to consider returning to the family home. Even if the wife no longer had a living *paterfamilias* (father in legal authority) and was legally independent (*sui iuris*), she would have to work out how and where she was going to live. She would regain her dowry, but she would need it to find herself a new husband. And if she had given birth to children she would be doubly penalized. She would have to leave them with their father to the eventual mercies or malice of a stepmother, and she would have to forfeit a portion of her dowry to cover the upbringing of each child.[19] This would be enough to keep most mothers in a marriage which was not actively humiliating but merely lacked affection and companionship. Then, as was true even fifty years ago, women generally initiated divorce only if they had already found themselves a lover or aspiring lover and could hope for the security of a new marriage.

Julia's childhood in context: the new Augustan society and culture

This would not be a real biography of Octavian/Augustus' daughter if it did not set her against the extraordinary cultural and economic revolution that took place in the generation of her birth. As Pompey had used the conquered wealth of Mithridates and other Asian states to finance his amazing theatre complex, centred on the temple of Venus Victrix and surrounded by pleasure gardens adorned with fountains and statuary,[20] so Caesar sent back the spoils of Gaul to finance land purchases for his projected new forum and the temple of Venus Genetrix. He had other ambitious projects that would make Rome the counterpart of grandiose and extravagant Hellenistic cities like Alexandria and Pergamum. These included a second great theatre and a double library of Greek and Roman literature, to be under the direction of the great scholar Varro, but with Caesar's assassination neither project would be begun until his adoptive son Octavian constructed first the porticoes of the library and later the theatre, named in memory of his nephew Marcellus. But even before Octavian had defeated Antony and Cleopatra and taken personal possession of Egypt and the city of Alexandria, he was busy with plans to enrich Rome with new temples that would give a religious sanction to his victories and publicize his reformist ideals. Once he became owner of the royal wealth of Egypt after 30 BCE, not only Octavian/ Augustus, but his wife and sister, his colleague Agrippa and many of his generals gave lavishly for the erection of new secular buildings and even temples.

It is against this background of great public monuments that the child Julia grew up. We can go further. Excavations at Rome itself, Pompeii and Herculaneum have revealed the sudden exuberance of private domestic architecture and schemes of decoration which passed during this generation from what is known as second style design to the third style, provoking indignant protests from the traditionalist architect Vitruvius. Vitruvius had been a military engineer and dedicated his ten volumes *On Architecture* to Augustus.

The age of Augustus has traditionally been called the golden age of literature, beginning with his slightly older contemporaries Virgil and Horace.

Virgil was the first poet to celebrate the new age, and among the ten Bucolic poems published as the *Eclogues*, two (*Eclogues* 1 and 9) portrayed the painful realities of contemporary civil-war confiscations, but one poem, the *Fourth Eclogue*, dedicated to Virgil's patron Pollio (to be discussed in the next chapter), looked forward to a new golden age, associated with the birth of a wondrous child. The inspiration for this Messianic poem with its palpable resemblance to parts of Isaiah, must have come from the Sibylline prophesies, which have been preserved in Greek but reflect Jewish and Middle Eastern thought. But the events of 40 BCE made it particularly opportune to speak hopefully of a wondrous child, for in this year the political compact between Octavian, Antony and Sextus Pompeius was sealed by two marriages: that of Antony to Octavian's full sister, the younger Octavia, and that of Octavian himself to Scribonia. Heirs could be expected from both unions, but Italian hopes would focus on Octavian. Unfortunately, both unions produced girls – Antony's daughter Antonia the elder, and the Julia who is our subject. The *Fourth Eclogue* could of course be read allegorically, in more visionary terms, and both Virgil and Horace came to enjoy the encouragement of Octavian's friend Maecenas long before Octavian emerged the victor of Actium and conqueror of Alexandria in 30, and 'restored the commonwealth to senate and people' earning his new quasi-religious title Augustus, 'The Revered One.' Both poets produced major works – Virgil's *Georgics*, published in 29 and Horace's *Epodes* and *Satires* – before Julia was old enough to appreciate poetry, and Livy too had published the first five books of his *History of Rome* from its foundation by 25 BCE. It is more likely that the adolescent Julia read the first three books of Horace's *Odes*, and the elegies of the new younger poets Tibullus, who died when she was twenty, and Propertius, who eulogized her stepsister. We shall need to set her tastes and personality against a more detailed exploration of the themes and professed values of these love poets. The *Aeneid*, which used the legend of the Trojan hero Aeneas to glorify her father, may have had only a mixed appeal to Julia, but, as she reached womanhood, a younger poet than any of these began to recite and then publish elegiac poems which were less poetry of courtship than witty analyses of love, lovers and their absurdities. Ovid's first poetry book – *Amores* or 'Love Affairs' – cannot really be dated (but the poet himself was only four years older than Julia) and reflects a similar indifference (even antagonism) to the solemn ideals of the older generation.

While the end of civil war had brought peace and relaxation of anxiety, it also brought a relaxation of morals which the newly transformed Augustus could not accept. Through his restoration of decaying republican temples, through his systematic renewal or invention of religious observations, through the devising of cults such as that of the Arval Brothers to create new elite priesthoods and of ceremonial occasions such as the Secular Games[21] which provided new solemnities, the Revered One set about providing a framework of religious activities for the elite. Not content, he disciplined public pleasures, devising regulations to control attendance at the theatre and public entertainments, and took up the moral supervision of the republican censorship, imposing a framework upon domestic morality by legislating a programme of benefits (and corresponding penalties) for marriage and paternity, and severe new laws to take the punishment of adultery out of family control and into the public domain. In all these areas, architecture and city planning, the visual arts, literature, religion, public order and domestic morality, the life of the Roman elite underwent an unparalleled intensity of change, a revolution in many ways more radical than the breakdown of republican government, which had been to some degree eased and extended by debate and compromise between rival power groups.[22] It was Julia and her generation who lived to enjoy the new flowering of the arts, but who would bear the brunt of her father's repressive vision.

2 Julia's parents and childhood

It was certainly political interest, rather than any personal affinity, that brought Julia's parents together in marriage. They probably did not meet until 40 BCE, but to understand their careers will require us to go back to the outbreak of the civil war ten years earlier. Let us begin with her mother Scribonia, since even if she was not, as Syme 1939: 229) unfairly described her, Octavian's 'senior by many years and a disagreeable character',[1] Scribonia began adult life somewhat before her new husband. So how old was Scribonia? She is usually identified as the younger sister of the Pompeian Scribonius Libo, who must have been born around 90 BCE, since he had reached the praetorship before the civil war broke out in 49 BCE. Libo was not important in his own right, but in the years after Caesar's murder, Octavian had to keep on good terms with Libo's son-in-law, Pompey's younger son Sextus Pompeius, who controlled Sicily and was in a position to starve Italy of essential food supplies. As Libo's sister, we would expect her to be quite close to him in age – perhaps over forty in 40 BCE. But since we have evidence that Scribonia was still alive and in full possession of her wits in 16 CE, she must have been born after 70, and at least twenty years younger. More recently John Scheid, noting that she is referred to as the aunt, not the great-aunt, of Libo Drusus, has suggested that Scribonia was an otherwise unattested second daughter of this Libo, rather than his sister. Her formal name would have been exactly the same. But this in turn seems to conflict with her marital history: certainly Suetonius attests that she had been married twice before the union with Octavian, first to the Consul of 56 BCE, Cn. Cornelius Lentulus Marcellinus. However, given his seniority and probable age, it is most unlikely that she was his first wife. In fact it is also quite unlikely that she was the mother of his son, Lentulus Marcellinus, named by Caesar as the quaestor put in command of his fortifications at Dyrrhachium in 48 BCE.[2] Quaestors were usually at least twenty-five years old, so for this young man to have been Scribonia's child, she would need to have married Marcellinus by 74 and so be born at latest soon after 90 BCE. On the other hand, an inscription by a group of freedmen records the joint patronage of Scribonia and a Lentulus Marcellinus, identified as her son. Perhaps this man was only a younger half-brother of Caesar's quaestor.

A further problem is that Suetonius claims that Scribonia had children by only one of her previous husbands,[3] and there is no doubt that she had two children by her second husband, P.Cornelius. This man is usually identified as the P.Cornelius (Scipio) who would become Consul Suffect in 35 BCE.[4] The poet Propertius wrote a funeral elegy in 16 BCE for Cornelia, Scribonia's daughter, which addresses her widowed husband L. Aemilius Paullus and speaks of the consulship held by her brother, P. Cornelius Scipio, in that year. To be Consul her brother would have to have been at least thirty, which puts Scribonia's marriage to his father in or before 47 BCE. It is most likely that the elder Marcellinus died soon after his last known activity as a supporter of Pompey in 49 BCE, and that Scribonia's subsequent marriage to Cornelius Scipio was ended by divorce before 40 BCE. (It is even possible that the divorce was forced upon her to enable her last and least happy marriage to Octavian.) All these problems arise from the fact that Roman historians were essentially uninterested in mothers and daughters unless their husbands or fathers were exceptionally powerful figures.

Our best portrait of Scribonia and her family comes from the same elegy of Propertius already quoted briefly in our Introduction (4.11):

> If anyone has drawn fame and glory from ancestral trophies, our bronze inscriptions speak of ancestors who conquered Numantia: another group claims parity for the Libones of my mother's side, and each family is raised up by its own triumphal titles. Soon, when my maiden's toga gave way to bridal torches I was joined in marriage to you Paullus, so that I left your bed only to be named on this stone as wife of one man alone. I bear witness by the ashes of my ancestors revered by Rome, under whose triumphal claims you lie beaten, Africa, and he who broke the dynasty of Perseus, provoked by the pride of its ancestor Achilles, and made arrogant by him, that I never weakened the censor's law, nor did any hearth blush at shame of mine.
>
> (29–42)

> I never did anything to hurt you, sweet mother Scribonia: what would you wish changed in me except my death? I am praised by my mother's tears and the laments of the city, and my bones are vindicated by Caesar's groaning. He laments that I ended this life, though a worthy sister of his daughter, and we saw tears coming from this god. I saw my brother repeat his curule office, and I, his sister, perished at the time he was made consul.
>
> (55–60, 65–66)

Thus, Scribonia's daughter lays claim to Scipio Aemilianus, conqueror of Carthage and Numantia in Spain as her paternal ancestor, and to his natural father Aemilius Paullus, who defeated Perseus of Macedon. We have less evidence for the achievements of the Libones on her mother's side. But equal time is given to her link with Octavian through her mother's later marriage, and to Julia, her stepsister. In the later part of her imagined speech, when Cornelia addresses her husband Aemilius Paullus, she names her sons, Lepidus and Paullus, and her daughter Aemilia, all still children living in the marital home. All of them will reappear as adults in our narrative.

In his later study, Syme (1985: 248) spoke more euphemistically of Scribonia as 'now well past her first youth', but also as approximately the same age as her second husband, the Consul of 35. We seem to know that she bore three living children between, say, 48 and 38 BCE, unlikely if she herself was already over thirty-five when she married P. Cornelius. But if Cornelia's 'brother', the Consul of 16 was not Scribonia's son but a stepson by an earlier wife, Scribonia need not have been more than thirty when she was offered to Octavian – after all, Cicero's daughter was only thirty when she married her third husband Dolabella, and Scribonia's own daughter Julia would be under thirty when she married her third husband, Tiberius, in 11 BCE.

Now for Julia's father. Young Octavius was the child of Julius Caesar's niece Atia and M. Octavius, who died after governing Asia as Propraetor in 58. Atia remarried, to the Consul of 57, Marcius Philippus, and brought her son up in his home. It is not clear how early Caesar began to concern himself with his niece's son, but he took young Octavius with him on his Spanish campaign against Sextus Pompeius in 45, and sent him to Apollonia in Greece to be tutored, but also to await the expected time in spring 44 when he would accompany Caesar and the legions waiting in Apollonia to join Caesar's campaign against Parthia. This does not seem to have attracted much attention at Rome, where Caesar had given noticeable promotion to Mark Antony, as his second in command in charge of Italy during his absence from 48–46, and as his consular colleague in 44 BCE. When Antony as Consul took charge and agreed to an amnesty for the conspirators after Caesar's death, he may have been surprised and dismayed to find that Caesar's will had adopted Octavius and named him as his heir.

The young man came to Italy and made himself known to Caesar's veteran legions. He had his adoption ratified and began to call himself Gaius Iulius Caesar Octavianus.[5] In the appalling complexity of the situation at Rome, the rivalry between the Consul Antony and Caesar's eighteen-year-old heir would be prolonged by an alternation of hostility and temporary reconciliation spread over the next thirteen years.[6] Armed by the Senate to fight against Antony, and reluctantly honoured with a highly irregular consulship,[7] Octavian made common cause with Antony and Lepidus, the Governor of Africa, to declare themselves *tresviri* (a board of three) to reorganize the state. After defeating the republican forces of Brutus and Cassius at Philippi in 42, Antony went to his high command in the East, leaving Octavian to cope with the affairs of Italy and the western provinces.

It was obvious that Antony was Octavian's most serious long-term rival for power, but he was understood to be preoccupied with his hopes of winning military glory in the East by mounting a major campaign to attack Parthia. Octavian had more immediate anxieties at home. Italy itself was deeply troubled, not least by the rebellion of cities whose land Octavian had earmarked for confiscation to reward his demobilized troops. The year 41 saw him besieging Perusia (modern Perugia) and he is reported to have followed its capture with a massive slaughter of 300 of the surrendered, both senators and knights. Worse, Sextus Pompeius, supposedly defeated by Caesar in 45, had reorganized, built a large fleet, and made himself master of Sicily. Not only was Sicily one of the main sources of the necessary grain supplies for the city of Rome, but with Sicily and his warships, Sextus also commanded the sea routes by which Rome received imports of wheat from Alexandria and North Africa. For a brief period, in fact, Sextus also had control of Sardinia and Corsica. Since Octavian did not have the naval strength to defeat Sextus, he would have to be bought off. It was in this situation that the Consul Asinius Pollio, a supporter of Antony, and Octavian's agent, Maecenas, came to Brundisium in 40 BCE to negotiate a treaty between Antony and Octavian. By this treaty, Octavian added Gaul and Illyria to his areas of provincial control, but he had still to settle with Sextus Pompeius. Both agreements would be confirmed by close marriage alliances.

The first marriage solemnized was between Antony and Octavian's sister, the younger Octavia, newly widowed by the death of her husband C. Marcellus. Indeed, Octavia was still within the ten months' mourning period during which it was against custom for a woman to remarry, and according to Plutarch a decree of the Senate had to be passed to legitimize their union, for which both Antony and Octavian came to Rome. This irregularity gives some indication of the political importance attached to the rapid cementing of this union, designed to serve, to quote Syme (1939: 217–18) as a 'public token' of the actual political agreement, whose terms could not perhaps usefully be made fully public.

Antony had already been married twice – first, to his cousin Antonia, child of Antonius Hybrida, Consul of 63, by whom he had a daughter. (The daughter may not have reached adulthood – nothing more is known of her). Antony divorced Antonia in 47, and married Fulvia soon after. This marriage had ended in her death.

The second marriage, between Octavian himself and Scribonia, was negotiated by Maecenas with Libo, Sextus Pompey's brother-in-law, brokering the marriage as part of the settlement achieved by Octavian with Sextus. This was the occasion of Maecenas' journey to Brundisium, with a retinue of friends, including the young ex-republican poet Horace, who describes the first stages of the trip in the fifth poem of his first published book of *Satires*. Maecenas and Libo, with the non-partisan Cocceius Nerva (and Antony's mother Julia looking after both his and Sextus' interests) brokered a separate political agreement soon after the meeting at Brundisium. In these negotiations at Misenum, Sextus was recognized as administering both Sicily and

Sardinia, in return for his guarantee to keep the seas free of pirates (his own warships!).

At the time of his marriage to Scribonia, Octavian was only twenty-three, but had already been betrothed twice, briefly to Servilia, daughter of Servilius Isauricus, and on his first reconciliation with Antony in 43, to Antony's stepchild, Claudia, the daughter of Antony's wife Fulvia and her first husband P. Clodius, the demagogic tribune of 58. Claudia had not reached puberty and was a virgin when the betrothal was broken off, according to Suetonius, after Fulvia and Antony's brother Lucius quarrelled with Octavian over his veteran settlements in 41. Essentially, Octavian had no experience of married life.

The binding effect of such unions stemmed not from the marriage alone but from the heirs common to both families which they were expected to produce. This is at least part of the explanation for the brilliant poem with which the still unknown Virgil now honoured the consulship of his patron Asinius Pollio as the occasion of a miraculous birth.

> Now a new child shall be sent down from high heaven, if only you, chaste Lucina, will be kind at his birth to the boy under whom the age of iron will come to an end and a golden race arise over the whole earth. Your brother Apollo is already reigning. And just so this glory of our age will come into being with you as consul, Pollio, and the great months will begin to advance. With you as leader, if any traces survive of our wrongdoing, they will release the lands from fruitless terror. He will receive the life of the gods and behold the heroes mingled with gods, and himself be seen by them, and rule a world pacified by his father's valorous achievements.
>
> (Virg. *Eclogue* 4, 7–17)

While the body of the poem was undoubtedly inspired by the kind of eastern prophecy that has now been preserved in Greek among the Sibylline books, the miraculous child whose father is marked by such Roman military greatness is best seen in the context of this treaty: not, alas, Pollio's own son Asinius Gallus, already born in 40, or his next, short-lived, child Saloninus, but a child of one of these power-broking marriages. Given Antony's seniority, we may share Syme's interpretation (1939: 218–20) that if anything the secular saviour was meant to suggest the expected child of Antony, ruler of the eastern empire, and Octavia, rather than that of his junior, Octavian. As we have already mentioned, the Fates voided the prophecy when both the children produced by Octavia and Scribonia in the first years of their marriages were daughters: Antonia[8] was born first, then Julia, daughter of C. Iulius Caesar Octavianus, in the last weeks of 39 BCE.

But Scribonia's marriage was damned even before Julia could be born, and damned for two reasons. Early that year, 39 BCE, Sextus Pompeius' admiral Menodorus deserted, handing over Sardinia and Corsica into Octavian's control. Restored confidence and access to the trade routes made Octavian careless of retaining Sextus' goodwill, and in late summer a young woman had come to Rome who would infatuate Octavian and make him impatient to end his marriage. Livia Drusilla was born on 30 January, 59 (or perhaps 58) BCE to M. Livius Drusus Claudianus, who was born a member of the Claudian family, and then adopted by the reformist tribune Livius Drusus. Claudianus is first heard of in 59, as a supporter of the triumvirs Pompey, Crassus and Caesar. Praetor in 50, he seems to have given his support to Caesar's assassins, as he is recorded in 43 as sponsor of a decree transferring two legions to the command of Decimus Brutus.[9]

It is not surprising, then, that Claudianus died that year, proscribed by the triumvirs. His daughter Livia had married Ti. Claudius Nero as soon as she was of age, in or soon after 44,[10] and their first son, the future Emperor Tiberius, was born in November 42, the year when her husband was Praetor. Unfortunately, in the following year, Tiberius Nero sided with Fulvia and the Consul L. Antonius in opposing Octavian, and had to escape from Octavian's siege of Perusia early in 40 BCE. From there he fled to Naples, and from Naples to Sextus Pompeius in Sicily, who snubbed him. Luckily, although he had now been proscribed, Tiberius Nero was able to escape under the protection of Antony's mother Julia (such were the intricate family connections of the aristocracy) to Athens, where Antony found him a home in Sparta. Only the reconciliation between Octavian and Antony made at Brundisium created the new circumstances that enabled Tiberius Nero to return to Italy and Rome late in the year. His wife, Livia, was already pregnant with her second son Drusus, but Octavian fell in love with her so rapidly that they were betrothed within months, and he took Livia into his home.

The date of Octavian's divorce and remarriage are disputed, but it seems Drusus, born 14 January 38, came into the world not three months after the marriage of Octavian and Livia, as some sources suggest, but three months after their betrothal. As Barrett has recently argued,[11] our sources have been confused by the fact that Octavian did not wait for marriage to take Livia into his home, but did so on their betrothal. In the scandal associated with this rapid divorce and remarriage it was natural that sources should disagree about the timing. As it was, Tacitus (*Annals* 1.10.5) and Dio (49.44.1–2) both report[12] that Octavian consulted the Pontifices for their opinion on whether it was right for him to marry a pregnant woman and received their approval, provided the pregnancy was already established. He then went to Tiberius Nero and obtained his cooperation; indeed, Tiberius 'gave away' his ex-wife to Octavian and attended the wedding feast. It is not clear whether Octavian took any pains to look after the future of his former wife in consultation with her father or brother Libo (still alive), nor where Scribonia went after Octavian had divorced her and excluded her from his home. Where would she go now? The home of her first husband Marcellinus would have been inherited by his eldest surviving son, and her second husband may have remarried or died. If Libo had a house in Rome she will naturally have gone there until she could establish her own household. Octavian had the Roman father's right of taking his children with him after divorce, but it seems unlikely that he would want to exercise it by taking the small baby into the home he now shared with his new wife. Julia would remain his only child, but in the excitement of his mating with Livia he may have counted on sons to come and looked on the female baby with indifference.

Julia's childhood, the early fortunes of her family, and her playmates

There is unfortunately no evidence of how Julia spent her infancy. She would probably have been suckled for more than a year by a wet nurse. We do know that Octavian scrupulously returned the newly born Drusus to his father, who would have kept his older son Tiberius with him according to Roman practice. Dio apparently quotes from a memorandum of Octavian: 'Caesar returned the child borne by his wife Livia to his father Nero' (48.44.4) and notes that when Ti. Claudius Nero died, he left Octavian as guardian to both Tiberius and Drusus. It was, of course, essential to reaffirm that the boy was in fact the son of Claudius Nero. But when would Octavian and Livia have been ready to welcome the growing daughter of his discarded wife? Perhaps Julia was allowed to stay with her mother until it was convenient for her father to take her into his household. This in turn might have been affected by the constant crises which took him away from Rome to southern Italy. We shall see that besides his concern over Antony's behaviour, Octavian was very much preoccupied with Sextus Pompeius and constantly engaged either in naval warfare or negotiations (which called upon Scribonius Libo as intermediary) until his final victory over Sextus at Naulochus in 36. A brief survey of his fortunes over the five years after 40 BCE may suggest that if Octavian had not yet taken his daughter into his home, he would find himself in a more assured position at Rome by 35. Tiberius Nero's death seems to have occurred in 33 or 32, but once Octavian and Livia had assumed charge of her sons, they may have felt no urgency to add another infant to their household.

There is only one straw in the wind that might suggest Julia spent the later years of her childhood with her mother. We know from Suetonius' historical list of Roman teachers of *grammatike* [13] that after her divorce from Octavian Scribonia purchased from the *grammaticus* Orbilius a learned Greek, whom she later freed, giving him the name Scribonius Aphrodisius. This man wrote challenging the work on orthography of Augustus' protégé Verrius Flaccus. Why would Scribonia have acquired a learned slave? It is most likely that she wanted him as a tutor for one of her children. Kaster (1995) suggests her son by Cornelius Scipio, but the boy's education would have been determined by his father unless Scipio died soon after his consulship in 35. Could Scribonia have wanted Aphrodisius to teach her daughter?

The years after 40 BCE, so full of both diplomacy and campaigning for Octavian, also deeply involved his sister Octavia, the closest member of his family. Octavia's experiences as wife to Antony will not only help to illustrate patterns of marriage and motherhood in the Roman elite, they will demonstrate how much elite women could be actively involved in political negotiation, which in her case was inseparable from the vicissitudes of her marriage. Her movements will also throw light on a question that will be relevant to Julia's future life as wife of Agrippa and Tiberius: to what extent did Roman wives in this generation accompany their husbands on official tours of duty as governors and commanders?

Although Octavia was the younger of Octavian's two sisters, she seems to have been about seven years older than her brother. When he offered her to Antony in marriage, she already had three children by her first husband Marcellus. Since most of our knowledge of her character and actions is derived from Plutarch's *Life of Antony*, we come closest to her in the period from 40–30 BCE. The tradition has made her a model of loyalty both to her brother and to her husband(s), a fine foil to Fulvia, Antony's wife from about 48 to her death in 41,[14] or to his foreign mistress Cleopatra. According to Plutarch, Octavia was very dear to Octavian, who certainly respected her judgement in political matters. Plutarch's explicit praise of her gravity and good sense is born out by the narratives of our other sources. After her marriage, she accompanied Antony to Athens, which was his base for the next two years, taking with her his two children by Fulvia, Antonius Antyllus and Iullus Antonius as well as her own three. Although Antony had treated his liaison with Cleopatra as marriage[15] and she had borne him twins in 40 BCE, in the next two years, he seems to have left Athens only to direct his largely unsuccessful campaigns against Parthia. During this time Octavia bore him two daughters, both of whom would in due course be ancestors of emperors.

The treaty of Brundisium secured little more than a temporary calm. Even when Octavian and Antony showed their reconciliation by coming to Rome together, Sextus' naval campaigns brought renewed famine to Rome, and Octavian had to be rescued by Antony when he was personally attacked by a rioting populace. The settlement with Sextus at Misenum later in 40 did not prevent him from naval raids the following year, and both Libo and Antony's mother Julia were called upon to secure Sextus' goodwill by recognizing his control of Sardinia and Corsica as well as Sicily. In addition, his legitimacy as a Roman statesman was confirmed by conferring an augurate upon him, and guaranteeing him a consulship for the year 34 – one he would not live to hold.[16]

The same year also saw Antony and his fleet make a futile journey from Athens to Brundisium for a consultation with Octavian, who failed to appear. Yet when Maecenas travelled to Antony in 37 to seek his help for Octavian against Sextus, Antony again sailed to Italy, taking Octavia with him.[17]

He came with a fleet of 300 ships, ready perhaps to change peace for war if he was not satisfied, but although he was turned away by the people of Brundisium, he was welcomed to Tarentum where he met with Octavian to renegotiate their relationship. From Plutarch's detailed account in his *Life of Antony*, it seems Octavia herself met her brother and his advisers Agrippa and Maecenas before he consulted with Antony and was instrumental in smoothing their conflicts. Now, officially as a courtesy to Octavia, her brother agreed to be the guest of Antony and to transfer legions from his own command for Antony's Parthian campaign in return for one hundred of Antony's warships, while Octavia personally negotiated supplementary ships from Antony for her brother in exchange for further infantry. Since Antony was ready to embark on his expedition against Parthia in the Asian hinterland, he sent his wife and children back into the care of Octavian at Rome, but Octavian himself went south to conduct a naval war against Sextus. Octavia again persuaded her brother to let her return to Athens, taking with her military reinforcements and supplies for Antony. But Antony, who had renewed his association with Cleopatra (another son was born in 36), was now planning another expedition against Armenia. At first he simply asked her to remain at Athens, which was to be expected while he was in the field, but perhaps at his suggestion, she would return in 35.

After formally renewing the triumvirate for the years 36–32, both Antony and Octavian would achieve military success, Antony in a campaign against Armenia that enabled him to wipe out the failure and losses of the previous year, and Octavian in a final confrontation with Sextus. With Lepidus, based in the province of Africa, and the general Statilius Taurus, Octavian and his admiral Marcus Agrippa mounted a threefold attack on the three coasts of Sicily. Agrippa defeated Sextus' admiral Papias off Mylae in the north-east, while Lepidus attacked and occupied part of western Sicily. But the decisive battle came at Naulochus, when Agrippa commanded Octavian's forces and annihilated Sextus' navy. Sextus himself fled eastwards, hoping to make an arrangement with Antony, but he was not seen as worth any concessions and after futile attempts to negotiate with Parthia was captured and killed by Antony's lieutenants. The year 36 also saw another beneficial consequence of the Sicilian naval victories. When Lepidus, still nominally an equal member of the triumvirate, demanded control of Sicily as his reward for participating in the campaign, Octavian challenged him by marching into his camp and addressing his legions, who immediately gave him their allegiance. Lepidus was deprived of his old command in Africa and forced into private retirement.

Now Octavian could return to Italy with a secure and lasting victory, and he advertised that peace had been restored by land and sea. In 36 he was hailed at Rome with a public celebration (a simple declaration of praise, or *ovatio*, since triumphs were not awarded for civil-war conflicts), with extravagant honorific statues and with the new honour of tribunician sacrosanctity for life. When Octavia left Antony's home in Athens for the last time to live in Rome this year, she was well aware of Antony's public recognition of his children by Cleopatra, but she was still anxious to observe her role as his wife, and we are told that she would not leave her husband's house, although her brother ordered her to live in a house of her own, but stayed there and continued to care for his children.[18] It was probably for her protection and as propaganda against Antony that Octavian now obtained from the Senate decrees awarding both his sister and his wife Livia the sacrosanctity which he himself held, a totally unprecedented status for any woman.

I have provided these details to illustrate the choices available to a wife in this social class when her husband went abroad: Octavia's choices indicate four possible options, three of them compatible with continuing her marriage. First, the unlikely one of accompanying her husband into contested territory; next, the option (which she had taken) of accompanying him to his seat of government or any other settled provincial city; or, third, of staying at his town house at Rome. The fourth option – to leave her husband's house, as Octavia was forced to do when Antony chose to divorce her in 32 – was either the consequence or occasion of divorce. Octavia's residence in Athens in fact is the first instance of a change in pattern. The wives of republican generals and governors had not left Rome to follow their husbands until the understandable exception of Pompey's wife Cornelia, who left Italy with him in the civil war to stay at the naval base of Mytilene in Lesbos. But under the principate, the wives of imperial commanders generally went with them to their provincial commands, like Agrippina the Elder, who accompanied Germanicus not simply to Lyons but to his camp near the Rhine on the edge of hostilities.

As for Scribonia's position, it would now be contingent on the prestige of her brother Libo, which seems to have been undamaged. We should note that in 35 he held the consulship which had been promised him four years earlier; so, too, did the son of Sextus Pompey's paternal cousin, though there is no evidence that this man was ever associated with the rebel Sextus Pompeius. The year after, both Scribonia's ex-husband P. Cornelius Scipio and her son-in-law Aemilius Paullus were among the supplementary ('suffect') consuls. It did not affect the extended family of Sextus Pompeius that this former ruler of Sicily and Sardinia was first a fugitive, then executed as a traitor.

Let us assume that Julia, now aged five, had now been taken into her father's household. She will have wanted to associate with other children, and her father will have seen the proper companions as coming from his own extended family. From 33 or at latest 32, Octavian's house on the Palatine would have been the home of Tiberius, three years older than Julia and no doubt mildly contemptuous of the little girl, and Drusus, so near her in age. The children would be watched by numerous slave attendants and elementary teachers in a large household where there would be less consciousness of deviation from the nuclear family, and we should probably not expect in these siblings the inherited hostility one might find between the modern child of a rejected wife and her stepbrothers or sisters. Even so, one would look for playmates outside the immediate family, and these Octavia's household would supply in abundance. Julia had even been promised in betrothal as an infant to Antony's eldest son Antyllus (seven or eight years her senior?), but as relations between Octavian and Antony cooled, this had lapsed.[19] After 35, Antyllus stayed with his father in Egypt. As the boy approached puberty, his father would treat him as a future soldier, and this very fact would ensure his betrayal and murder on Antony's defeat and suicide in 30 BCE.

Octavia, too, will surely have lived on the fashionable Palatine, near her brother's house, and some at least of her mixed brood of children will have been of an age to associate with Julia. In 35, this meant her son Marcellus, born in 42, and his two sisters, who may have been slightly older than him; the younger one could have been born between 42 and 40, and so little older than Julia. It also meant Antony's son by Fulvia, Iullus Antonius (born before her death in 40), and Octavia's own children by Antony, the elder Antonia, born in 39, and her sister (also Antonia) born 31 January 36 BCE, Antonia the Younger, future mother of the Emperor Claudius, who would add the celebration of her birth to the official Roman calendar. In addition, Octavia took on responsibility in 30 for the three surviving children of Cleopatra. Of the twins born in 40, Selene lived to be given in marriage to young Juba of Mauretania: was she, too, part of the household on equal terms with the Roman children? Selene's brother, Alexander Helios, walked in Octavian's triumph in 29 but probably died soon after, while Ptolemy, the youngest, is not heard of again.[20]

We hear much less of Octavian's elder sister and her family. She married a Sex. Appuleius, whose sons, Consuls in 29 and 20 BCE, must have been born around 60 and 50, and so twenty years older than Julia. We saw that in 16 BCE Cornelia spoke with pride of Julia as her (half)-sister, but she and her brother would have been more than five years older, and there may have been little contact between their families.

By 30 BCE, Julia's stepbrother Tiberius and cousin Marcellus would have moved on from instruction by a *grammaticus* functioning as private tutor – something that could also be enjoyed by the daughters of a Roman family – to working with a *rhetor* on composition and training for public speaking in both prepared and extempore oratory. This was the age when declamation became fashionable, and the young men would have trained on both *suasoriae* (speeches advising a historical figure on his decision in a crisis) and *controversiae* (simplified and fictionalized court cases). They would also have been prepared for military service by training in equitation, athletics and wrestling. An ode of Horace shows that young men of this time usually exercised on the Campus Martius, although the area would gradually be occupied by public monuments under the peacetime regime of Octavian.

After his victorious return from the campaigns of Actium and Alexandria in 29, Octavian celebrated a triple triumph: the first day for his (and Agrippa's) victories in Aquitania, Pannonia and Illyria (where he had successfully conducted three minor campaigns against the Delmatae and other tribes), while both the second day, celebrating the naval victory at Actium, and the third were presented as victories over Egypt, which supplied a far greater display of wealth and exotic objects of art and luxury.[21] While poor Alexander Helios and his sister Selene had to walk before Octavian's chariot along the triumphal route to the temple of Jupiter Capitolinus, Octavian could have followed the Roman custom by which the victorious general took his son into his chariot, but of course he had no son. Instead, we are told that Marcellus had the position of honour riding the right-hand trace horse, while Tiberius was mounted on the left-hand horse. Julia presumably watched with Livia and Octavia from a special stand, erected for the women of the family.

Octavian surely recognized by now that he and Livia could not hope for a child and looked for an heir from his own kin to be his successor in the family if not yet in the commonwealth and as ruler of empire. No one had a stronger claim to be his heir than Octavia's son Marcellus, and he would have been the prime candidate when the newly exalted Augustus began to consult with Octavia and Livia about his daughter's future marriage, even before the children themselves realized that Julia and Marcellus were marked down for each other.

For the time being, Octavian shared the consulships of 28 and 27 at Rome with his trusted friend Agrippa, who had taken Octavian's niece, the elder Marcella, in marriage.

Together, they reviewed the bloated membership of the Senate and reduced its active membership, permitting those now dropped to retain the public symbols of senatorial rank. Octavian needed the cooperation of the old elite families and fostered this by elevating new families to the patriciate (Augustus *Res gestae* 8) and by creating or recreating a prestigious priest-hood, the twelve Arval brethren whose only duties were the cult of Dea Dia on his, Octavian's, behalf. On 13 January 27, he made an official gesture of restoring to the Senate the government of empire and control of all the provinces that did not require a military presence. This division of responsibility was understood to constitute the *Res Publica* (Augustus *Res gestae* 34.1–2) and Octavian declared his intention of working with and through the Senate as nothing more than the First Citizen among them. In return, he added to his existing honorific title of Imperator[22] the unprecedented epithet Augustus: 'The Revered Leader'. Revered at home and supreme commander abroad, he claimed to surpass other citizens only in authority. These titles, reminiscent of those offered to Hellenistic kings, will have pointed the way to founding a dynasty on the model of the Seleucids or Ptolemies, whose representatives he had now conquered.

Tu Marcellus eris: the short-lived prince and consort

Marcellus was probably no more modest and prudent than any other young prince – we can imagine, if we like, behaviour comparable to some of the follies of two recent generations of British princes or scions of the Kennedy family. But Augustus, as we shall now call him, started Marcellus on his political career with a decree of the Senate making the fifteen- or sixteen-year-old prince a member, with the status held by ex-praetors. The candidates nominated by the Princeps were guaranteed election, and so Marcellus was elected to the office of Aedile, one technically junior to that of Praetor, but more promising as a source of public popularity, for it was the Aediles who presided over the public games and distributions, as well as Rome's public monuments.[23] We know of only one act by Marcellus during his year of office, the provision of movable canvas awnings (*vela*) to shield the audiences of the games from the sun in the theatres and perhaps also the circus. Although the theatre that would later bear his name had been planned by Julius Caesar and was being pushed forward by Caesar's heir, it was not yet under construction, and would first be used, still incomplete, in the Secular Games of 17 BCE.[24] Tiberius was the same age as Marcellus, but was given noticeably lesser honours. In 25, when Marcellus was Aedile, Tiberius was Quaestor and honoured only with the privilege of standing for other offices five years before the regular age. Many quaestors served abroad as assistants to a governor, but one of the most responsible and demanding functions was supervision of the public grain supply for Rome, and success in this would bring Tiberius goodwill.

In 24 or perhaps 25, Marcellus and Julia were married. Augustus himself was concerned with campaigning in Spain and delegated Agrippa to preside over the festivities – an irony that would only be appreciated later. We do not know where they lived, but it was not for long. In 23, both Augustus and Marcellus were seriously ill. Augustus had been sick on several occasions before, but this nonetheless alarmed both him and the people of Rome. There was a new fashionable physician, a Greek of course, called Antonius Musa, who advocated the cold-water cure. It worked for Augustus – or maybe he recovered in spite of it – but failed to help Marcellus, who grew sicker, left Rome for the healthier climate of Baiae, the resort on the bay of Naples, and died there in 23.

The young prince was honoured by a public funeral in the Campus Martius before his body was laid to rest in Augustus' new Mausoleum, the first member of his family to be buried there. Italian funerary reliefs, such as the relief of Amiternum, show the deceased's grieving widow and children visibly lamenting at the public exsequies. Was this expected of the Princeps' daughter too? Nothing is said of the role played by women, but we do know that Augustus himself delivered the funeral eulogy, which must have been published, since both Servius, the fourth-century scholar of Virgil, and Plutarch quote the text of Augustus Caesar's praise of M. Claudius

Marcellus. It was Roman custom that eulogies should celebrate the ancestors of the deceased who had held public office and, even more, those who had won military honours. A famous ancestor of Marcellus had won Rome's greatest military honour, the Spolia Opima, by killing a Gallic chieftain in single combat. This man, M. Claudius Marcellus, had gone on to hold five consulships and recapture Syracuse for Rome during the war against Hannibal. Another ancestor had been Consul three times. These figures would be even more prominent since young Marcellus died before he could add any achievements of his own.

This would be an occasion for massive public mourning, and we can sense its dramatic intensity from the reactions of two Roman poets.[25] The younger, Propertius, produced a rather frigid but circumstantial lament, exploiting the historical monuments of the area and its proximity to Lake Avernus, believed to be one of the accesses to the Underworld:

> Where the sea kept apart from shady Avernus beats on the steaming pools of Baiae's warm water, on the sands where Troy's bugler Misenus lies buried and the Way constructed by Hercules' labour resounds, here where the cymbals clashed for the Theban god as he came propitious to seek the cities of men, – but now Baiae has incurred loathing for its great offence, what hostile god came to rest in your waters? Marcellus lowered his gaze to the Stygian waters, and that spirit wanders in the infernal Lake.

> What availed him his race, or excellence, or gracious mother, or that he had embraced (in marriage) the hearth of Caesar? Or the awnings recently fluttering over such a crowded theatre, and the festive omens given by admiring applause? He perished, and his twentieth year came to an end, unhappy youth; the day cut off in its cycle so many merits . . .

> But as to you, Marcellus, may the ferryman who takes across the pious shades of men convey your body now empty of its soul. Where Marcellus, victor over the land of Sicily, and where Caesar passed on, your soul has departed from human commerce to reach the stars.[26]

> (Prop. 3.8.1–16 and 31–4)

But Virgil, who had just finished his sixth book of the *Aeneid*, now added the young Marcellus to the parade of great Roman heroes described by Anchises – or did he only change a celebration of the young prince's future into a lament? As Propertius notes, Marcellus' most famous ancestor, M. Claudius Marcellus, had won back Sicily from Hannibal and celebrated a triumph for taking Syracuse by storm. Anchises comes to this man last in his enumeration of the heroes:

See how Marcellus comes forward, glorious with the spoils of single combat, and as victor towers over all men! He will restore Rome's fortune with his cavalry, and lay low the Carthaginians and rebellious Gauls, and hang up the third votive offering of arms to Father Quirinus.

(*Aeneid* 6.855–9)

At this, Aeneas spies the young prince 'a young man of exceptional beauty in glittering armour, but with a sad brow and eyes cast down', and asks his father who the young man is, and why his companions are making such cries: why is his head surrounded with the grim shadow of black night? Virgil represents his own grief through the tears of Anchises, as he replies:

My son, do not ask about the immense grief of your kin; the fates will only show this man to the earth, and not allow him to live on. Gods above, it seemed you thought Rome's descent would be too powerful if these gifts had been hers to keep. What mighty groans the Field will utter by the great city of Mars, what a funeral you will witness, god of the Tiber, when you glide past his fresh burial mound! No boy of the Trojan race will exalt so greatly his Latin forefathers, nor will Romulus' land ever boast so proudly of such a nurseling. Alas for his piety, his old fashioned integrity and his valour undefeated in war. No man would have confronted him in arms without suffering, whether he advanced against the enemy on foot, on spurred the flanks of his foaming horse. Alas, pitiable boy, if somehow you might break through the harsh fates, you will become Marcellus. Give me lilies to fill my hands, let me scatter brilliant flowers and at least honour my distant child with these gifts, performing a futile service to him.

(6.867–886)

We are told in Donatus' life of Virgil that an impatient Augustus asked the poet to read to him the three books of the *Aeneid* that he had just finished, and Virgil broke his journey northwards from Tarentum to read his work to the Emperor. But when he came to this passage, Octavia, who was present, broke down. Her grief would never end, according to Seneca. He warns his friend Marcia in his *Consolation* not to be like Octavia, who did not learn to bear a mother's grief. Seneca claims that for the twelve years between Marcellus' death in 23 and her own she never smiled again, nor allowed anyone to mention him, and ceased all public appearances.[27]

There is no report of how her young husband's death affected Julia. If they were happy together, this loss would only be the first of the sorrows to be expected in her life. But she would guess it was only the prelude to another political marriage. We must assume that she was now shrewd enough to know that her father would choose her next husband for the sake of the State and not for her happiness.

3 Tensions of Julia's youth
The poetry of pleasure and the legislation of morality

If Julia's father and stepmother followed the initial scandal of their precipitate marriage with an exemplary life and a strict parental model for their assorted children, they were probably exceptional. We cannot judge high society by the exaggerated gossip that circulates, as anyone will know if they read accounts in the newspapers of the supposed behaviour of their own acquaintances. But if we cannot know what Julia saw of high society in the years just before and during her first marriage (or until the birth of her first child in 20 BCE), we do know what she is likely to have read about the lives of her peers. One major source of personal poetry was the household and circle of friends of the conservative aristocrat M. Valerius Messala Corvinus (64 BCE–8 CE) who fought for Brutus and Cassius at Philippi, then transferred his allegiance to Octavian. He seems to have been appointed as Praetor in mid-year 40 after the treaty of Brundisium, and served Octavian as Agrippa's deputy in the campaign of Naulochus in 36. He was made Consul Suffect in 31 BCE in Mark Antony's place when Octavian declared against his fellow triumvir and deprived him of his expected magistracy. One of Octavian's leading generals and most respected supporters at Rome, Messala was associated with the old republic, and would be the symbolic spokesman who offered the Princeps the title of *pater patriae* on behalf of the Senate in 2 BCE.

But Messala was also a lover of *belles lettres*. A fastidious orator and literary patron of the elegiac poet Albius Tibullus (perhaps ten years older than Julia), he would also be patron of Ovid's early career. Messala's niece Sulpicia, orphaned daughter of Servius Sulpicius (perhaps the son of Cicero's friend Servius) also wrote elegiac poetry, and the subject of these poems was chiefly love. Tibullus was the first of the three Roman elegists to become known (probably chiefly from recitation before the publication of his two written collections), and if we take the poems with which he opened his first book, they will provide a portrait of how he wished to appear to his readers – young men and women of his own class. This portrait has so much in common with the self-representation of the other contemporary elegiac poet Propertius, and even of their younger peer Ovid, that it can fairly serve as a model for the kind of behaviour Julia will have grown up to admire.

Tibullus starts from his origin as a peace-loving country gentleman, though one apparently in reduced circumstances, probably because of confiscations of land from his property. However, he rejects the option of acquiring new wealth by military service overseas, preferring a devout life on his now straitened estate, where he can enjoy the love of his *domina*,[1] addressed as Delia. In this he contrasts himself with Messala, whose position makes it proper for him to wage war and bring triumphal spoils to his ancestral home (Messala did in fact triumph over the Aquitanians in 27 BCE and is honoured for it by Tibullus 1.7). Tibullus himself is not free to leave his mistress's doorstep (55–56) but loves her more than glory; it is his hope that he will gaze on her when he dies and she will tend his grave. Surely this is a premature anxiety, unless he really did enjoy ill health, but the theme lapses in the second elegy, which exposes the illicit nature of this sentimental romance. He seems to be speaking at a party, and is already half-drunk, in despair because his beloved girl has been put under lock and key by someone identified only as the master of the house (*ianua difficilis domini*). But Venus teaches lovers tricks, and as Tibullus wanders the streets by night, he is not afraid, so long as Delia can unlock the door and slip out to join him. He addresses himself to Delia and calls the master of the house 'your partner' (*coniunx tuus*), but he has enlisted the help of a witch to prevent this man detecting Delia's infidelity. He had gone to this old witch not to be cured of his love but so that she would make it reciprocal. But there is another rival, seemingly, a cavalry officer, who has left Delia to go on an expedition against the Cilicians (in southern Turkey), whereas Tibullus will be happy enough to farm his land in Delia's company. He falls to wondering how he has offended the gods that he should be shut out from where Delia lives and mocked for it. Whoever laughs at him (perhaps the man in possession of Delia?) should fear the onset of old age when he in turn will love unrequited.

The third elegy returns to Tibullus' patron Messala, whom he had clearly accompanied on campaign or at least on the way to his command. Tibullus has fallen sick even before Messala reaches mainland Greece and is left behind in Corcyra, far from Delia. We learn that she worships Isis and has been making vows and prayers for him. Returning to the opening theme of the first elegy, he now longs to be back on his family estate and muses on the joys of the good old days when there was no corruption, no wealth and no war (and not much else – such as agriculture or riding, or house doors and property boundaries! [1.3.41–44]). The poet provides his own epitaph, which represents him only as Messala's faithful follower, then consoles himself that Venus will guide him among the lovers in Elysium. The final picture of this elegy is equally imaginative, of Delia spinning late at night among her maids (like Lucretia or some chaste old-fashioned matron) and rushing to greet him when he arrives unannounced.

Did elite Romans read these outpourings as based on fact? That this wellborn young officer of Messala was in love with a woman who apparently passed from one protector to another, and, so it appears, was influenced by their wealth? This clearly was no senator's virgin daughter or citizen wife. Delia's Greek name can be read as a poetic pseudonym, but her lifestyle cannot be explained away. She is represented as a kept woman, and these midnight assignations with his great love can have nothing to do with the kind of marriage his late father would have wanted Tibullus to make. But perhaps no one expected the audience or private readers of this poetry to treat it as fact. Certainly, Tibullus' next elegy (with two others, 1.8 and 9) is concerned with a different orientation – the love of boys. In fact, he contrasts his own love of the boy Marathus with the love life of his friend Titius, now under the thumb of a new wife (1.4.73–5). As if to confirm that this is all fantasy, Tibullus will pass within ten lines from begging this boy to spare him (a euphemism for gratifying his sexual demands [1.4.83]) to begging the same mercy from Delia, in the name of their secret lovemaking (*furtivi foedera lecti*) and in return for his vows and prayers when she lay sick (1.5.9–17). But no! Another is enjoying her favours.

Tibullus' elegies are particularly kaleidoscopic in their discontinuous sequences of vignettes and their pretence of three diverse love-objects: the half-faithful Delia, the boy Marathus and the shamelessly mercenary Nemesis of his second collection. Other elegies present his patron Messala and friends Cornutus and Macer (compare Titius mentioned above) in the normal social context of marriage and a life of politics or military service or land-owning. In contrast, the love elegies of his near-contemporary from Assisi, Sextus Propertius, name only one beloved, Cynthia, and tend to presuppose shifting phases in a single affair. Cynthia too dominates her lover, but Propertius also has a prominent patron. This man, the aristocratic careerist Volcacius Tullus, can be contrasted with a number of named companions whose interests are limited to partying and love affairs. Far more than Tibullus, Propertius makes it explicit that his desires determine his lifestyle and the values that have led him to reject a respectable career. He not only refuses to marry some respectable young woman to satisfy current legislation, but sees his possession of Cynthia during a night of love as a conquest greater than the triumph of Agamemnon over Troy.[2] Not any the less for that, these elegists thrive on rejection. They share a yearning for a woman who is sexually available – but not to them, or not now, though she has once been theirs. How would an impressionable teenaged girl react to hearing or reading such erotic tales? Would she not feel that she was excluded from a more exciting world and doomed to be treated without passion as some husband's fixed and obligatory companion?

We seem to know how one teenaged girl reacted. Certainly the six poems of Messala's niece, the girl Sulpicia, copy in mirror fashion the despairs and (much less frequent) ecstasies of the male poets. They are very short, little more than forty lines in all, and seem to me so emotionally immature in their rapturous exhibitionism that if they were not written by a young girl they must have been composed 'in character' to impersonate one. Sulpicia[3] scorns a pseudonym: she names herself as her father's daughter, but adopts the male practice of giving a pseudonym to the beloved. She loves Cerinthus and is bitter and angry when her guardian insists on taking her to the country to spend her birthday away from him, then overjoyed because they have come together and she is now his. In fact, she is ecstatic just because she is now known and said by others to be his.

Is this the daughter of a noble Roman family? Why would her guardian allow her to write or recite such things (let alone actually consummate an extramarital affair)? Who would marry her after reading her poems? One strangeness is the name 'Cerinthus'. The many foreign women who lived by their sexual charms regularly adopted elegant Greek names (if they did not have one of their own), but they had no male counterparts apart from the sexy boys like Marathus who lived by appealing to men. So Cerinthus should surely be read as the nom de plume of some young student or officer such as Tibullus. Various explanations have been offered – of which the easiest to accept may be that she is writing as a married woman, and the man here called by the Greek name 'Cerinthus' is in fact her Roman husband, the friend addressed by Tibullus as 'Cornutus'.[4] Her readers would know she was merely adding the spice of clandestine romance to celebrating the joys of her marriage bed. We could then relate this romance to the Cornutus whose birthday Tibullus himself celebrates in 2.2, and whose birthday wish is that his wife may stay faithful to him, as she surely will, since he has wearied the gods with such wishes (2.2.11–12). Surely any girl who read such poetry would be envious of this young woman's liberty and set up a private standard in her heart of the emotions and experiences she aspired to?

Given the ambiguous status of Sulpicia's poems, it may be more informative to consider the larger body of Propertius' elegies. The opening elegy of his second book of love poetry, dedicated to Maecenas, shows that his first book, the *Monobiblos* written around 29 BCE, had won the patronage of Augustus' great friend and cultural adviser. It would be easy for this poetry to reach young Julia. Even if she was too young to read Propertius' first book on its publication, she would be old enough to want to read his second and third books, published between 27 and 25 BCE. From Propertius she would have come to know a more sociable, party-going world of sexual freedom than Tibullus' rather private dream of living for his beloved Delia and his patron Messala.

The very first poem of Propertius opens with the name of his beloved, Cynthia, and confesses his enslavement to his young patron Volcacius Tullus (addressed in four poems of Book 1). The same poem, designed as his self-presentation, appeals to his friends to rescue him from his crazy passion, if only by sweeping him away from Cynthia and Rome. Book 1 is full of friends such as the poets Bassus and Ponticus and Gallus – or even two men called Gallus (the addressee of 1.20 may well be a different man from the close friend addressed in 1.5, 10 and 13), but while Propertius contrasts his own abject submission to love with Tullus' service as a dutiful aristocrat pursuing his political career as aide-de-camp to his uncle as Governor of Asia

(1.6), he associates his other friends only with his or their love life: Bassus' denigration of Cynthia; the epic poet Ponticus' early contempt for love, followed by his surrender to passion (1.7, then 1.9); Gallus' attempt to seduce Cynthia (1.5) and later involvement with an unnamed beloved. These men seemingly live in a world of parties (*convivia*) that the modern popular press might have called voyeuristic orgies. Twice Propertius speaks with sympathetic relish of observing Gallus' lovemaking with the unnamed girl (1.10 and 13). While these parties are most often the site of malicious gossip (2.9.22, 2.16.5–6, 2.30.1), they involve heavy drinking by both sexes that may turn men and women alike to jealous violence, as in 3.8, when Cynthia curse Propertius and throws her wine cup at him.

Outside the parties, the city itself is the setting for both rendezvous and actual intercourse. A great favourite, later celebrated by Ovid, was Pompey's portico

> with the shade of its colonnade, glorious with brocaded awnings, and the dense avenues of matched plane trees and streams springing from sleepy Maro, with the plash of waters splashing around the basin when the Triton suddenly spills back the fountain.
>
> (2.32.10–16)

For more clandestine night escapades, Propertius' last book recalls Cynthia escaping through her window to range around the low-class Subura and mate with him under his cloak at street intersections (4.7.15–20). This woman is not hampered by a stern father, or indeed any family, and can go off with young men on trips to nearby Tibur and Praeneste, Tusculum, Aricia and Lanuvium (2.32.1–10, 4.8.3–18). An early elegy (1.15) imagines Cynthia at the pleasure resort of Baiae, swimming and boating, no doubt in male company, and another, more in the vein of Tibullus, reports that she is in the country, where he hopes she is safe from other men and intends to join her. Later elegies are concerned with love between Roman husbands and wives: Propertius celebrates a military expedition setting out for Arabia (3.4–5), but later in the same book reproaches a husband, Gallus, for going on campaign and leaving his loving wife (3.12). The third elegy of Book 4 is a reproachful letter from a Roman wife under the Greek nom de plume of 'Arethusa' to her husband who has already been away for three years campaigning against the Parthians.[5] While young Roman gentlemen served as army officers or travelled on tours of duty, as Tullus did, or went east to Greece and Asia Minor as cultural tourists, the elegist also writes, as did his predecessor Cornelius Gallus,[6] of his beloved leaving Italy for wilder lands. In 1.8, Cynthia is about to set off for Illyria, but is persuaded by his pleas to stay behind. Why would any woman go to unpacified and undeveloped Illyria? The answer seems to come in Propertius' next book, where his starting point in 2.16 is the return from Illyria of Cynthia's rich protector, the Praetor, bringing her luxurious gifts and occupying her bed. (If she had gone, it would have been as this man's bed-mate.) In this poem, Cynthia is abused as a gold-digger, indifferent to men's status and interested only in weighing their purses. How real is this? Certainly Illyria was the scene of military campaigning in the late 30s and early 20s, and such campaigns would be commanded by a man of praetorian rank. There were few enough praetors fighting in Illyria that it might seem possible to identify this rival. In other elegies, more like romantic fantasy, Propertius himself is marooned on a deserted shore, (1.18 and 19) or Cynthia is shipwrecked and near to drowning – he delights in imagining a romantic sharing of death before settling for a happy ending in which a cultured and poetry-loving dolphin emerges to rescue her (2.26a).

Was Cynthia an actual woman of whom some or all of this was true? It is most unlikely. The key may lie in Elegy 2.7, which opens

> Surely Cynthia rejoiced that the law has been repealed which made us both weep long in the past when it was decreed, for fear it should sever us. And yet not Jupiter himself can separate lovers against their will. But Caesar is mighty! Yes, Caesar is mighty in warfare; but conquered nations have no power over love.
>
> (2.7.1–7)

For a century or more, scholars tried to explain the elegy in terms of either an early Augustan law on marriage, decreed and then repealed under pressure of public resentment or a law merely proposed and withdrawn – something that Propertius' language does not permit. (We will discuss what this law could have been in the second part of this chapter.) The other issue, which concerns us more closely, is to understand why Propertius could not marry Cynthia herself. In the second part of the elegy (8–14) the poet assumes that if he married he would have to wed some other woman, and that the law is designed to produce legitimate sons to fight for Rome. He angrily rejects the idea of bearing children to serve in the army and shed their blood for Roman triumphs.[7] He protests that for him a marriage that forced him to pass by her door would be worse than death (2.7.10–11) and their love is worth more to him than the name of father.

This goes against the most solemn of Roman elite values: to perpetuate the family by bearing a son. Here is a poet advocating 'making love, not war', seeing the campaign of love for his girl as the 'real' military service; disgusted by past civil conflicts, he chooses to live for pleasure – what stern fathers called *nequitia*, worthless indulgence. And the survival of his poetry shows that his message was as welcome to many readers as his talent. But why couldn't Propertius marry his Cynthia? Either she was one of the many unattached women legally ineligible for marriage because they were from Greece or the Near East, without Roman citizenship, or perhaps she was a citizen but had earned a reputation for promiscuity that made her socially ineligible. Far more likely, however, is that she was in fact married, and that this relationship was adulterous. Do we have a hint of this in the one elegy of Book 1 that seems totally detached from either Propertius or his friends? This is Elegy 1.16, the lament of the door to an aristocratic house:

> I who was once opened for great triumphs, dedicated to Patrician chastity, whose threshold gilded chariots thronged, and most with the pleas of suppliant prisoners of war, am now abused by the brawls of drunken men and beaten by unfit hands. Shameful garlands are constantly hung from me, with torches left to witness the men shut out. I cannot defend myself against the slander of my dishonoured mistress, noble as I am but abandoned to dirty songs; she cannot be reformed to spare her reputation by ceasing to live more disgracefully than the low morals of our age.
>
> (1.16.1–10)

The door then reports a sample lament by a lover, excluded, not because this woman is faithful to her husband, but because she is sleeping with a rival (1.16.31–32). This kind of door song (*paraclausithuron*) had become traditional in Rome and Italy with Plautus and Catullus,[8] but the tradition, which came from Greek comedy and epigram, had normally presupposed that the lady of the house was a professional courtesan, not a wife. The change to explicit or implied adultery was new with Catullus' love for Lesbia in the generation before Propertius. Can we imagine how a girl like Julia, with a sternly omnipresent and omnipotent father, would feel reading about the liberty of these contemporary men and their women? She may not have known Propertius' early poetry, since she was a pre-teen when this elegy was written and most likely published.[9] But his third book affirms his fame and his popularity with precisely her kind of reader – with young men and girls awaiting a rendezvous.[10]

Did Julia hear this poem recited, or even read it in secret? Nothing could come closer than Elegy 1.16 to the reputation that she would leave behind her at the time of her disgrace. Propertius speaks more than once of a society in which adultery is pervasive, and his older contemporary, the unmarried Horace, makes female adultery with the connivance of indifferent husbands the key to Roman decay.[11] We will see in the next section that once adultery was made into a public offence, it would be necessary for poets (and less poetic members of the elite) to disguise the nature of their own love affairs in order to avoid prosecution.

Legislating morality

One reason that scholars reading Propertius 2.7 were so quick to deduce early Augustan legislation penalizing those slow to marry must have been the tone and preoccupations of Horace's collection of three books of odes. Horace begins the last of his 'Roman Odes', composed before 23 BCE, by warning his Roman audience that they will continue to suffer divine punishment for their ancestors' sins (of civil war) until they have restored the temples of the gods. It was much easier to restore temples than restore morality and family values. Octavian set about rebuilding even before he became Augustus. By the time he composed his *Res gestae* (*Record of Achievements*) he could claim to have restored some eighty-two temples. But Horace's central theme is moral decay. This is seen most strongly in *Odes* 3.6, where the opening motif is the guilt of civil war, but the message turns to an indictment of women and their sexual behaviour: 'generations fertile in guilt first polluted marriage and descent and families'. The fertility should of course have produced legitimate sons to fight for Rome, but

> as soon as she is grown, the young girl delights to learn suggestive Ionian dancing and moulds herself to trickery: already she is preoccupied from top to toe in plotting impure love affairs: soon she seeks out younger adulterers during her husband's drinking parties, not fastidious about the men to whom she gives forbidden pleasures once the lights are removed: instead she openly leaves the room with her husband's connivance, whether it is a workshop manager or the master of a Spanish ship who invites her, lavish purchasers of her shameful behaviour.
>
> (*Odes* 3.6.21–32)

Here something not far from hypocrisy is compounded with snobbery, as if it were morally worse for the bride to commit adultery with a man below her own class. But did Horace know people who behaved like this? Well, yes, and in the best circles. According to Antony, quoted by Suetonius, the young Octavian had openly led a consul's wife away from her husband's party to a bedroom, bringing her back to her husband blushing and dishevelled. Indeed, the wife of Horace's own friend and patron Maecenas, Terentia, is one of the four matrons named by Antony as Octavian's mistresses within the first decade of his marriage to Livia.[12] Suetonius has just declared in his own person that not even Augustus' friends denied his adulteries but explained them as politically necessary means of obtaining knowledge of conspiracies! The following chapter (70) in which Suetonius reports Octavian's 'Dinner of the Twelve Gods', at which he dressed up as Apollo, will give some idea of the future Pontifex Maximus' respect for the gods of Rome.

We saw that Propertius was alert to rumours that the newly glorified Augustus was planning to suppress immorality by legislation. These plans may be the occasion for another Horatian ode focused on the theme of sexual licence. *Odes* 3.24 begins with the theme of the noble savage, praising the simple morality of the nomadic Scythian in whose homes innocent wives gently guide motherless stepsons, and no dowered woman controls her husband or boasts of a sleek adulterer:

> The integrity of parents is the greatest dowry, as is chastity in a firm
> marriage bond, shunning contact with another man, the fact that sinning
> is evil and its penalty death. If any man will put an end to impious
> slaughter and civil rage, if he desires the name of Father of Cities
> inscribed upon his statues let him dare to curb untamed wantonness.
>
> (3.24.17–28)

Was Horace encouraging the ruler? Or responding to the ruler's own
request for public support? Despite Propertius' Elegy 2.7, there is no evidence
for any moral legislation in these early years, but Augustus may well have
followed up his purge of the Senate in 28–27[13] by circulating the possibility
of morality laws to gauge public response. If so, he was clearly discouraged
from immediate action. The most thorough reconsideration of the Propertian
elegy, by Ernst Badian,[14] has offered a relatively simple explanation of the
newly repealed law. This was not, Badian argues, a recent law of Augustus
– indeed, the Latin words *qua quondam edicta* ('when it was once decreed')
put the law into the distant past – but one of many triumviral laws repealed
en bloc when Augustus 'restored the republican constitution' in 27. Among
the various laws decreed by triumviral edict to raise funds for warfare,
Badian suggests the revival of an old republican tax on unmarried men, the
aes uxorium. Such a tax would be applied only after the normal age of
marriage (around twenty-five for men) and so might not initially have
affected young Propertius. But Badian's re-examination of the apparent
references to early legislation in Dio, Velleius and other historians has made
it clear that no legislation was formally proposed or passed by decree in
the decade before 20 BCE.

There is one less stringent form of moral legislation that may have been
enacted before the main legislation of 18 BCE. As Ovid makes clear, young
men used to go to the theatre and chariot games to pick up women,
especially the free-living foreign girls. But while seating in the circus was
'general admission' and the would-be lover could hope to meet a charming
companion there, Augustus had regulated seating in the theatre (and
probably Rome's new amphitheatre as well). The architecture of his new
theatre of Marcellus and the refurbished theatre of Pompey was clearly
articulated by gangways and tiers, allocated on principles of social hierarchy, with senators and other office-holders seated in the front rows or
orchestra, followed by fourteen rows assigned to the *equites* (wealthy
businessmen or landowners). There were also wedge-shaped units (*cunei*)
assigned to boys below the age of manhood, with another unit alongside for
their escorts (*paedagogi*). Other units were allocated to the Praetorian
guard[15] or to important men for their distribution to favoured supporters.
Women, on the other hand, were seen as a distraction and relegated to the
high tiers at the back of the auditorium, involving a strenuous climb and an
inferior view to that enjoyed by their husbands. There is no evidence that the
new *Lex Iulia Theatralis* separated senatorial wives, mothers and daughters

from humble but respectable citizen wives or even from the provocative ladies of pleasure, but given the moral principles involved, there surely must have been a separation. So when Ovid recommended attending the theatre to pick up a new girl,[16] he had in mind only the period when they were entering or leaving the show. But Augustus may have gone further in his prohibitions: the marriage legislation of 18 BCE is usually taken to have excluded those who persevered as bachelors and unmarried women beyond the age of marriage (twenty-five for men, twenty for women) from attending all public shows (*spectacula*).[17]

By 19 BCE, when Augustus was offered the supervision of laws and morality (*cura legum ac morum*), an equivalent to the republican censorship,[18] he had more drastic measures in mind, perhaps working with a timetable that required enactment of the 'reforms' before he could hold the great Secular Games of 17. Although he was undoubtedly concerned with larger questions of military manpower, Augustus did not envisage measures to reinforce the rural peasantry from which, as Horace assured his readers (*Odes* 3.6.33–40), the best soldiers would come. Every clause of his legislation *De maritandis ordinibus*, 'on marriage within (or among) the Orders' that is known to us was concerned to preserve the *ordines*, the ranks of senators, wealthy *equites* and freeborn citizens, from contamination. Since the jurists and legal codes that are the sources for Augustus' laws all date at least a century after his death, we must reckon that some provisions represent later modifications. But, as we shall see, Augustus himself had to dilute his more stringent requirements some twenty-five years after the original morality laws. First came the question of rank. There was apparently a shortage of young women (although Dio attests this only for the upper classes), so citizens were allowed to marry freedwomen, that is, women probably of other ethnicity, who had been born slaves – apart from senators and their families. Any son or grandson of a senator who went through marriage with a freedwoman would find his marriage invalid and suffer the new penalties imposed on those who remained unmarried during their reproductive years.[19]

This period was defined as being from age twenty to fifty for women, and twenty-five to sixty for men. While there was no penalty attached to divorce, those divorced within these age limits would have to remarry within a year to escape the penalties attached to celibacy.[20] The new penalties and rewards went hand in hand. Citizens were also prohibited from marrying members of the dishonourable professions (prostitutes, procurers, actors, slave merchants, auctioneers, undertakers, etc.), or rather, if they contracted such marriages, these were not accepted as valid. In contrast, by marrying respectably, a man made himself eligible to be nominated for office, and fatherhood of three children gave him priority over his peers. But by staying celibate he would rule himself out from office and from receiving legacies from friends or inheritances from any but the closest relatives. Sources for both the late republic and early empire show that such legacies were a very important component of any elite man's income – the penalty could have been significant. Wives who gave birth to three children (even if these did not all live beyond infancy) were rewarded with legal and financial independence from the guardians normally imposed on women.[21] This *ius trium liberorum* was also a privilege that could be accorded to men and women regardless of their parental status.[22] When Octavian gave legal and financial independence to his wife Livia and sister Octavia, Octavia had already reared five children, but Livia had only her two sons by Claudius Nero. This may be why some sources believe she had given birth to a still-born child by Augustus.[23]

Of course, it was easy enough to marry without committing oneself to parenthood. Suetonius reports that men evaded the requirement by engaging themselves to girls below puberty and divorcing to suit their convenience, until Augustus restricted the length of betrothals in the later legislation.[24]

Adultery was a different matter. It is clear even from Horace's lurid example and Antony's accusations that much of the problem was the sexual indifference of husbands, who had probably married women for their dowry or their family connections. In the republic, adultery or illicit intercourse by unmarried or widowed citizen women was usually private business handled by family councils, although there are records of public trials, presumably for flagrantly public displays of immorality. Now, however, Augustus made the punishment of adultery the husband's responsibility. If the husband who discovered his wife's adultery did not divorce her and prosecute the woman and her lover within two months of the divorce, any citizen could bring a prosecution both of the guilty parties and of the husband for the offence of pimping.[25] But the woman was the main target; prosecution of the lover depended on the prior conviction of the adulterous wife. The penalties for the convicted wife were exile to an offshore island with confiscation of half her dowry and a third of her other property; she was also rendered *infamis*, that is, disqualified for any valid marriage (to her lover or to any other man). For the lover, the penalty was also exile and confiscation of half of his property. Such legislation would expose any member of the elite with enemies to slander and denunciation, so that it is rather surprising that we hear of so few accusations in the next ten to fifteen years.[26]

Since punishment of guilty women had previously been the province of fathers (if the wife was still under *patria potestas*) or less often of husbands, Augustus left carefully calibrated provisions under which either man could avenge adultery with death. The father could kill the lover on the spot if he caught the couple in the act either at his own home or the marital home, but only if he also killed his daughter. The husband's vengeance was more limited: he could not kill his wife, or even her lover, unless the man was from the dishonoured and disqualified professions, such as an actor or gladiator. It is easy to see why there was this distinction between the rights of father and husband. Not only would a father be more reluctant to kill what might be his only child, but a husband with personal or financial incentives to get rid of an unwanted wife might have found it more convenient to silence her than to divorce her with falsified allegations about money or behaviour.[27]

But as Horace sadly noted in *Odes* 3.24.35, laws without corresponding public moral values – *leges sine moribus* – were ineffective. As with modern laws prohibiting the use or sale of marijuana or anti-abortion laws, once the public ceases to endorse a moral or 'lifestyle' policy, violation of the laws is overlooked by all except personal enemies seeking an excuse for prosecution. A year after this legislation, Horace invoked Diana in the hymn commissioned for the Secular Games to bring forth a new generation and 'favour the decrees of the Senate on marriage, and the law fertile in producing lawful children' (*Carmen Saeculare* 17–20). In a later stanza, he seems to answer that now honour and old-fashioned modesty and neglected virtue were daring to return (57–60). But it is only in his last book of *Odes*, composed between 13 and 8 BCE that Horace reverses his pessimism: 'now no family is polluted by fornication, morality and law [*mos et lex*] have suppressed dirty wickedness, and mothers earn praise for bringing forth children that resemble their fathers, since punishment inevitably overwhelms guilt' (4.5.21–24).[28]

No other source registers a change for the better in smart society, and it is more likely that the poet's proud statement reflects either wishful thinking or the mellowing of perception that should come with age.

It would be satisfying to believe Augustus' laws had been effective, but although ambitious men and families may have taken advantage of the easily won privileges from earlier marriage, historians and biographers have given us no evidence of any pattern of change in public behaviour. On the contrary, Tacitus, writing about the modifications introduced a generation later by the Consuls Papius and Poppaeus,[29] reports in 21 CE (*Annals* 3.25) a further motion to ease the conditions of this law 'which Augustus had passed in his old age after the Julian bills to stimulate penalties for the unmarried and reinforce the treasury'. 'Marriages and childrearing', Tacitus adds, 'had not become more common, with childlessness predominating; instead the crowd of those threatened with prosecution swelled, as every household was undermined by the claims of informers, and society suffered from the laws as it had previously suffered from scandalous behaviour.'

After an interpretive history of previous legislation, the historian returns to the *Lex Papia Poppaea* to stress the law's financial aspect, and its impact on private life. He notes that the rewards it offered imposed spies on any individual who shirked the privileges of parenthood. Although he mentions as a kind of rationale for the legal penalties that the Roman people could claim the disallowed legacies by virtue of the people's role as universal parent (*Annals* 3.28), Tacitus' language could not express more severely the conservative historian's protest at this invasion of privacy and citizen rights. When every prosperous Roman family had households of slaves, privacy was probably an alien concept, but protection from false accusations would be in inverse proportion to the importance of the victim, and no members of any family would be more exposed to such malicious allegations than those closest to imperial power.

4   The rise of Marcus Agrippa

Once young Marcellus had been buried, his widow would be expected to pass the next ten months in mourning, but the daughter of Augustus Caesar could not be left long unmarried. Her father would clearly be taking private thought for this and there are stories that Augustus actually considered avoiding the risks of conferring the unique status of son-in-law on any potential successor by marrying her off to his private friend Proculeius, a man who had held aloof from political life.[1]

Instead, he decided to take as his son-in-law his most long-standing political and military supporter, Marcus Agrippa. After a first marriage to Caecilia Attica, daughter of Pomponius Atticus, the wealthy banker and friend of Cicero,[2] Agrippa had been brought into Octavian's family in 28 BCE as husband of the elder Marcella, by whom he had at least one, if not two daughters. These would still be small children when Augustus and his sister Octavia, Agrippa's mother-in-law, decided on the divorce from Marcella to make him free for remarriage. Marcella was offered to Antony's son Iullus Antonius, whom Octavia had brought up after his mother Fulvia's death and his father's affair with Cleopatra. The stage was now clear.

But who was this Marcus Agrippa? He was not from a senatorial family and probably came from outside Rome itself. In fact although his father's name is recorded as L. Vipsanius Agrippa, no one knew anything about him, not even the kind of crude allegations of low origin or vulgar trade that were common at Rome, and were even broadcast against the father of Octavius himself, a conventional senator who had held a praetorship and provincial governorship before he died. Young Agrippa was already the close friend of Julius Caesar's great-nephew Octavius when Caesar took him to Spain on what would be his first campaign, and he seems to have been with Octavius at Apollonia when the news came of Caesar's assassination. Perhaps Agrippa came from the same small town of Velitrae or had met Octavius at school, but we do not even know whether Octavius was educated at home by a private tutor or attended a local school. If any *grammaticus* like Orbilius had been put in charge of educating the future princeps, we would have expected the man to boast about it in later years. In fact, nothing is known of Octavius' education before Caesar sent him to Apollonia with a Greek philosopher to supervise him while he (and Agrippa, it seems) waited for Caesar to join his legions on the first stage of the campaign against Parthia.

Julia's future husband Agrippa was a man of amazing talent and even more amazing loyalty throughout his life to his friend, the mutating Octavius–Octavian–Augustus. It is only his loyal willingness to support Octavian and the glamour consequent on Octavian's adoption that led contemporaries, and still misleads students of Roman history, into regarding Octavian, rather than his humbler friend, as the architect of Rome's military, economic and social renaissance in the years between 43 BCE and Agrippa's death. Although the *Res gestae*, Augustus' retrospective record of achievements, does not mention Agrippa in reporting his military successes, Agrippa contributed more than his share in the history of those years, and his career as a commander on land and especially on sea, as well as his services to the city of Rome, deserve a chapter of their own.

In 43, before Julia was born, the twenty-year-old Agrippa had shown his loyalty to Caesar's memory by prosecuting Caesar's assassin Cassius for parricide as defined under the *Lex Pedia*:[3] we know this only because the historian Velleius Paterculus proudly reported (Velleius 2.69.5) that his senatorial uncle Capito acted as Agrippa's secondary prosecutor. Cassius himself was safely out of reach in Asia, so we can treat this as a political act – a show prosecution. What the episode does suggest is that Agrippa as tribune of the people was demonstrating the people's desire to avenge Caesar's murder. This office and this prosecution would be his first step on the political ladder. He was still too junior to hold a command in the campaign of the triumvirs Octavian and Antony against Brutus and Cassius which ended in the victory of Philippi, but by 41 Agrippa was acting as one of the commanders of Octavian's forces in the civil conflict against Lucius Antonius and Antony's wife Fulvia, and modern historians[4] claim that it was Agrippa's strategic occupation of the town of Sutrium that drove Lucius Antonius' forces to take refuge in the city of Perusia, which Octavian besieged and finally took by storm.

Octavian executed many of the Roman supporters of Lucius and more or less destroyed the city, confiscating its lands. Indeed there were rumours that he had made a human sacrifice to the shades of his father Julius of some 300 senators and knights. The episode left bad memories, not least for the poet Propertius who had lost kinsmen and probably property in the defeat of his townsfolk.

Since Caesar's first dictatorship, the magistracies at Rome had been largely predetermined: Caesar had decided who should become Praetor or Consul for up to three years ahead of the elections, and this pattern seems to have continued. Agrippa was nominated as a candidate for the praetorship of 40 BCE and duly elected. In fact, a happy coincidence found him Urban Praetor, the magistrate with the most power to affect life in the city, not just through presiding over the courts but through his presidency of the more important public games. This position must certainly have made Agrippa's name and won him immense popularity. Of course, he would have to spend his own fortune on providing the most lavish games, but this fortune had been considerably increased by his acquisition of the confiscated property of Brutus after Philippi, and would be lavishly supported by his wealthy father-in-law Atticus. Indeed, Agrippa may already, as some historians report, have been able to finance the renovation of some aqueducts and the construction of the new Aqua Julia. We know that in July he celebrated the Games of Apollo (*Ludi Apollinares*) with two whole days of chariot races in the circus, and revived the antiquarian *Lusus Troiae*, the supposedly traditional Trojan Show, an equestrian display by elite boys below the age of manhood (who would later form Rome's cavalry commanders). But unlike the urban praetors of the late republic, Agrippa was also needed to deal with military emergencies outside Rome. This was the year in which Sextus Pompeius used his official naval command in southern Italy to make pirate attacks on ships carrying the grain supply and raid Italian coastal towns, and Sextus was joined in this by Mark Antony, who attacked and seized Sipontum. It was Agrippa who confronted both enemies and restored sufficient control of the coastal waters to make possible the agreement of Brundisium that reaffirmed the division of the eastern and western empire between Octavian and Antony and secured the supposed cooperation of Sextus. As we showed in the previous chapter, this agreement was confirmed by the marriages of Antony with Octavia and Octavian with Scribonia.

With calm apparently restored, Agrippa could follow his praetorship with a proconsular command in Gaul in 39 BCE, where he operated in both the south-west and the central-eastern area, crossing the Rhine. But although his campaigns were successful, he chose not to send dispatches to the Senate that would justify requesting a triumph.[5] In fact, despite his successful independent campaigns and his collaboration in all Octavian's major battles, Agrippa avoided any hint of competition with his great friend: he would never celebrate a triumph of his own. In the complex pattern of Octavian's and Agrippa's provincial campaigns, the two were usually complementary. Octavian conducted operations in the province briefly this year but had to return to Rome to deal with new troubles from Sextus in Italy. This was the year in which he met Livia, the wife of Tiberius Nero, and would initiate divorce of his new wife Scribonia when she delivered her daughter Julia.

But Octavian's personal life was necessarily confined to the winter, before the renewal of military operations in spring 38. Relations with Sextus Pompey again broke down in 37, when Agrippa was Consul for the first time. He had realized that it was essential for Octavian to control his own fleet, and for this he had begun, probably in 38, to construct a new harbour and naval facilities relatively near to Rome in Campania. At whatever date Agrippa was actually given official appointment as Admiral (*Praefectus classis*), he had begun to organize the creation of the new fleet and was training its sailors in Campania. Velleius, who pays tribute to Agrippa's energy and urgency, reports that he was commissioned to construct ships and collect marines and rowers, training them in naval exercises and manoeuvres.[6] For this purpose, he had begun engineering operations near Cumae, north of Naples. Felling the forests around Lake Avernus, where he built the new fleet of warships, Agrippa used both Avernus itself for naval drills and the Lucrine lake, which he expanded and shaped by raising moles between this coastal water and the sea and cutting a canal for naval access. Augustan writers such as Virgil and Propertius[7] remember this more as a daring feat of engineering than for its service to the naval programme that Agrippa had in mind. To this day, visitors to the area (still subject to slow shifting of ground levels) can visit the *Piscina mirabilis,* or Marvellous Pool, an immense underground fresh-water reservoir constructed by Agrippa to supply the naval base at Misenum. Without these preparations, the struggle against Sextus Pompey's naval raids would never have ended in victory. But with his new fleet of 300 ships, Octavian could even survive the serious losses of a storm off western Sicily, and the threefold attack that he mounted on all three coasts of Sicily in 36 was successful, thanks above all to Agrippa's interim victory at Mylae and his strategy for their joint victory at Naulochus. Sextus Pompey knew he could not survive his losses in wrecked and captured ships and abandoned Sicily to die a fugitive in Asia. Octavian himself recognized Agrippa's role in planning (and winning) this victory with an entirely new honour, the golden Naval Crown which is often featured on coinage honouring Agrippa.[8] The Senate would later decree that Agrippa could wear this crown in all military ceremonies.

This victory was decisive. The removal of Sextus at last freed Octavian from the political nightmare of famine at Rome, and the year 33 saw the first of his minor campaigns in Illyria. (There were always tribes to fight in Illyria with what Syme has called 'the promise of cheap blood' (Syme 1939). Besides, Illyria was on the edge of the agreed boundary between Octavian's and Antony's areas of responsibility and near enough to Antony's base in Athens, should he decide to direct his energies westwards.) What was Agrippa doing? He had, after all, been Consul in 37 and exercised command in 36. He chose a position that would surprise students of republican politics, the ostensibly backwards step of becoming Curule Aedile. But this office, while it called upon the holder to spend considerable funds on games and urban monuments, brought with it enormous scope for popularity.[9]

Agrippa had already earned this kind of goodwill from his year as Urban Praetor in 40. In fact, historians admit they cannot be sure which of Agrippa's benefactions to Rome belonged to that earlier office. More than anything else, Rome was suffering from neglected and damaged water supplies. Just as the water and sewage systems of London and New York, dating from the turn of the nineteenth century, now regularly spring leaks, flooding subways and streets, so Rome's four existing aqueducts had become silted up and the supply weakened by illicit diversion into private houses.

The *Encyclopedia* of the elder Pliny is perhaps the earliest source for Agrippa's aedileship, but it seems Pliny did not consult Agrippa directly.[10]

Thanks to Frontinus, who was Water Commissioner (*Curator Aquarum*) a century after Agrippa, we know how Agrippa now set about repairing these aqueducts. Even before election to office, he had restored the Aqua Marcia at his own expense. He now restored the Aqua Appia and Anio Vetus. Either in 40 or this year, he drew on a series of sources along the Via Latina to supplement the Aqua Tepula and construct his new Aqua Julia. From the restored aqueducts, according to Pliny (*Natural History* 36.21), he supplied the city with 700 open pools, 130 reservoirs and 500 fountains. To ensure that, henceforward, water supplies would be well maintained, he created and took on the post of Water Commissioner and organized crews of 200 public slaves to supervise the maintenance. The same work crews would surely also maintain the drainage system that he had overhauled, giving special attention to the centuries-old Cloaca Maxima.[11] Thirteen years later, Agrippa would again create a new aqueduct, the Aqua Virgo.[12] Perhaps this was the occasion when Augustus retorted to an urban crowd demanding free wine, 'Hasn't my son-in-law supplied you with enough water?' (Suet. *Augustus* 42.1). Thanks to Agrippa's work as Water Commissioner both in 33 and in the years after Actium, Rome would be reorganized into fourteen districts, each well supplied with pure water.

Besides this radical improvement to the water supply, Agrippa also took care of the safe storage of the public grain supply in the new warehouses (*Horrea Agrippiana*) that he constructed between the Forum and the Vicus Iugarius. And anticipating the traditional slogan of 'bread and circuses', Agrippa now remodelled the Circus Maximus, Rome's favourite show-place, with new fountains in the form of dolphins and a new mechanism for counting the laps. He himself recorded in his memoirs that during his aedileship he had given public games lasting fifty-nine days and paid for free entrance to 170 public baths, though Pliny, who is our source, regards this number as small in comparison with the number of baths in his own time.[13]

As the next year began, Octavian made the political schism with Antony so apparent that the Consuls Sosius and Domitius Ahenobarbus, both partisans of Antony, left Rome and moved to Egypt followed by several hundred senators. Agrippa's popularity had assured Octavian of the support of Rome itself, and the year 32 was devoted to securing the loyalty of the Italians with an oath sworn first by *tota Italia*, then by the western provinces.[14]

But it was again Agrippa who won the decisive victory, first by his strategy in systematically excluding Antony's fleets from the west-coast harbours of Greece. He seized Methone, the southernmost port of the Peloponnese, sailed north to occupy Corcyra, then took possession of the island of Leucas, which almost closed the mouth of the gulf of Ambracia, and made a rapid expedition to secure Patras and Corinth.[15] Thus, the fleets of Antony and Cleopatra were virtually trapped in the gulf. What would later be portrayed as their flight was in a sense their escape from this trap. On 2 September (some say 3 September), the wind rose, favouring an engagement. Agrippa was officially the Admiral on the flagship of Octavian's fleet, facing Antony's own squadron, while it seems that Octavian himself sailed on a smaller and more nimble Liburnian ship that would not expect to engage. It was by enticing Antony's left wing northwards away from his centre and right wing that Agrippa created the space through which Cleopatra and her sixty ships now escaped – or fled – followed by Antony himself. But the official version recorded by Virgil is far more memorable: in the god Vulcan's depiction of the battle on the shield of Aeneas, Augustus' four lines (678–81) are almost matched by the next three lines (682–4) giving (not quite) equal prominence to Agrippa:

> You would see all Leucas seething with arrays for combat and the waves glittering with gold. On this side Augustus Caesar was leading the Italians into battle, with senate and people, Rome's Penates and the Great Gods, standing on the lofty bridge, as his joyous brow emitted twin flames and his father's comet was revealed at his head. On the other side Agrippa with winds and gods favouring him, aloft and leading his battle line: his brow crowned with the ship's beaks gleams with the proud adornment of war.[16]

But while the flames of the future Augustus' brow are poetic and supernatural, Agrippa was indeed wearing the naval crown that he had earned at Naulochus. Antony himself, clad in barbarian finery, is soon eclipsed by the poet's description of the Queen summoning up with her foreign rattle (the sistrum) and zoomorphic Egyptian gods (695–8), her battle lines of sinister foreign peoples instantaneously routed by the archer god Apollo from his temple high on the promontory of Actium (704–6). As Cleopatra sails away, the poet stresses her pallor and panic, then cuts to Egypt itself and the god of the river Nile opening his many arms to welcome and protect its queen. Propertius too, writing after Virgil, focuses on Apollo, who alights on the prow of Octavian's flagship, uttering a long speech of encouragement to his protégé (Propertius 4.6.27–54). In Propertius' panegyrical fantasy, the opening shot from Apollo's bow is followed by the cast of Caesar's spear: 'Rome triumphs through Apollo's guarantee and the woman is punished as her shattered sceptre floats on the Ionian waters . . . and she makes for the Nile, mistakenly relying on her fugitive vessel' (4.6.55–8, 4.6.63).[17] There is no mention of Agrippa, only of the god Julius looking down from his star and confirming his son's divine status.

In fact it would take Octavian another year to establish his authority over Roman Asia and Syria and the various royal protectorates before he entered Alexandria on 1 August 30 BCE.

Agrippa did not follow Octavian through Asia to Egypt but returned to Italy, because Octavian could not be sure that his forces would accept his authority if it were only delegated to the civilian Maecenas.[18] Neither man held office, but, as Roddaz (1984) argues, they controlled affairs only because they were accepted as representatives of Octavian himself. Even so, Agrippa had to urge Octavian to return to Italy early in 30 to appease the potential mutiny of his veterans. He dealt with this crisis at Brundisium with promises of land settlement. It is difficult to see how Maecenas was valuable, except as a recognized mouthpiece of Octavian in the private lobbying that dominates most oligarchies; the senators may have been more willing to take guidance from a blue-blooded Etruscan 'born of ancestral kings' than the military commoner Agrippa. On the other hand, Agrippa, as an ex-consul, could speak early in any senatorial debate and was no doubt invited to give his official opinion first, since he was understood to represent the wishes of Octavian. Certainly, Agrippa and Maecenas administered affairs at Rome without further trouble until Octavian's return for his triumph in August 29.

His triumph did not extend to include a partner, but Agrippa was now officially honoured with a naval standard and would be rewarded both by his later representation on Octavian's coinage and more concretely with Antony's possessions, including the former mansion of Pompey which Antony himself had received after Pharsalus.[19] Something of the importance of this house can be seen from the fact that Octavian encouraged Agrippa to move into this residence in 29, jointly with Rome's most senior republican figure, Messala Corvinus. Exactly what did this mean? These wealthy men did not need houses: both Agrippa and Messala already had mansions in Rome; Agrippa had a home on the Campus Martius and, as we shall see, may have already owned a more expansive villa on the original site of the Renaissance Villa Farnesina in Trastevere. Presumably the house, especially since it was to be shared with Messala, was kept available for Agrippa's use rather than his main domicile. He had married Octavian's niece Marcella in 28, and it seems hardly likely that the couple would want to live in such an arrangement. It is more significant that when the house burned down in 27, Agrippa was invited by the newly renamed Augustus to move into his own Palatine home as *synoikos* (house-mate).[20] The eleven-year-old Julia was presumably living with her father and stepmother in this palace complex, but it is most unlikely that she took any interest in her father's 'middle-aged' friend.

We should think of Rome in these years as full of excitement but also of noise, dust and disorder arising from large construction projects. In particular, the temple of Palatine Apollo,[21] which Octavian had vowed in Spain in 36, had begun to rise alongside Octavian's own residence in 36 and would be dedicated along with its porticoes and Greek and Latin libraries in 28 BCE. This will have been taking place under young Julia's eyes until she reached the age of ten.

But while Agrippa did not share the glory of Octavian's three days of triumph, or his consulship of 29 BCE, he was now treated by Octavian as his collaborator on equal terms and chosen as his colleague in the consulships of both 28 and 27. Dio stresses the symbolic alternation of the fasces between the two Consuls and their collegial role in conducting the census. The future

Princeps wanted a colleague of equal seniority to affirm his republican spirit, but he also needed someone who would share his policies. Without holding the actual censorship, Octavian and Agrippa now exercised the powers of censors to conduct the first genuine census of citizens and their property status for over forty years, but this process also had a political purpose and effect: part of the censors' duties consisted in reviewing the fitness of individual senators to serve in the Senate, and Octavian needed to do this in order to purge the Senate's accumulation of followers of Antony and probably of Sextus Pompeius. But on this occasion he does not mention this or any act he imposed on the Senate, his supposed partner in government. Only the creation of new patrician families, which probably included Agrippa and his descent, and the universal census of citizens are listed after the report of his triumviral powers early in the *Res gestae*.

> In my fifth consulship I increased the number of patricians on the instruction of both people and senate. I revised the roll of the senate three times. In my sixth consulship *with Marcus Agrippa as colleague* I carried out a census of the people and I performed a lustrum after a lapse of forty-two years.[22] [emphasis added]

This was the first census completed since Julius Caesar's enfranchisement of Cisalpine Gaul – roughly equivalent to modern Lombardy and Veneto – and Augustus proudly records a total of over 4 million citizens.

The year 28 also saw Agrippa as co-president with Octavian over the Actian Games, adding circus races, a gymnastic contest and gladiatorial contests. It was one of the frequent occasions on which Octavian himself was taken ill, and Dio records that Agrippa took over the duties of both presidents. In 27, however, Octavian staged his grand formal restoration of the republic to the Senate (and of course the Roman people). This consisted chiefly of giving responsibility to the Senate for the government of the non-military provinces. Receiving in return the carefully chosen new title of Augustus, he soon left Rome for the provinces of Gaul, which needed a reorganization of their administrative structure, and Spain. Agrippa would have been the only consul functioning at Rome, but he was content to remain at Rome without office for the year 26 and two further years. He had his own agenda of completing an expansion of the monumental core of the city on the relatively undeveloped area of the Campus Martius.

Augustus himself boasts of completing two of Julius Caesar's projects: first, the new Forum Iulium containing the temple of Venus Genetrix (Venus as ancestress of the *gens Iulia*), planned by Caesar as early as 54, and dedicated by him in 46, but still incomplete, then the Basilica Iulia (*Res gestae* 20.3). He also saw to completion and dedicated a few days after his triple triumph, on 18 August 29 BCE, the temple of the Deified Caesar in the republican forum that had been vowed by the triumvirs in 42 BCE.[23] In 27, Agrippa took on the completion of two secular projects begun by Caesar on the western part of the Campus Martius before adding his own imaginative complex. The first Caesarian project was the vast marble porticoed space called the Saepta Iulia, which Julius Caesar had begun to plan well before the civil war. It had been partially constructed by the unlamented Lepidus before his disgrace, but remained incomplete. This was originally designed to provide voting enclosures for the public assemblies, but these now met seldom and had little effect on political elections or decisions. After Agrippa completed and dedicated the building in 26, it would usually function as a magnificent site for concerts and public occasions. Agrippa also began the Diribitorium, the building originally intended for the counting of votes and situated next to the south face of the Saepta, but did not live to see its completion.[24]

However, if young Julia was allowed to leave the Palatine under safe escort to walk as far as the Campus Martius, she must have been fascinated by Agrippa's most spectacular project of civic planning. Echoing the splendid projects of Pompey who used part of the Campus Martius to give Rome both its first monumental theatre and splendid parks lined with Greek statuary in the 50s, Agrippa now undertook a larger complex of parks and buildings. For its effects, this depended on the increased supply of pure water from the Aqua Virgo, whether he had actually completed that aqueduct in 33, or was only now carrying it to completion. Agrippa now laid out a huge ornamental pool, big enough not only for swimming but also for pleasure boats, the Stagnum Agrippae, fed by the Aqua Virgo and drained by an ornamental canal, the Euripus, that led to the bank of the Tiber, surrounded by tree-lined walks.[25] The pool was placed alongside the magnificent baths, the Thermae Agrippae, of which the *laconicum*, or hot chamber, was the first part to be built, its foyer and steam rooms lined with marble panelling and precious statues and paintings.[26] When the exiled Ovid looks back sadly to the Rome he will never see again, he speaks longingly,

> now my mind sees with the eyes of the imagination the forums, the temples, the theatres covered with marble, each portico raised on levelled ground, now the lawns of the Campus [Martius] that gazes on the beautiful gardens, the pools and Euripus canal and the waters drawn from the [Aqua] Virgo.[27]
>
> (*Ex Ponto* 1.8.35–6)

Between the pool and the Saepta with its Portico of the Argonauts, recalled by Horace as the fashionable Porticus Agrippae,[28] Agrippa erected two other buildings: the Basilica of Neptune,[29] to recall his naval successes to the public, and the original structure of the shrine of all the gods, the Pantheon. Although the entrance porch of the present-day domed rotunda bears the inscription of Agrippa in the pediment, neither the porch nor the rotunda are the buildings he erected: the domed building we see is Hadrianic, and Agrippa's temple was more conventional in plan. Recent excavations suggest that it was a regular rectangular temple twice as long as it was broad, oriented with its entrance porch on the opposite wall to the present entrance. Ancient sources add that it contained caryatid pillars modelled on those of the Athenian Erechtheum, with bronze capitals.[30] It had been Agrippa's intention to honour Augustus by calling this the Augusteum and placing a statue of Augustus in the inner temple (the *cella*) alongside the statues of Rome's ancestral gods, Mars and Venus. When Augustus would not allow his statue to be placed in the shrine with the gods, Agrippa set up statues of Augustus and himself on the inner wall of the entrance porch, on either side of the door to the shrine itself. Dio is at pains to explain that Agrippa did not do this to aggrandize himself or make himself equal to Augustus, but only out of modesty and loyalty. In this and his earlier description of Agrippa's new public buildings, Dio stresses the popularity that Agrippa earned by his generosity in choosing humane and brilliant projects to do honour to Augustus and to provide enjoyment to the public.

It must have been early in this lavish and glamorous programme of public building that Agrippa made a famous speech reported with admiration by Pliny: 'there is preserved', he says, 'a speech of Agrippa, generous and worthy of Rome's greatest citizen, advocating making all statues and paintings property of the People, which would have been far better than removing them to country mansions' (Pliny *Natural History* 35.26)[31] Agrippa, his older contemporary Asinius Pollio and many members of Augustus' family would adorn the public porticoes and basilicas with famous statues and paintings, many of them from earlier centuries, some seized as spoils after recent victories, others actually bought from or given by Greek cities. At this time, when Augustus himself was occupied in campaigning in western Spain (Lusitania), there was probably no man at Rome more admired than Agrippa: it was Agrippa whom Augustus entrusted with presiding over the marriage of his daughter to Marcellus. When the Princeps returned from Spain in 24 – the occasion celebrated by Horace in *Odes* 3.14 – Marcellus was already his son-in-law and not yet ailing, but it was Agrippa to whom Augustus entrusted his signet ring when he was again taken ill in 23.[32] Clearly, if he was to die at this time, it was not yet safe either to trust affairs of state to a twenty-seven-year-old or to ask the Senate, people and legions to accept such a youth as their supreme authority.

There is one more event during these crowded months in which Agrippa's behaviour has provoked both ancient and modern speculation. In 23 while Marcellus was still in good health, Agrippa suddenly left Rome for Mytilene without any official status or mission. Did he leave in resentment of Marcellus' privileged position? It hardly makes sense in view of Augustus' manifest trust in Agrippa. Or was he anxious to avoid obstructing Marcellus' influence and exercise of authority? Was it, like Tiberius' behaviour in 6 BCE, an act of self-exile?

Hardly. Historians tended to let their perceptions of later episodes (see Chapter 7) affect their judgement of this unexplained departure. Too much has been made of Marcellus and court gossip. A better explanation was offered by David Magie in his study *Roman Rule in Asia Minor*.[33] Rome still suffered the embarrassment of the standards captured by the Parthians from Crassus at Carrhae in 53 BCE and from Antony. As Augustus would show by his diplomatic manoeuvres and Tiberius' expedition in 20 BCE, it was preferable to recover the standards without expensive warfare, but this involved discreet negotiations to save the face of both parties, something that could not be proposed to the Senate and labelled as an eastern command. It still is a matter of continuing dispute whether Agrippa was given in 23 the geographically unlimited and overriding proconsular command that he would receive for five years in 18 BCE and again in 13. But we have seen how much Agrippa (and Maecenas too) acted without official positions. At the naval base of Mytilene on Lesbos, Agrippa was little more than 5 miles or so from the province of Asia, ready to take action if it were needed.

Instead, as we know, Marcellus first contracted a winter fever, then failed to recover and died in Campania early in 23. Augustus was faced not just with a crisis in marking his successor, but a crisis of public anxiety, marked by both popular protests and, as it appears, aristocratic conspiracies. We will see in the next chapter how Augustus resolved both the public and private aspects of the new and evolving situation.

5   Old enough to be her father
Marriage to Agrippa

The year 23 BCE left Julia already a widow in her sixteenth year, but we do not know enough about her relationship with her deceased nineteen-year-old cousin and husband Marcellus to help us understand whether this caused her personal grief or anything more than social inconvenience. She had grown up in the Princeps' household – may indeed never have been allowed to leave it, if she and Marcellus were housed in the Palatine complex – and must have realized that widowhood for the daughter of Augustus meant remarriage, and remarriage on her father's terms.

Augustus himself had been seriously ill in 23, and must have provoked speculation, if not alarm, about the continuation of stable authority at Rome. With the loss of his nearest male kinsman and chosen successor, Augustus had to reconcile the restive nobility and reassure the people of Rome. His own priorities were clearly abroad on the frontiers of the empire, but for the Roman people, he was virtually the only leader to be trusted – whether for military or social protection. When Augustus resigned his consulship prematurely in 23, securing his replacement by the old republican P. Sestius, this was more a response to the discontents of the nobility than of the common folk. It is difficult to make sense of the alleged conspiracy of Marcus Primus and Licinius Murena, designated for the consulship of 23, but it may reflect a challenge to his autocratic exercise of control over commands in both 'imperial'[1] and 'senatorial' provinces. Once condemned, the two men were quickly forgotten, but the people's grievances were more difficult to calm. They seem to have refused to elect both consuls for 22, reserving one of the positions for Augustus. The protests continued and perhaps increased before the elections of the following year,[2] and were only resolved when Augustus adopted a new basis for his powers in 19, combining his proconsular *imperium* in the provinces with a new tribunician power that represented his concern for the city and its people, as well as a formal sharing of public appearances with the consuls.

It was easier to resolve his family problems. Agrippa was admittedly the same age as Augustus but enjoyed better health and would be the best person either to represent Augustus or to take over control if he should die. Maecenas supposedly told Augustus that he had made Agrippa so powerful that Agrippa must either become his son-in-law or be eliminated by murder (Dio 54.6). If this comment reached Agrippa, it may well have helped him to take the next step. Now, with Octavia's consent, he divorced her daughter, the elder Marcella, to free himself for marriage to Julia. Tradition required widows to wait ten months before remarriage, but if it took Agrippa and Julia almost two years, this was more due to his public duties than to any personal issues.

It is frustrating to depend on Cassius Dio for the sequence of events, since he tends to group them by topic or sphere of action, but his narrative is probably correct in putting the marriage of Agrippa and Julia before Augustus himself departed to the East to back up the simultaneous diplomatic and military manoeuvres to achieve a satisfactory settlement with Parthia. Where was Augustus? Apparently in Sicily; according to Dio, he 'sent Agrippa to Rome immediately [after the divorce?] to see to the wedding and to take in hand affairs in the city' (54.6.5–6). Once again, it seems, Augustus himself did not attend his daughter's wedding, and it was left to Agrippa to deal with disturbances over the excessive growth of the rites of Isis and the aborted election of the city prefect.

The following year, 20 BCE, Julia gave Agrippa a son, Gaius, and Agrippa himself set out for the Gallic provinces, although the chief emergency to be dealt with was the unfinished 'pacification' of north-west Spain. Augustus had supposedly reduced the Cantabri before he left in 25, but they had rebelled and it is clear that Agrippa had to conduct a fierce campaign with heavy casualties before he could confirm their conquest in 19 (Dio 54.11.1–5); the very difficulties may have motivated his unwillingness to send the dispatches to the Senate that might have earned him a triumph. But he was probably more moved to avoid any step that would impugn his responsibility to the Princeps himself, or set him on an equal footing with him – who had after all 'pacified' the Cantabri five years earlier. Agrippa also took steps to reorganize the situation in Gaul and put a stop to inroads by the German tribes across the Rhine.

By this time, a pattern was developing in which Augustus and Agrippa took turns to visit and control the western and eastern provinces. Agrippa's two campaigns in Spain and Gaul were more or less simultaneous with the actions of Augustus and his stepson Tiberius in the East. Thus, Augustus went east to Greece in 21, wintered in Aegina, visited the provinces of Asia, Bithynia and Syria in 20 and spent the next winter (20–19) in Samos.

Gaul was, of course, nearer. Did Agrippa return to Julia in either of these winters between his changes of province and military front? It is time to admit the kind of information we cannot derive from our historical sources. Suetonius as a biographer is sometimes more helpful. Since we are writing about a woman's experience, we would like to know when she and her husband were together, either on his return to Rome or because she had followed him at least as far as a central community in his area of provincial command. During the republic, wives had never accompanied their husbands until the flight of Pompey and the Senate from Rome and then the entire Italian peninsula in 49 BCE forced at least some wives to follow their husbands.

Cornelia followed Pompey, but only as far as his naval base at Mytilene, a technically autonomous city. But Cornelia was not only wife but also daughter of a general commanding the opposition to Caesar and could have found herself a kind of political hostage if she had remained in Italy once it was under Caesar's control. Cato's wife Marcia stayed behind to manage his household. Forty years later, Julia's daughter Agrippina accompanied her husband Germanicus to Gaul and even into camp on the Rhine, but for at least some of the time left her infant children behind. Early in the principate of Tiberius, Tacitus presents a formal senate debate on the issue of provincial commanders' wives, arguing the advantages and disadvantages of having women with their husbands, since this might also bring them close to the military zone, where they were seen as interfering with discipline.[3]

It is worth reviewing the arguments of both sides in this debate, for a sample of Roman aristocratic prejudices against women. It was argued that the company of women associated with a governor's wife would contaminate peace with luxury and war with fearfulness, making a Roman military body resemble a barbarian migration. Women were not just weak and unequal to hardship but, supposedly once given access to licence, would also be cruel, ambitious and greedy for power, intruding upon the officers and men. Indeed, whenever governors were accused of peculation, most charges were against their wives, who attracted all the worst provincial followers to handle their affairs. The result, it was claimed, was a double burden, in which the orders imposed by the women were more persistent and excessive than those of their menfolk. There was an old Roman tradition that women had once been disciplined by sumptuary laws such as the *Lex Oppia* and now that they were exempt they would dominate their husbands, the city and even the armies.

On the other side, women are first defended on the grounds that their husbands behaved worse, in greed, ambition and lust, then their champion exploits the same mistrust of women conveyed by the speaker who had proposed banning governors' wives from the provinces:

> marriages were barely surviving undamaged when a husband's super-vision was on hand, what would happen if they were cancelled [by the husband's absence] for years at a time like an actual divorce? The speakers were attacking offences committed abroad as if they had forgotten the scandals of the city itself.
>
> (Tacitus *Annals* 3.34)

This argument may have clinched the Senate's decision: the motion was defeated.

Given the later allegations against Julia of infidelity to Agrippa, one would like to know how much time they had to spend apart. There is only scattered data for Julia, as for any imperial woman, and no evidence to show either that she joined her husband in Gaul or that Agrippa returned to Rome over the winter of 20–19 BCE. This has one further consequence – that we have no basis on which to calculate the conception or birth of any child between that of Gaius in 20[4] and his brother Lucius in 17. Authorities still differ on the birth-dates and relative ages of Julia's two daughters. It seems likely that the elder was conceived and born during 19–18, while the younger must have been conceived and born after Lucius, while Julia accompanied Agrippa to the East, most likely in 15 or 14 BCE. But which was the elder daughter? Vipsania Agrippina, named after her father, who would marry Germanicus (born 15 BCE) or Julia, named after her maternal grandfather, who married her maternal half-cousin, Cornelia's son Aemilius Paullus? It would help to know when they married, but it is only an inference that this was in 4 BCE rather than later (see Chapter 9). It seems that once adult, the two daughters followed separate destinies; they are not mentioned together. We cannot deduce priority from their names, which could reflect either the traditional privilege of the father (with Agrippina the elder child) or the unique importance of the Julian, maternal, line. The seniority of Agrippina perhaps gains further support from the survival of a statue base at Thasos inscribed in honour of Livia and the younger Julia alongside other statue bases for Agrippa and his wife. Rose has argued from the small size of this base that it depicted one standing figure, Livia, holding the infant Julia in her arms.[5]

Nothing can be inferred from the fact that no statue base of Agrippa himself or of his other children have survived. Even if they survived, we would not be compelled to infer that the children (or Julia their mother) actually visited Thasos with their father. Certainly Livia did not. The statue was erected to recognize her importance (and power to benefit the community). On the other hand, as we shall see, there is a fairly consistent pattern of statue bases in mainland and Asiatic Greek cities erected to honour Agrippa and Julia, with some also inscribed in honour of Gaius and Lucius.[6] To what extent are the surviving bases evidence for determining which members of Agrippa's family travelled with him, and where?

From Agrippa's return in 19 to his departure for the East either in late 17 or the following spring was the longest period that Julia and her husband spent together in Rome. It would be sentimental to imagine her delighting in her new baby boy like a modern mother who has usually spent a decade or so as a single adult and knows she can only afford one or two children, but Julia could at least treat Gaius as her child for the first three years. When his brother Lucius was born in 17, her father formally adopted both boys as his own children. There was no precedent for the adoption of infants; indeed, most parents were too uncertain that their infants would survive to consider adopting or letting them be adopted. But a Roman adoption was total – and seemingly irreversible. When Aemilius Paullus let two of his four sons be adopted by Cornelius Scipio and Fabius Maximus, and then lost his two younger sons to fever, he did not try to reclaim the other two. It is more than likely that the possessive and authoritarian Augustus would want to remove his grandsons from their parents' care – the more so as Agrippa and Julia were about to leave Rome for Greece and the provinces of Asia Minor. But Augustus himself was planning an extended period in Gaul from 16 BCE, which would surely postpone any plans to take over his new 'sons'. There is no evidence for the boys' infancy – Romans were not interested in unformed children – but such information we have for the boys' later upbringing is entirely concerned with their (grand-)father Augustus' reactions to their behaviour and the training for public life that he chose for them.

It may have been some compensation to Agrippa for the loss of his legal heirs that Augustus now elevated him to be his colleague in tribunician power for a five-year period from 18 to 13 BCE, and gave him *proconsular imperium*, legalistically defined as not less than that of any governor in whatsoever province he was allotted as his sphere.[7] Augustus was already planning Agrippa's next tour of the eastern empire.

In 19, Augustus modified his own role in the city to include visible signs of his parity with the Consuls. He was now seated between them and accompanied by his own fasces. It was more significant that he claims to have accepted (and no doubt initiated) a version of the proposal from the Senate and people that he should be appointed supervisor of morals and legislation with supreme power (*curator legum ac morum summa potestate* [*Res gestae* 6.1]) for both 19 and 18. Although he insists in the *Res gestae* that he held no unconstitutional office, he comments that he carried out the request of the Senate and people on the basis of his tribunician power. His most intrusive moral legislation, rewarding and defining 'proper' marriages, penalizing men and women of fertile age who shirked their reproductive duty and imposing punitive sanctions on adultery and the condoning of a partner's adultery, was enacted in 18 and perhaps 17 BCE, and will be discussed in detail in Chapter 7.

One motive for this onslaught of moral legislation was his desire to celebrate a new age – a new *saeculum* – in 17 BCE.[8] This was to be a demonstration of renewal, and the new enhanced version of the traditional rituals occupied five days from 31 May to 3 June, followed by a further seven days of theatrical and other entertainments.

These games were conducted by the priestly Board of Fifteen for the Performance of Rituals (*Quindecimviri sacris faciundis*), in which Agrippa stood second only to Augustus himself, and the inscribed record of the ceremonies[9] shows Augustus and Agrippa each sacrificing a bull to Jupiter the Greatest and Best on 1 June, and two more to Juno the following day. On 3 June they again jointly made a bloodless sacrifice to Apollo and Diana of nine sacrificial cakes, and two more groups of nine Greek ritual cakes. This was only a part of the complex celebrations that involved both the Capitoline and Palatine hills (where a choir of fifty-four boys and girls sang

Horace's 'Secular Hymn' in front of the Palatine temple of Apollo), performances of plays in Greek and Latin (some without a stage, some in temporary theatres), equestrian displays and even chariot races.

But Julia was probably no less busy than her husband. For three successive nights, 110 married ladies, chosen by the *quindecimviri*, offered a ritual *sellisternium*, or offering, to seated statues of the goddesses Juno and Diana, with prayers whose words are recorded by the inscription. Can we imagine that Augustus and Agrippa and the other thirteen members of the Board failed to choose Livia and Julia? For the second of these ritual *sellisternia*, indeed, it seems to have been Agrippa who intoned the prayer they made to Juno, asking her blessing for the fortune of the Roman people, the Quirites. Modern comparisons (I think of Queen Elizabeth II, or the First Lady in the USA) suggest that such public exposure in model roles would be a recurrent and time-consuming burden of imperial power. Julia was probably in advanced pregnancy with Lucius, and the ceremony must have been an ordeal.

But the time approached for Augustus and Agrippa to leave Rome for the western and eastern provinces. Agrippa may have left for Greece before Augustus made his departure for Lugdunum (Lyons) in Gaul. The evidence for Agrippa's itinerary reflects a kind of imperial progress, no doubt to meet the eagerness of each city to receive as much attention as its neighbours and rivals. There was no reason why Julia would not have accompanied him on the first leg of his journey through mainland Greece, and there was something to be gained by an appearance of the Emperor's daughter as guarantee of the self-made general's high standing. Reinhold (1933) traces Agrippa's journey from inscriptions in his honour at Corcyra (the eastern end of the crossing from Italy) through Taenarum, Gythium, Sparta and Corinth in the Peloponnese to Athens and Oropus. The larger cities received benefactions and returned the favour by honorific coinage bearing Agrippa's bust or by setting up social structures in his name such as the college of Agrippiastae at Sparta. At Athens, Agrippa was honoured by a colossal monument in front of the Propylaea to the Acropolis showing him driving a four-horse chariot (the quadriga was as much a symbol of Greek Olympic victories as of Roman triumphs),[10] and by the naming of a new auditorium in the Ceramicus as the Agrippeion. Unfortunately, the late literary source does not indicate whether it was simply named after him or funded by his gift.[11]

It was also customary for prominent Romans travelling in Greece to attend any of the major athletic festivals that occurred during their visit and to seek initiation in the Eleusinian mysteries. But Agrippa was not on holiday. (He had, for example, to help administer the new colonial settlement of veterans at Patrae.) The only festival he seems to have attended was the Festival of the Muses at Thespiae, the nearest village to Helicon. Our evidence is, again, inscribed statue bases.[12] That Agrippa and Julia went to Thespiae is almost guaranteed by the statue bases; that they actually attended the festival is only an inference, from the addition 'To the muses' and from the unlikelihood that they would visit Thespiae for any other occasion. Clearly Livia was not with them, so it would be overconfident to infer from the statues of the three children that Agrippa and Julia took them on his tour of Greece.

As might have been expected of any important Roman official on tour, Agrippa also visited the shrine of the healing god Asclepius at Epidaurus and left an inscription thanking the god. This Reinhold (1933) connects with a notice in Pliny that Agrippa suffered terribly from his feet and resorted to baths in hot vinegar. Was this gout? It was a common Roman ailment, since wine was the only drink available besides water. If we are reconstructing the experience of husband and wife, Agrippa's sufferings will obviously have caused some hardship and anxiety to both himself and to Julia, even if the inconvenience was eased by the use of attendants and litters. His affliction may also have been the reason for a dedication made by Julia to Asclepius at Mytilene.

Mytilene, on the fertile island of Lesbos, is only a few miles from the coast of modern Turkey and has a fine harbour. Through its leading diplomat Theophanes the city had become a favourite with and strong supporter of Pompey during his eastern campaigns in the 60s. When Pompey withdrew from Italy to gather his eastern allies in the civil war against Caesar and the two armies were about to join battle at Pharsalus in Thessaly, he sent his wife Cornelia to Mytilene for safety and visited the city to retrieve her after his defeat. But Caesar did not hold this against the city and confirmed its alliance with Rome, as did his 'son' Augustus in 25 BCE.[13] Agrippa had made Mytilene his headquarters during his curtailed tour of duty in the East (23 BCE), and Julia and Agrippa wintered in the city more than once between 16 and 13. Indeed, she may have given birth to her younger daughter Agrippina there. It was a wealthy and cultured community that manifested its loyalty to Augustus and his family with fulsome decrees, as is borne out by an inscribed decree of the city council offering a thanksgiving to him and his wife Julia (an error) and sister Octavia and children and relatives and friends.[14] The reference to Octavia puts the decree earlier than her death in 11 BCE, and to his children might suggest a date after the adoption of Gaius and Lucius, but the lack of specificity suggests that it was composed and erected before Agrippa and Julia visited the city. The preamble of this decree is damaged, and the first part of the text suffers gaps, but what is preserved begins by mentioning a hymn to the ruling house, also theatrical and other shows with prizes – clearly at honorific games. There is a chief priest of the imperial cult and annual sacrifices and offerings to Sebastos (Augustus) on the same scale as regular offerings to Zeus, each month on his birthday. The decree sends envoys to Rome with a golden crown and promises any such future honours as may be devised.[15] There was already a cult of the god Augustus at Pergamum on behalf of the province of Asia, and such decrees with their various forms of tribute (chiefly temples, festival games and sacrifices) would become standard in the Greek East. We can assume that much of Agrippa's time, and Julia's too, would be spent like a modern head of state in ceremonial appearances, both at Mytilene and when they visited other cities. The pattern of honorific statues is again attested by surviving statue bases, honouring Agrippa (as the city had honoured first Pompey, then Caesar, and now honoured Augustus), and other later bases to Gaius and Lucius and even Agrippa Postumus. The city did not give cult honours to Julia, but other statue bases commemorated her and Agrippa as human benefactors, and an undated dedication to 'Julia' as Thea Aphrodite (*IGR* 4.114) may come from this time.[16]

Agrippa's official command and destination was the major military province of Syria, which he was administering in the Emperor's name.[17] Reinhold (1933) suggests that rather than crossing to Asia Minor from Greece by sea (which was often easier), he may have chosen to visit the Thracian Chersonese, which Dio (54.29.5) reports as his property at the time of his death. The land had belonged to the State by right of conquest (*ager publicus*), presumably ceded by defeated communities that had supported Antony. Scholars differ on how it could have accrued to Agrippa, whether by gift of Augustus or purchase, even a nominal purchase at a convenient price. Four cities on either side of the Hellespont, Sestos in Chersonese and Cyzicus, Lampsacus and Parium in the Troad were visited either now or on Agrippa's return journey. It may be a confirmation of Julia's presence with her husband that Sestos erected a statue to Julia as well as to Agrippa. It is, of course, lost – so are they all – but she is described on the base as 'the divine Julia, daughter of the sole ruler Caesar Augustus son of the god Caesar'. These journeys could bring both profit and loss to cities. While Agrippa restored its independence to Cyzicus, which had offended Augustus on his earlier visit, he purchased for a conspicuously high price famous paintings of Ajax and Venus that the citizens of Cyzicus might have preferred to keep.[18] Such purchases were often coercive even when generously paid, and he may have put the same pressure on nearby Lampsacus from which he took Lysippus' *Dying Lion* back to Rome.[19]

From this point I will focus on what is historically attested – Agrippa's actions and whereabouts during the years in the East, leaving open during this narrative the question of where Julia was, with or apart from him. When Agrippa had first gone as Augustus' governor of Syria in 23, the serious illness of Augustus had precipitated his return from his base at Mytilene before he could visit the mainland; whatever he had achieved had been done by remote diplomacy. This time, however, he spent time both in Syria and outside it, in the established provinces of Asia and Bithynia and on the outer edge of Roman rule, north of the Black Sea. Our knowledge of his actions is skewed by the interests of the main sources: the history of the fifth-century Malalas of Antioch in Syria, and the discursive *Antiquities of the Jews*, composed in the 70s of our era by Flavius Josephus.

The Roman province of Syria corresponded roughly to modern Syria, Lebanon, Israel and Jordan and consisted of the highly populated and fertile valley of the Orontes, dominated by Antioch, the former capital of the

Seleucid Empire, and the other cities of the Tetrapolis, Apamea, Seleucia and Laodicea, the rich coastal cities of former Phoenicia, (Tyre, Sidon and eight others), a less fertile hinterland and a number of politically independent states under client kings: Commagene to the north-east, Arabia Petraea to the south-east, Emesa, and Judaea, about which we are best informed. Until 30 BCE, the region had been under the control of Mark Antony, who had both attempted and failed in the attack on Parthia originally planned by Julius Caesar. Augustus kept at least three, often four, legions concentrated in the north, not only to deter or confront Parthian invasions, but also for potential campaigns of expansion such as the expedition led into Arabia by Aelius Gallus in 26–25 BCE.

Antioch itself was a great conurbation of several hundred thousand citizens, second in size only to Alexandria in the east and splendidly equipped with civic buildings and monuments from the Seleucids and from Julius Caesar, who gave it a new basilica (the Caesareion) and theatre. The population was a mixture of Greeks, Syrians and Jews, who even had their own community (*politeuma*) and magistrate (*archon*). Although any hybrid city of this size was prone to rioting, there is no evidence of trouble in Antioch itself during Agrippa's time in the East, and no reason why he (and his wife or family) should not have lived there in security and enjoyment. Certainly, he presented Antioch with a whole new suburb that took his name, expanded its theatre by an additional tier and erected two public baths and an aqueduct to service them. Herod, too, King of Judaea since he overthrew the high priests to conquer Jerusalem in 37 BCE, gave generously to Antioch, paving its main street and furnishing it with 2 miles of colonnades to shade the citizenry from the summer heat. But although Malalas is informative about Antioch, he does not report Agrippa's movements or actions. Instead, we must depend on Josephus, who in turn relies on the historian and diplomat Nicolaus of Damascus, friend of Herod and biographer of the young Octavian. The effect of reading the fifteenth and sixteenth books of Josephus' *Antiquities* is to believe that Agrippa did nothing without Herod and depended upon him for advice and diplomatic negotiations. Herod is described as his intimate and greatest friend after Augustus himself, and greatest friend of Augustus after Agrippa (*Antiquities* 15.350, 15.361 ff).

Herod himself was, by Jewish standards, an outsider, since his father was an Idumaean (from Edom outside Judaea), and he depended for his survival on being perceived as the Romans' chosen ruler. His policies were to secularize and Hellenize the kingdom. Herod seems to have had unlimited funds not only for benefactions to Antioch and Athens, but also to remodel his own cities: he gave Jerusalem a theatre and an amphitheatre, set up a festival in honour of Augustus and provided Roman-style chariot races, gladiatorial games and wild-beast hunts (*Antiquities* 15.268f), but he also constructed powerful fortresses such as Antonia, beside Jerusalem, and a new city, Caesarea, with an artificial harbour and a dominant temple of Rome and Augustus (15.331–41).

Although Herod had been a loyal ally of Antony until the campaign of Actium, he ingratiated himself with Augustus and sent his two sons by Mariamne to Rome to be educated. When Agrippa began his journey towards Syria, Herod was in Rome, and occupied in bringing back his now adult sons and arranging their marriages. So when (according to Josephus) he discovered that Agrippa was in Asia, a year or more had passed since Agrippa left Rome. It was late in 15 BCE that Herod came to Agrippa and persuaded him to visit Jerusalem. There, Agrippa stayed long enough to order the offering of a huge sacrifice to the Jewish god, and to hold a feast for the city populace, before he left 'making the return voyage to Ionia' before winter set in. In spring 14, Herod left his kingdom to support Agrippa in the expedition he was planning to settle affairs in the Bosphorus.

The Asian command itself was predominantly a diplomatic responsibility, rather than one requiring military action or providing military opportunities. This minor campaign north of the Black Sea was potentially the most exotic episode in Agrippa's command. When Pompey had put Rome's old enemy Mithridates on the run in 63, he had found his last refuge before killing himself in the Bosphoran kingdom of the Crimea, and in Augustus' time this kingdom was still in the hands of Mithridates' descendant, queen Dynamis. But she in turn had allied with a mysterious usurper called Scribonius, who also claimed to descend from Mithridates. According to Dio (54.24.5–7), Rome had already sent the client king Polemon from an adjacent region of the Bosphorus against him, and Polemon had killed Scribonius and married Dynamis but had not yet reduced the tribes still in revolt. But the news that Agrippa was at Sinope (on the south coast of Black Sea) was enough to subdue them, and Polemon and Dynamis received the approval of Augustus. It seems then that Agrippa did not have to leave Asia Minor to secure this peace. As a coda to the episode, Rose (1990) has recently argued that the beautiful diademed woman depicted on the south side of the Ara Pacis with the two little boys wearing torques is Dynamis, with her sons kept in Rome as hostages for her loyalty.

Josephus describes Agrippa's return through Paphlagonia and Cappadocia to Phrygia and thence to Ephesus and Samos (*Antiquities* 16.23). In spring 13, deputations of Jews from the diaspora came to Agrippa with protests against the Greek cities that were denying them their recognized rights of immunity from military service and civic duties that would violate observance of the Sabbath and of paying their taxes in the form of tribute to the High Temple in Jerusalem. Josephus' source is Nicolaus of Damascus, who spoke on their behalf, and he reports that when Agrippa had confirmed the privileges of the Jews, he returned to Lesbos. Was this then the approach of winter 13? When Josephus returns to this theme at *Antiquities* 16.160, he is detailing the abuses suffered by the Jews of Asia and Libya, who sent envoys directly to Caesar himself. He includes in his dossier of imperial letters to various governors, two letters from Agrippa (presumably when he was on the spot?), one to the magistrates, people and council of Ephesus, and a similar letter to the people of Cyrene in Libya. If one factor in Augustus' scrupulous treatment of the Jews was the tradition begun by his father Julius Caesar, another was no doubt the trust he and Agrippa placed in Herod, ironically because Herod himself was not devout, but secular in outlook.

Josephus follows Herod's actions to Agrippa's return to Rome 'after ten years', (that is, in 13 BCE, ten years after his first visit in 23). Herod sailed from Judaea to meet him and himself went to Rome taking his son Antipater whose intrigues had now driven his older sons from his favour. One of the strangest aspects of the supposed close friendship of Herod and Agrippa is their difference of temperament and behaviour within their families. Herod seems to have been passionate, easily besotted (one source records ten wives), but jealous and foolishly suspicious. In contrast, none of the Roman sources record any act of ill will or suspicion between Agrippa and his wife of nine years whom the same sources accuse of blatant infidelity.

To return then to Julia's experiences during these three years: if we have no statements to document her presence in Antioch or even Mytilene, there is one surprising but unambiguous witness to her visiting Troy, or Ilium, as it was then called. This was not when Agrippa himself was visiting Troy, but while he was returning from Sinope and in Paphlagonia. Apparently Julia had tried to cross the flooded Scamander on her way to Ilium and was almost drowned. This was recorded by Nicolaus because Agrippa in anger fined the people of Ilium 100,000 drachmae, and they sent an appeal to meet him on his route at Amisus but could not face his anger. It was inevitably Nicolaus of Damascus and Herod who interceded and secured the cancellation of the fine.[20]

This clear evidence that Julia made this inconvenient journey in the direction in which Agrippa was campaigning, and did so in difficult weather, seems a guarantee that we should assume far more travel on her part. But her second daughter, Julia, must have been born either late in 14 or early in 13, since she was already pregnant with Agrippa's posthumous son (Agrippa Postumus) at the time of his death in March, 12 BCE.[21] Pregnancy and a very young baby were presumably deterrents to any unnecessary travel. Reinhold adduces a number of inscriptions in honour of Julia from the islands. Besides Mytilene, where she is flatteringly honoured as the New Aphrodite, inscriptions honouring her as daughter of Augustus and wife of Agrippa survive from Andros, Delos, Samos, Cos, and Paphos in Cyprus, but only one from the Asian mainland – from Ceramus on the gulf of Cos. Although Fitzler, writing on Julia (RE XI.I Julia No. 550, 896–906, suggests she may have toured the western coast of Asia Minor while Agrippa was in Syria and on his expedition to the Black Sea, this can only be hypothesis.[22] The lack of statuary inscriptions even from Ephesus, where the names of both Agrippa and Julia were inscribed on the entrance to the Agora, is discouraging.

This was, in fact, the period from which the only coin types showing Julia are known. Pergamum issued coins honouring both Agrippa and Julia, but separately: one issue paired Agrippa with Augustus, another, Julia with Livia,

Figure 5.1 Denarius of C. Marius Tromentina, 13 BCE. Obverse: Augustus, bare-headed (DIVUS AUGUSTUS); Reverse: head of Julia, flanked by Gaius and Lucius Caesar.

thus marking recognition less of Agrippa and his wife, than of the Princeps' family as such.[23] Ephesus instead honoured Agrippa and his wife together.[24]

Back in Rome, Augustus had revived the mint, and one of the *Tresviri monetales* (Board of Moneyers) for 13 BCE, C. Marius Trio of the tribe Tromentina, issued a coin with Augustus (inevitably) on the obverse, and honouring Gaius and Lucius with their mother on the reverse. None of the three is named, but despite their miniature size, the young men's profiles resemble Augustus so strongly that they can only be his 'sons', and their mother is there to serve as blood link between the Princeps and his heirs.

For Agrippa and Julia, the last months of their marriage entailed a period of separation: Agrippa's powers and position as equal to Augustus were renewed in 13, but trouble in Pannonia (roughly corresponding to parts of Austria and Hungary) called him, and he set out to the chilly northern province even though winter was underway. The news of his approach seems to have calmed the rebellious tribes, but Agrippa himself fell sick and returned without any campaigning. Once again, Julia's husband was sent to Campania to recover, and, like Marcellus, Agrippa failed to survive. Whatever her personal feelings towards her relatively elderly husband, Julia can only have faced the future after his loss with extreme anxiety.

6 Julia's homes
A domestic interlude

We do not know where Julia's mother Scribonia lived after Octavian divorced her, nor when her father took his child to live with her new stepmother in his house on the Palatine. But we do know quite a lot about the house where Julia spent much of her childhood both from texts and from archaeological excavations. Perhaps it would be best, however, to begin with some comments about the difference between elite Roman attitudes to their town and country houses and the expectations and the preferences of present-day political leaders.

Andrew Wallace-Hadrill has reminded us first and foremost that Romans did not share our modern concepts of domestic privacy: the town house of a politician or banker was also his place of business and was expected to reflect his importance in the size and decoration of its public rooms.[1] These were predominantly the atrium, containing family monuments – the shrine of the Lares, the painted stemmata of ancestors who had held office, and the formal marriage bed or *lectus genialis* – and the rooms associated with it, the side rooms or *alae* and the *tablinum*, literally the record room, beyond which lay the various dining rooms (*triclinia*) and *cubicula* (smaller rooms used not only as bedrooms but also as offices and studies). Both friends and clients were received in the atrium for the morning salutation and other business, and these seem to have been ranked. We are told by Seneca that the Gracchi brothers, a century before Octavian's rise to power, were the first to distinguish between their closer friends admitted to the first audience and more insignificant clients admitted in larger groups. But, as Wallace-Hadrill makes clear, we should not envisage the Roman statesman's house as a clear sequence of public rooms grouped around the Atrium, with private rooms ranked behind them around the open courtyard modelled after the Greek peristyle. The wealthiest houses might not include a peristyle and were not designed as a linear sequence, but were far more complex, containing a number of separate suites, each combining dining space and *cubicula* – not bedrooms in our sense, but private spaces used for intimate business and for study as well as for sleep. In a sense, nowhere in a public man's town house was private or secluded solely for family use. Indeed, even the country villas of a statesman such as Cicero were open to uninvited visits from both citizens of the local community (say Puteoli or Formiae) and Roman friends and acquaintances.[2]

There was another difference in attitude. Romans were very much aware of the famous figures who had owned a house, which might continue to be called the house of Crassus or Catulus decades after the owner's death. And politically minded Romans all wanted to live in the same elite area. Besides Cicero's teacher L. Crassus and the aristocratic brothers-in-law Lutatius Catulus and Hortensius, Cicero and his enemy Clodius, Licinius Calvus and Mark Antony all owned houses on the Palatine. But some kind of respect for original owners seems to have prevented new owners from demolishing in order to rebuild on a grander scale. Instead, demolishing a house was a political gesture, echoing the legends of the early republic which marked Spurius Maelius or Manlius Capitolinus as would-be tyrants and enemies of the people whose houses were razed to the ground by public decree. Clodius had repeated this gesture in 58 BCE, razing Cicero's Palatine home and attempting to pre-empt the ground by declaring the area a shrine of liberty. Owners might block in doorways or move entrances to their homes, or enlarge them by incorporating adjacent properties, as Clodius had incorporated the Porticus Catuli with Cicero's town house into the ground plan of his shrine, but they seem to have avoided substantial rebuilding. Still, Octavian himself was to initiate a whole new phase in Roman domestic architecture, one we can encapsulate by noting the change from his home on the Palatine to the new imperial sense of *palatium*, the name given to the residences of subsequent Caesars and origin of the modern word 'palace'.

Suetonius' *Life of Augustus*, written over a century after the Princeps' death, stresses the simplicity of his living quarters. He first occupied the house near the forum of the orator Licinius Calvus (who seems to have died before 47 BCE), then moved to the Palatine in or just before 36 BCE, purchasing the relatively modest house of Hortensius, not remarkable either for spaciousness or ornament.[3] To Suetonius, this house, which had only a small portico of local Alban peperino stone and rooms without marble facing or pavements seemed unpretentious and modest. And yet Hortensius, Consul in 69 BCE, was known as a dandy and a lover of luxury, a connoisseur eager to acquire Greek sculptures for his home, such as the sphinx that his client Verres had stolen from the Sicilian Greeks.[4] Romans of the next century, like Pliny, would have a choice of suites facing north and south to counteract the heat of summer and cool of winter, but Suetonius adds that Augustus kept to the same bedroom all the year round for the forty years that he lived in the house and never left the city during the winter, although the climate was hard on his health. For absolute privacy, he used a special room above the main house (*in edito*) which he called Syracuse, or by the Greek name *technophuon*, or he took refuge in the house of a trusted freedman. When he was sick, he might convalesce in the more luxurious house of Maecenas in the new Esquiline quarter of Rome.

This house was first tentatively identified almost 150 years ago, as the archaeological remains on the south-west ridge of the Palatine, overlooking the river and Forum Boarium, set between the foundations of the second-century temple of Magna Mater and Augustus' own great temple of Apollo (to which we will return).[5] There are two detached domestic buildings, which seem to form a family compound: the House of Augustus, as it is now confirmed to be, and the smaller mostly underground house usually called the House of Livia.[6] Neither can be completely exposed by excavation because of subsequent imperial building, but enough has been discovered of each to demonstrate the amazing, even revolutionary, transformation in decorative styles that took place in the first twenty-five years of Augustus' dominance in Rome. Yet there is another factor that leaves open to doubt whether the child Julia saw the brilliantly decorated rooms that have been uncovered. Fires were common in Rome: in 31 BCE, a serious fire, apparently started by arson among disgruntled freedmen, ravaged the Circus Maximus district, destroying the Temples of Ceres (with Liber and Libera) and Flora in the Forum Boarium. Another fire in 25 destroyed the house of Mark Antony on the Palatine, which Augustus had given to Agrippa and Messala.[7] Dio reports that a fire damaged (or destroyed?) Augustus' own house in 3 CE. How did these decorations survive the fire? The house was apparently abandoned after the death of Augustus but left intact until Domitian filled in the rooms that archaeology has now brought back to light. Because the style of decoration in both the House of Augustus and the smaller 'House of Livia' seems to belong to the 30s and 20s BCE, we must assume these rooms survived.

As a child, Julia would have lived in the larger House of Augustus but no doubt visited the smaller house quite often. It was identified as the House of Livia because of a lead pipe found there and stamped with the name IULIA AUG[USTA], which she was given in 14 CE by Augustus' testament. Admittedly, it may not have been inhabited by Livia before that time, but it was the nearest house to that of Augustus and clearly part of the family compound. Although it seems to have been below ground level, this may have been a matter of choice: Romans did not want the heat of direct sunlight and avoided windows, letting light filter indirectly through porticos and doorways. Beneath the stucco of its rooms has been found masonry datable to the house's first occupancy around 75–50 BCE. Several rooms were richly decorated. In one particularly rich room, the mythological paintings of the central frames have faded since their discovery, but both the scene of Mercury with Argus guarding Io, and that of Polyphemus and Galatea (favourite Hellenistic myths that Ovid would later make famous) were copied by nineteenth-century artists and are reproduced by Galinsky (1996).[8] Galinsky also reproduces a drawing of the decorative scheme in another room, in which columns resting on fantastic animal bases articulate spaces filled by swags of flowers and fruit topped by a yellow frieze of Egyptian genre scenes at eye level[9] and symmetrical fantasy figures sustaining balanced pairs of griffins in the upper register. This is a full-blooded example of the new (third) style to which the Augustan writer on architecture, Vitruvius, objected so violently. Since almost every piece of wall decoration from Julia's Augustan context is in this new style, it time to consider how Vitruvius described – and condemned – the new fashion. After remarking in 7.5 ('On Wall Painting') that the old architectural, mythological and genre scenes 'which were based on reality' have now been discarded, he denounces the monstrosities favoured by corrupt modern fashion (*iniquis moribus*):

> Instead of columns men paint thin stalks, instead of painted pediments, panels containing curling foliage and tendrils, candelabras support representations of shrines (*aediculae*) with other outlines above their gables rising from roots, with tendrils and producing a number of irrational little figurines, and stalks sustaining half-figures with assorted animal and human heads.
>
> Such things neither exist nor could exist nor have done. . . . how can a reed support a roof or a candelabrum the decorations of a gable, or some soft and slender stalk bear a figurine, or flowers and half-figures sprout from roots and stalks?
>
> (*On Architecture* 7.5)

To Vitruvius, it is a perversion to reject the old realistic paintings for these whimsies, which are so far from reality, and to praise the new images because they are skilfully painted. Yet it is just these new fantasy combinations, with their sophisticated detail, that now began to prevail in all the most luxurious rooms that have survived from this generation.

The house of Augustus contains splendid examples of both the waning second style and the burgeoning third style. The Room of the Masks, with vivid perspectival painting of red and yellow walls, surmounted by masks and theatrical symbols flanking gabled *aediculae* containing mythological scenes, is surely second style. Coarelli (1974)[10] dates the room to 30 BCE and notes the painted architecture in realistic perspective. But the painted architecture is already adorned with fantastic griffin-like creatures, and the predilection for such fantasies is conspicuous in the Princeps' private study with its undulating swans in flight, Egyptianizing lotus buds and anchors and other non-natural symbols subtly shaded on a black background against red or alternating bands of red and yellow.[11] From the same study, Galinsky (1996) has illustrated the programmatic nature of Augustus' taste with pastel Victories offering garlands, again alternating with lotuses in the ceiling frieze (Galinsky, Plate 5a) and with a pastel-toned wall painting in another room in the house that depicts the Princeps' new patron god Apollo in his guise as *citharoedos*, with flowing hair and clad in a long robe, leaning back on his throne as he tunes his lyre (see Galinsky, Plate 5a).

This study and these rooms declare the Princeps' own taste and chosen representation of his role, including the association with Apollo, which goes back long before the victory of Actium so opportunely won beneath the temple of Actian Apollo. As early as 36, after Octavian's naval victory over Sextus Pompey in Sicily, he had designated for a new Temple of Apollo, an area on his own plot that he claimed had been marked by a lightning strike for this purpose.[12] There was already a Temple of Apollo Medicus, just outside the ritual boundary of the *pomerium* (near what is now the Theatre of Marcellus) which would be restored and dedicated during the 20s by Sosius, the Antonian admiral and Consul of 30. But Octavian's project outshone it – almost literally, for his new temple, with its unusually high proportions, was built of Carrara marble from Luni and was no doubt as crudely conspicuous as the monument of Vittorio Emmanuele remains to this day.

The temple may have taken nearly eight years to construct, and the building works must have filled the air all round with noise and dust, blighting the nearby ground and bushes during the operations. The finished building was close enough to the house of Augustus to be connected by a ramp, and we still have an immediate record by the poet Propertius of the impression it created. One of his elegies (2.31) excuses himself to his girl Cynthia for arriving late at a rendezvous because the Emperor himself had been opening the portico that surrounded the new temple:

> The whole portico was set out as a promenade with columns of Punic marble, between which stood the throng of daughters of old Danaus. Here the marble image of Phoebus seemed to me more handsome than the god himself, as he mouthed a song to his silent lyre; and around the altar stood Myron's herd, four oxen, statues brought to life by the artist. Then in the centre rose the temple of brilliant marble, dearer to Phoebus than his native Delos; upon it above the gables was the chariot of the sun, and before it the doors, a famous work of Libyan ivory. One door displayed the Gauls cast down from the peak of Parnassus, the other mourned for the deaths of mother Niobe. Then within the Pythian god himself, between his mother and his sister, is seen clad in long robe uttering his songs.
>
> (2.31.3–16)

The poem is quite strange, partly because it marks with temporal connections elements that are spatially distinct. It starts, not from the temple, which had been opened earlier, in 28 BCE, but from the framing porticoes. These led to the new imperial Greek and Latin libraries, which are not mentioned (they may have not yet have been completed). There follows an array of exotic adjectives from Rome's empire, starting with the Punic marble columns, yellow veined with red (Numidian or *giallo antico*) and praising the doors made from the ivory of Libyan elephants, but also invoking the Apolline sites of Delos (Ortygia) and Delphi (on Mount Parnassus, where the oracle was delivered by the Pythia).

The colonnade was remarkable for the statues of the fifty daughters of Danaus sworn by their father to slay their cousins, the sons of Aegyptus, on their bridal night, and a later reference by Ovid[13] shows that there was also a statue of Danaus himself. This is a strange myth to honour in so significant a place. In Greek thought, the girls (except Hypermnestra who warned and spared her husband) had committed a crime against marriage, for which they were punished in Hades by being forced to carry water in leaking sieves, though Aeschylus in his *Suppliant Women* had them pardoned by the State of Athens. And yet their name 'Daughters of Danaus' made them Greeks (*Danai*) who had slain Egyptians. Were they featured, then, as ethnic models of patriotism, or as bad examples of gendered behaviour? While the poets Horace and Ovid honoured the one daughter, Hypermnestra, for loyally refusing to slay her husband, it seems that Octavian had chosen the women to prefigure his own defeat of Egypt. It has even been suggested that each of the fifty girls was shown with sword drawn in the act of assault.[14]

Such a bristling array would constitute an aesthetic nightmare. Besides, the black basalt statues found near the temple site which have now been identified as Danaids are immobile, almost like squared-off Greek herms, their rigidity only broken by the hand that grasps a fold of their skirts. But it is equally strange that Octavian should have chosen this myth. What sort of image of fatherhood (or of marriage) would a suggestible young girl receive from such a parade of violence outside her backdoor?

Propertius passes on to the colossal statue of Apollo in front of the temple, 'more handsome than the god himself', because, as some sources tell us, it had been given the facial features of Octavian, and to the group of bronze heifers by the Hellenistic sculptor Myron, so lifelike that, according to Greek anecdote and epigram, a thirsty calf had tried to obtain milk from the udders of one cow. Behind the altar rises the temple, surmounted by the Sun God's gilded chariot and team, and bearing on its doors scenes of divine vengeance exacted on the Theban queen Niobe who boasted that her fertility was greater than Apollo's mother Latona, and on the sacrilegious Gauls who raided and plundered Delphi in the third century. Finally, we follow the poet into the shrine, occupied by the statues of Apollo, flanked by Latona and Diana, products (as Pliny tells us)[15] of three different Hellenistic sculptors. Propertius does not mention either the pediment or the frieze, and it is not clear whether the terracotta panels showing the contest of Heracles and Apollo for the tripod, and female devotees garlanding *baetyls* (standing symbols of Apollo's cult) came from the temple or from its porticoes.[16] Sumptuous the temple certainly was, and it would dominate the view, even twenty-five years later when Augustus opened the other great temple – of Mars Ultor – in his new forum. But would it have inspired reverence for either the god or Octavian the son of the deified Julius? Or was this merely a source of patriotic pride, like some modern bank headquarters, built to rise higher than its rivals in other countries? And do we feel awe before a building we have seen in construction? For Julia, this monument must have been simply one more looming extension of the identity of her ubiquitous father.

The married woman

We do not know whether Julia and Marcellus occupied a house of their own after their marriage or were simply allocated an apartment (that is a connected group of rooms) in the large house of Augustus. But Agrippa at least will have shared his own home with his first wife Marcella, and could be expected either to bring his new bride to it or to set up a new establishment for her. And this may have been the mysterious villa across the Tiber, known to archaeologists as the Villa under the Farnesina. The evidence for ownership can only be circumstantial. The site was close to the Pons Agrippae, across from his major engineering and architectural projects on the Campus Martius. But it was also close to the tomb shared by his supporter M. Platorinus and the brick manufacturer A. Crispinus Caepio. Could the villa have been simply the home of Platorinus or the wealthy Caepio?[17] What has chiefly argued against this is the assumption that bourgeois owners could not have commissioned the sheer luxury and brilliance of decoration to be found in the rooms excavated. These rooms were unfortunately few, perhaps less than half of the original structure, not only because of the renaissance and modern over-building, but also because the villa seems to have been abandoned. It was no doubt situated so as to enjoy the wide views of the Campus Martius across the Tiber, but was too close to the river bank and was exposed to flooding. It seems that it was not inhabited beyond the first generation.

The area excavated consists of a long covered corridor or *cryptoporticus*, a *triclinium* with adjacent garden and three *cubicula*, two parallel in orientation around it, with one beyond, on the approach to the *ambulacrum*, whose initial straight section led to a curved promenade, shaped like the foyer of a modern theatre, or the ambulatory behind a cathedral choir, so as to fit within the building's apsed contour.[18] The wall paintings from all these spaces have been detached and can now be seen set in a likeness of their original positions, on the top floor of the Palazzo Massimo alle Therme. It is very tempting to imagine each of these rooms as chosen by the taste of the newly married Julia, but evidence only permits us to say with confidence that they represent the taste of her class and generation.

The highly decorated *cryptoporticus* was clearly no mere access corridor for the household slaves, but the public approach to the rooms beyond. It was predominantly a warm natural beige, articulated by a series of slender turquoise blue columns. Between each pair of columns, two smaller scenes at eye level flanked a larger scene of figures outlined in tones of brown against a blue background (many of these were of Dionysiac cult). At ground level, a low dado featured elegant fantasy creatures against a black background, set in orange-red frames; above the running sequence of eye-level pictures, an upper register silhouetted various Egyptianizing figures, with larger central figures freestanding on a pedestal flanked by winged figures supporting an orange-red architectural frame, topped by a sphinx. Visitors entering this broad corridor would take in the vivid colour contrasts and perhaps the exotic human and animal figures, but focus on each successive scene as they advanced into the building. The long *ambulacrum* would require the same kind of treatment to provide diversion for the guests as they strolled, and most of the monochrome sepia scenes that open up to the viewer are what art-historians call sacro-idyllic, illustrating 'harbours, headlands, shores, rivers, springs, artificial channels (*Euripi*), temples, groves, hills, cattle, shepherds; some have also the outline of statues in the likeness of the gods' (Pliny *Natural History* 35.116).[19] Two of the most remarkable vignettes along this promenade show a naval battle (Sanzi Di Mino 1998: No. 143), and what seemed to me, despite the Hellenistic temples, to be an African or Egyptian scene with men climbing a palm tree.

In contrast, the *triclinium* (see Plate 7) (probably one of several dining spaces in this grand house) features black walls articulated by slender uprights supporting male and female figures in the upper register, which is otherwise marked by purely formal designs. Beneath a turquoise band, a running frieze at eye level illustrates a series of miniature scenes of judgement or appeal to a seated authority; there seem to be as many as three or four related scenes with eight to ten brilliantly sketched figures in each section suggesting a continuous narrative. One example has a figure apparently attacking someone as he removes a heavy load from a row boat. From the frieze, single swags of ivy leaves hang (like natural stems) over the large continuous black surface between the frieze and the formal dado. Each expanse of black wall between the uprights contains scattered scenes, now too faint to distinguish. Diners would find such a setting restful, while enjoying the delicate details in moments of boredom or while awaiting the next dish.

The two *cubicula*, or private rooms, facing the dining room on either side are too richly painted for words to do them justice. The colour scheme in Room B is predominantly red, with black dado and upper register, but there are at least five levels of depiction going on. The intention is to suggest a kind of art gallery – a room both painted and displaying detached board paintings. Thus, the end wall is dominated by a full-height *aedicula* painted like the frame of a baroque altar structure, containing a lofty mythological scene of the infant Dionysus nursed by the nymphs; above it, a winged goddess balances on arabesques, while naked figures hold rods that support the higher architectural designs to right and left. The upper register is painted to represent figured divinities standing in front of the wall, and two different types of *pinakes*[20] suggest pictures hung on the wall, containing smaller winged deities and priest-like sceptre-bearing males. Beneath, square classicizing *pinakes* of standing and seated women at their toilette are framed in ochre against the largest expanses of red, but presented as if held up by winged and half-naked women balancing on elaborate foliate pedestals. Everything, the *aediculae*, the upright figures, the assorted framed panel paintings and their supporting figured pedestals are painted so as to deceive the eye while suggesting the physically impossible.[21] This room, and its companion piece, Room D, function like picture galleries, offering the viewer a choice of different scales and styles of painting. For example, both rooms contain an erotic scene of lovers embracing on a bed with attendants, and both have delicate monochrome stuccoed ceilings with idyllic landscape scenes of hunters and fishermen gathering around rustic shrines (Sanzi Di Mino 1998: 102–4), more specific scenes of cult (Sanzi Di Mino 1998: 105–8) as well as symbolic figures of Dionysus himself and a winged victory (Sanzi Di Mino 1998: 109, 110).

But rich as these private rooms are, they are, in my opinion, outclassed by the refinement of Cubiculum E. Although its end wall resembles that of Room B in design, and the large sacro-idyllic pictures framed by the *aediculae* on the left and facing walls of a man worshipping at the raised statue of a deity are conventional (and now faded), the overall natural honey-coloured tone of the room with its accents of red-brown and green is particularly delicate and harmonious. It may be that what impresses me as a woman is the exquisite draftsmanship of the individual women depicted in classicizing style at their toilette, and the evocative figures of the two aspects of the goddess Diana/Selene. There are still the same multiplicity and variety of figures, but the plainer organizing framework is more serene. Here, too, there is a stucco ceiling of the highest quality, this time with what seems to be Augustan symbolism. However, the figure of Mercury with the face of the mature Augustus and the beautiful winged Victory (Sanzi Di Mino 1998: 130, 131) share the ceiling with a winged human-faced lion, the head of an old lady, another sacro-idyllic landscape, a sun disk (Sanzi di Mino 1998: 135, to recall Apollo) and a mythological scene of Phaethon asking his father for his sun chariot (Sanzi Di Mino 1998: 132, 133). Surely, the patron who commissioned this ceiling must have been very close to the Princeps – Agrippa himself, or, if we see this as a woman's boudoir, his wife Julia. Would any citizen unrelated to the rising dynasty have claimed these symbols?

Did Agrippa and Julia have a summer home in Campania? It is generally thought that the villa at Boscotrecase, partially excavated in 1903 and subsequently buried, belonged to their family, because a brick stamp was found bearing the name of Agrippa's last child, Postumus. Had it passed into his hands from his father? The advanced third style of the wall paintings rescued from the excavated cubicula might suggest a later date, after 12 BCE, when the infant son was born his father's heir (since his brothers had been adopted out of the family), raising the possibility that on Agrippa's death it was his widow Julia who commissioned the decoration of the villa. But this is only one of several possible conjectures. What survives, divided between the Metropolitan Museum and the National Museum of Naples, are panels detached from four cubicula aligned along a walkway on the south side of the villa, sufficient to suggest reconstructions of their decor.[22] And, as with the Villa under the Farnesina, perhaps decorated by the same workshop, these are rooms of extraordinary and striking originality that bespeak the great wealth of the owner, whoever he (or she) was.

Ten years ago, one could see these panels for oneself, but both museums have currently closed access to their holdings[23] and my description is perforce based on the scholarly discussion of von Blanckenhagen and Alexander (1962) supplemented by scrutiny of the colour illustrations of Anderson (1987a, 1987b). Of the four decorated *cubicula*, the White Room (Room 20) only survives in two small but delicate panels of intricate incense holders rising at eye level from a black dado with an upper band of red. Room 19, the 'Mythological Room', is represented by two striking full-scale paintings, of Perseus rescuing Andromeda from a very baroque sea monster and of Polyphemus serenading Galatea: both are lofty and precipitous cliff scenes in predominantly dark blue-green tones, which contrast strongly with the background of red walls and the ochre-yellow frieze. The so-called Red Room (Room 16), preserved at the Museo Nazionale in Naples, is chiefly notable for its sacro-idyllic scene.[24]

This is similar to the vignettes of shepherds and shrines from the walls of the Black Room (Room 15),[25] and since the Black Room is by far the most distinctive of the four, it should be the focus of any detailed discussion. Although its walls are only preserved in a number of separate narrow panels (three of them stored away in Naples), this room emerges with a clear character. Against the prevailing black background, slender metallic-looking supports soar to the upper register, where they are topped by an elegant curved band, figured in grey-blue, red and gold. Above this band perch parakeets and gorgon heads on the east and west walls, while the focal north wall is divided into three panels (Anderson 1987b: Plate 48). The outer panels sustain *pinakes* showing worship of Apis and Anubis in a pastiche of Egyptian tomb painting, while at eye level on each side a pair of elegant swans holds up the ends of a ritual fillet. The central panel seems to soar to a pavilion roof, but at either end metallic rods support raised medallions containing portrait heads against a purple background (Anderson 1987b: Plates 56, 57); these are aligned so as to face each other. They are not unlike the portraits set on the obverse of coins, but there is no parallel for such images as part of a domestic decorative scheme. Anderson has argued that these are female portraits, of which one must be Julia and the other Livia (1987b: 127–35), but neither of them resembles any version of the much-portrayed Livia (we have no certain portraits of Julia). I would suggest returning to the older interpretation which read both portraits as male. They are in profile and resemble each other more closely than either resembles Agrippa, or indeed Augustus. It is, I think, futile to dream up reasons why these portraits should be the children Gaius and Lucius Caesar, or Tiberius and Drusus, or any other adult male members of the imperial family.

If it were not for the marked similarity of taste between the two villas, which has led to the suggestion that they were decorated by artists from the same Roman workshop, there would be small reason to argue that Julia herself ever saw, still less commissioned, the decoration of the villa. It might seem that there was little time for Agrippa to purchase the villa and to see to its redecoration before he and Julia left Rome for Lesbos in 16 BCE. He would return to Campania only when he was mortally ill in spring of 12 BCE. After his death, when the villa was apparently inherited by the child Agrippa Postumus, Agrippa's widow would have had even less time to visit Boscotrecase or to choose its decoration before her enforced marriage to Tiberius in 11 BCE, and Postumus himself would never be in a position to order renovation, since he was first adopted and then repudiated by Augustus while not yet eighteen years of age. But here are the memorable remains of a luxury home with third-style wall painting. Given the alternatives, it surely must have been decorated before the couple left for Agrippa's tour of duty in the Aegean and Asia Minor.

And after Julia's marriage to Tiberius? We will see in the next chapter that this time was too troubled to leave any evidence on where or how they lived, together and apart.

7   The fatal marriage

When Julia lost her second husband Agrippa in the spring of 12 BCE after almost ten years of marriage, she was already mother of four children and expecting his posthumous child. She had fully earned the honoured status and privileges of a 'mother of three' (*ius trium liberorum*) and would have been exempt from any coercion to remarry, had she been any other father's child. But the Princeps' only daughter could not be left unmarried. There were too many ambitious noblemen who would see marrying her as the key to manipulating power if Augustus should die and the succession fall to his 'sons' (really the sons of Julia and Agrippa) Gaius and Lucius, now aged eight and five. It would surely have been better for everyone concerned had Augustus married her off to a wealthy private person without political ambitions such as his friend Proculeius,[1] but he was more concerned with marking out the right person to hold authority in the State than the right man to marry Julia. Instead, he chose Livia's older son, Tiberius, already experienced in both warfare and senatorial business. This decision of the Princeps was, if anything, more cruel to his future son-in-law than to his daughter, for Tiberius greatly loved his wife, Agrippa's eldest daughter, Vipsania Agrippina, the mother of his son (Drusus), and now pregnant with his second child.[2] Suetonius (*Tiberius* 7.2) reports that after Tiberius had been forced to divorce her in order to marry Julia, he once accidentally saw Vipsania in the street and gazed after her with such longing and distress that efforts were made to make sure they did not meet again.

What sort of man was Julia's third husband? Even by the standards of the civil-war generation, Tiberius had had a troubled childhood, and Suetonius gives him 'an infancy and boyhood full of hardship and anxieties' (*Tiberius* 6.1). His father, Tiberius Claudius Nero, had brought proscription and exile on his own head by taking the wrong side when he fought for Lucius Antonius against Octavius in the Perusine war of 42 BCE, and had to flee, first to Naples, then to Sextus Pompeius in Sicily (who did not make him welcome), then to Achaea. There, accompanied by Livia and the babe in arms, he was sent on to Sparta, a community under the patronage of his family, the Claudii. As they fled through the wild woodland, the baby's cries when he was taken from his mother twice almost betrayed them, and Livia herself was scorched by a forest fire. True, they were able to return to Rome when Tiberius was three, but then Livia's love affair with Octavius took his mother from him, and he would lose his father when he was nine. From then on, Tiberius and Drusus must have lived in the residence that their mother shared with Octavian. Tiberius was the same age as Octavia's son Marcellus, but when Marcellus was marked with privileges and offices as potential heir to the Princeps, Tiberius had to accept secondary roles – riding on the left (inferior) side of Octavian's triumphal chariot in the procession after Actium and serving as Quaestor when Marcellus held the more prestigious office of Aedile. Whatever Tiberius' education, he proved himself in the forum, both as a defence lawyer and as prosecutor of Fannius Caepio on a charge of treason in 23. As Suetonius reports, Tiberius was given advanced access to the career magistracies, serving in turn as Quaestor, Praetor and Consul (for the first time in 13), taking on tough assignments as Curator Annonae (administrator of the city's grain supply) and inspector to redeem kidnapped citizens and free persons from the many unauthorized slave workhouses (*ergastula*).[3] He also did more than his share of military service, fighting his first campaigns as Military Tribune in Octavian's Cantabrian war (between 25 and 23) before receiving the Princeps' commission to lead an expedition to Armenia and negotiate the return of the captured standards from the Parthians in 20–19 BCE. (Augustus himself went east but maintained a dignified distance from the negotiations.)

Since Tiberius has been judged unfavourably by Tacitus and Suetonius (and will not come well out of this narrative either), let me provide an antidote in the flattering character sketch offered by one of his loyal officers, the historian Velleius Paterculus.

> Reared with the education of divine instructors [i.e. Augustus], the young man was gifted with birth, beauty, lofty stature, great intellect and high culture. One might have hoped for his present greatness even then; indeed he had the appearance of an emperor.[4]

It was after the Secular Games of 17 that Tiberius saw real fighting, first serving for a year as governor of Gallia Comata, based at Lyons, then mounting a simultaneous operation in attacks coordinated with his brother Drusus (now twenty) from the north and west against the Raeti and Vindelici, Alpine tribes of modern Tyrol.

We know something of these two major expeditions from Horace's *Epistles* and last book of *Odes*. *Epistles* 1.3 and 1.8 (cf. 1.9) are a kind of indirect homage to Tiberius on his eastern expedition, addressed to officers in his personal entourage, Julius Florus[5] (also the addressee of an important literary critical letter from Horace, *Epistles* 2.2) and Celsus Albinovanus, and mentioning other noble young associates of Tiberius. The *Odes* are a different matter. Suetonius' *Life of Horace* reports that Augustus actually commissioned this fourth book to honour the victories of the two sons of

Plate 1 Augustus in his moral role as Pontifex Maximus (Museo Nazionale alle Terme).

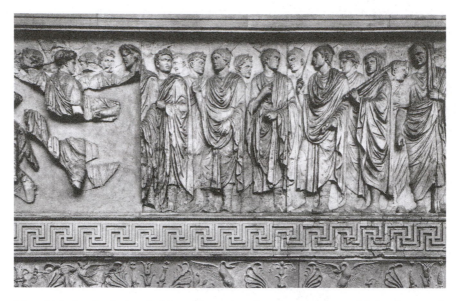

Plate 2(a) Ara Pacis, south frieze. Procession showing Augustus with head covered for sacrifice.

Plate 2(b) Ara Pacis. Agrippa with head covered for sacrifice, followed by Livia and Tiberius, Antonia and Drusus.

Plate 3(a) Ara Pacis (Louvre Panel). Damaged figure of widow, believed to be Julia, with child identified as Gaius dressed as a *camillus*, or altar boy.

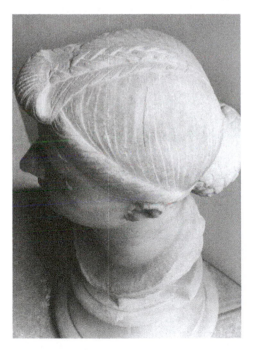

Plate 3(b) Bust of Julia from Baeterrae (Musée Saint Raymond, Toulouse).

Plate 4(a) Bust of Agrippa from
Baeterrae (Musée Raymond,
Toulouse).

Plate 4(b) Altar from Vicus Sandaliarius. Augustus as Augur (hen at his feet)
preparing Gaius for his great expedition to the East, with Livia (?) on
the right. (Uffizi Gallery).

Plate 5(a) Bust of Gaius Caesar
as a child (Pesaro, Museum).

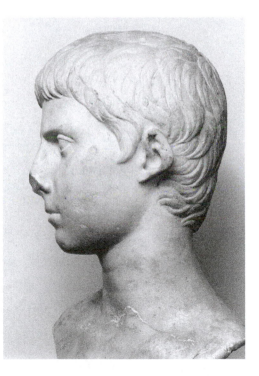

Plate 5(b) Bust of Lucius Caesar
as a child (Aquileia, Museum).

Plate 6(a) Agrippina the elder (Parma, Museum).

Plate 6(b) Germanicus (Parma, Museum).

Plate 7 Triclinium panel, from a villa under the Farnesina (Palazzo Massimo alle
Therme).

Plate 8 Sacro-idyllic wall-painting from the imperial villa at Boscotrecase (Metropolitan Museum).

Claudius Nero, and Horace juxtaposes the victory odes (4.4 and 4.14) with direct tributes to Augustus himself in 4.5 and 4.15 to form the nucleus of the book. Naturally, the lofty diction and loaded imagery of the two victory odes avoid any prosaic informative details of the Alpine campaigns, and the metrical awkwardness of the name Tiberius[6] leads the poet to speak first of Drusus, the younger Claudius, before praising 'the older of the Nerones' (*maior Neronum* in 4.14). Horace also had to calibrate his praise so as to maintain the myth of the young commanders' subordination to the strategy of Augustus, who no longer took the field, but under whose official auspices they and all other successful commanders fought. Thus, both odes address Augustus as the real victor. The second opens with lavish praise of the Princeps, then briefly honours Drusus before giving more attention to Tiberius:

> The Vindelici, ignorant of Latin law, recently learned how great was your power in war. For with your forces, fierce Drusus cast down the Genauni, that warlike tribe, and swift Brenni from their castles set on the terrible Alps in more than one reversal. *The elder Nero soon engaged in a mighty battle and routed the monstrous Raeti with successful auspices, worthy to be admired in Martian combat, for the vast downfall with which he overwhelmed hearts committed to death in liberty, just as the Auster harries the untamed waters . . . never tiring to assail the enemy squadrons, and to send his champing horse through the flames of battle.*
>
> (Odes 4.14.9–32, emphasis added)

By the time of his marriage to Julia, Tiberius had already fully established his credentials as a commander and Velleius, who had served under the future emperor, offers a detailed testimonial to his efficiency and concern for his men.[7] Tiberius had also held his first consulship, and could expect further years of military commands. He was called in to campaign in Illyria a year later (10–9) and would still be the man chosen to save Rome's north-eastern frontier almost twenty years later. But first, he had to adjust to this unwanted marriage.

Julia was now a sophisticated widow in her late twenties. The most specific and attractive picture comes to us through Macrobius. Although he is writing four centuries later, he has used a late Augustan source, Domitius Marsus' collection of witticisms of the great. Macrobius introduces his character sketch of Julia (*Saturnalia* 2.5.1–9) by describing her as being in her thirty-eighth year, but these witticisms are largely undatable, and he is probably citing her age from a biographical narrative in his source, which focused on the year when she suffered the worst crisis in her life. After some chapters stressing Augustus' patience in dealing with outspoken soldiers and civilians, Macrobius approaches Julia from the Emperor's point of view, as another test of his patience. He notes that she was approaching middle age (*senium*) but exploited the indulgence of both fortune and her father. She loved poetry and was very well-read, as was easy in that household, and her mild courtesy and good-humoured spirit won the woman immense popularity, as those who knew her vices marvelled at her contrasting merits.[8]

(*Saturnalia* 2.5.1–9)

He notes that Augustus repeatedly but tactfully warned his daughter to reduce her extravagant lifestyle and smart retinues, but was too conscious of her fertility and her children's resemblance to Agrippa to doubt her fidelity – a point which returns in an outrageous witticism attributed to her. When one of Julia's frivolous companions expressed amazement that she only produced children that looked like Agrippa, although she was so free with her favours, she retorted 'Ah well, that's because I only take on passengers when the cargo is already loaded!'[9]

Augustus supposedly told his friends he had to endure the caprices of two spoilt daughters – the State itself and Julia. The exchanges between father and daughter quoted by Macrobius deal with her coiffure, costume and companions. Thus, Augustus is supposed to have entered her room when her maids were obediently plucking out some of her grey hairs. When he discovered the reason. he asked her whether she would rather be bald than grey-haired. Here the wit is his, but in the other anecdotes it is Julia who has the retort. When she came to see Augustus wearing a risqué costume,[10] he kept quiet, but praised her the next day for appearing in a more modest outfit: 'Isn't this more becoming to the daughter of Augustus?' She answered that she was dressing 'today' for her father, but on the previous day for her husband. Again, when she appeared at the gladiatorial shows escorted by fashionable young blades, whereas Livia was surrounded by solemn middle-aged men, Julia answered her father's reproaches by pointing out that these young men would soon grow old along with her. But perhaps the most significant of her comments came as a reply to the admonition of one of those serious-minded family friends that she should adapt herself to the model of her father's frugality. Julia's words 'He forgets that he is Caesar, but I remember that I am Caesar's daughter', may be the real key to her character of pride and wilfulness and match Suetonius' judgement that her marriage to Tiberius failed because she despised him as her inferior (*ut imparem*).[11]

And yet Suetonius (*Tiberius* 7.2) reports that one reason for Tiberius' reluctance to marry Julia was his conviction that she had fancied him when she was still married to Agrippa. We might discount this as typical male vanity, if Suetonius had not added 'as was the general opinion'. Whether or not Julia had ever fancied Tiberius for an affair, they both realized they must try to make the best of this enforced marriage and managed to live in harmony at first, with apparent mutual affection. Julia even left Rome to follow Tiberius when he took up his next provincial command in Illyria. But two tragedies occurred to renew their mutual mistrust. The first was the death of their infant son, to whom she gave birth at Aquileia (probably the last settled community in north-eastern Italy short of the military front). But they were still on civil terms, and Julia joined with Livia in giving a dinner for the elite women to celebrate his triumphant return in Rome. But in 9 BCE Tiberius suffered a greater loss when his beloved brother Drusus, as Consul and commander in Germany, was fatally injured by a riding accident. Tiberius, who had rushed immediately to his brother's sickbed, escorted the body devotedly on foot through Gaul and northern Italy back to Rome and gave one of the public eulogies for Drusus, who was posthumously honoured with the title Germanicus. Now, indeed, Tiberius must have felt isolated and abandoned, and if we follow the sequence of Suetonius' narrative, from now on the couple slept apart. Historians note that when Tiberius was Consul for the second time in 7 BCE, Julia held aloof from the joint celebration by Tiberius and Livia of the new shrine of (marital) Concord. But divorce was out of the question.

The next year, Augustus offered Tiberius (as he had to Agrippa before him) the tribunician power for a five-year period, planning to send him to the East on a largely diplomatic mission. It seems that Tiberius was offended by popular demands for the early promotion of young Gaius as he came to puberty and the toga of manhood. According to Dio (55.9) the people actually voted Gaius Consul in the elections for 6 BCE (perhaps they knew better than Augustus how little power the Consuls now had?) and Augustus had to hold an assembly to rebuke them, explaining that this was premature. Indeed, he hoped the State would never again need an under-age consul (as it had done in 43 BCE when he was elected Consul at nineteen). Meanwhile, he would appoint Gaius to a priesthood and admit him to the Senate, designating him in advance for the consulship of 1 CE. Tiberius was certainly resentful that he was assigned diplomatic duties while the young men were earmarked for public promotion and privileges. And we cannot explain his next step by his weariness of the marriage to Julia, as some sources suggest, since the commission to the East would have enabled him to escape her. Instead, he announced that he wanted to lay down all public office and retire – to the same eastern provinces to which Augustus had planned to send him. As Agrippa had supposedly asked to retire to Mytilene in 23 in order to avoid clashes with the newly promoted Marcellus, so now, suddenly, Tiberius demanded to put away his office and retire as a civilian and *privatus* to Rhodes.[12] Despite Livia's attempts at persuasion and Augustus' complaints in the Senate, Tiberius was determined to abandon political life and to leave Rome. He actually went on hunger strike until he was allowed to set out for Rhodes, ostensibly to study, and when he left he took none of his previous retinue of aristocratic friends.

The large island of Rhodes was an autonomous state containing several cities and boasting a proud tradition of rhetorical and philosophical learning. In the previous half-century it had some famous teachers of rhetoric, such as Apollonius Molo, who taught Cicero and Caesar, and was the home of

Posidonius, the geographer and historian, philosopher and scientist, who enjoyed the friendship of Pompey and Cicero. The climate was mild, the island fertile and prosperous as a trading centre; one might envy Tiberius the seven years he spent there. If he had no young noblemen to converse with, he certainly had his astronomer Thrasyllus; he will have had learned Greek secretarial staff and *grammatici* to discuss the kind of erudite poetry and critical pedantry that he enjoyed. It would be a year or two before he felt the political dangers of Gaius' antagonism, or saw himself as a kind of exile instead of enjoying voluntary retirement.

He was not missed; strangely, there seem to have been no provincial uprisings or military losses during this period. It is less surprising that we hear nothing of Julia's activities in Rome for the next four years. But there was one way in which the departure of Julia's unloved husband would cause her great hardship. Augustus would not allow her to divorce him (he probably dreaded her becoming again eligible for marriage), and she found herself a virtual widow without hope of remarriage. Here is the first issue on which women in the Augustan age differed substantially from modern widows or divorcees.[13] While a woman in either category was free to remarry and, given position and wealth, would find a new husband, if she remained unmarried she would have no position in society. Indeed, she would have far less social and public life than a Vestal. We can see this from examples within Julia's own extended family. The younger women, like Agrippa's previous wife Marcella, were found new husbands. Romans like Seneca saw the refusal of, for example, Octavia or her daughter Antonia to remarry as almost perverse. Octavia at least had brought up five children and was over forty by the time of her divorce from Antony. She did not remarry and, on the death of her son Marcellus, withdrew completely from society. Her daughter, the younger Antonia had given Drusus three children before his death in 9 BCE and met the requirements of 'mother of three' privileged by Augustus' marriage laws, but she was only in her late twenties, and it was thought strange that she did not marry again.

Conversely, Julia's daughter Agrippina, who had borne nine babies and reared six adult children, would beg Tiberius for permission to remarry after the death of her beloved husband Germanicus, and it was thought cruel of Tiberius to deny it.[14] But any man who wanted to marry Julia, or Agrippina thirty years later, would be aiming for a political power the Princeps did not want to share or dilute.

Augustus had the heirs he wanted and made the gesture of holding the consulship in both 5 and 2 BCE, in order to introduce his 'sons' to the Senate. The year 2 BCE was a kind of jubilee. On 5 February, twenty-five years after he had restored the republic, he finally accepted the title of Pater Patriae, father of his country, at the request of Messala, the elder statesman who best represented the old republic. This is celebrated by Ovid in the February book of his *Fasti,* the calendar poem.

To you, holy Father of your country, the people and senate have given this name, and we, too, the knights, give you this name. But your achievements awarded it before us; indeed you have been late in winning these titles, since you were long since father of the world. You have the name on earth which Jupiter holds in highest heaven; you are father of men, and he of gods.[15]

(Ovid *Fasti* 2.127–32)

Unfortunately, Ovid also praises Augustus by contrasting him favourably with Rome's first founder, Romulus, and includes amongst the Princeps' superior achievements that 'he orders women to be chaste . . . he has driven away wickedness . . . the laws flourish under Caesar.'[16] Now, Augustus had indeed legislated some years before to make adultery a criminal offence punishable by relegation to an island, but it was a disastrous coincidence that Ovid should evoke this law so close in time to the terrible scandal that would mark the year 2.

In August, the Princeps solemnly inaugurated the Forum of Augustus containing the temple of Mars Ultor and transferred to the temple the standards that had been restored by the Parthians eighteen years before. It was after this celebration, and only then, that he sent a savage denunciation of his daughter to the Senate. He had just 'discovered' that his own daughter had been committing multiple adulteries and indulging in public debauches in the Forum 'from the very rostra where he had proclaimed the *leges Iuliae*.' Our authorities, from Velleius, a virtual client of Tiberius, to the moralist Seneca, to Pliny the Elder's encyclopedic *Natural History* and Dio, Tacitus and Suetonius, who usually share a common source,[17] differ only in detail about Julia's supposed activities, detail which probably goes back to the Princeps' original letter of denunciation.

Essentially, the denunciation took two forms. First, there was a generalized and undated list of her alleged partners in adultery. Second, there was an account of her alleged public misbehaviour which was the immediate occasion of her exposure.

What are we to believe? Velleius, the earliest source, names five men as Julia's adulterers (2.100): Iullus Antonius, the son of Antony and Fulvia, reared by Octavia, Julia's contemporary, Consul in 10 BCE (and married); Sempronius Gracchus; T. Quinctius Crispinus, (Consul with Drusus in 9 BCE); Appius Claudius Pulcher; and Cornelius Scipio, probably a kinsman of Julia through Scribonia's first husband. Iullus, in particular, and Sempronius are confirmed by later reports in Tacitus. But of the five, only Iullus was executed.[18]

We know from Horace (*Odes* 4.2) that ten years before this he considered himself a poet of Pindaric lyric,[19] but this may have been a face-saving pose. Iullus almost certainly cherished dangerous ambitions and the desire to avenge his father's fate. He was also to be feared by Tiberius if not by Augustus himself, because of lingering popular memory of his father. His full brother Antyllus had once been betrothed to the infant Julia, but was executed after the fall of Alexandria. Iullus had managed to outlive his brother by almost thirty years, but it is significant that he had never been trusted with a military command or even an administrative office supervising the corn supply or Tiber embankments. As for Sempronius Gracchus, he seems to have been an old suitor, since he is reported to have composed a letter for Julia to send to her father denouncing Tiberius.[20] Tiberius believed himself to have been personally wronged by Gracchus and would have his revenge once he became princeps. The less prominent men were treated as guilty of adultery and relegated.

More mysterious is the immediate occasion of the crisis. Seneca in *De beneficiis* (6.32, Appendix II, 2b) reports from Augustus that she 'scoured the city in nightly escapades, and had chosen the Forum itself and the platform from which her father had carried his laws against adultery for her fornications; that there had been a daily gathering by the statue of Marsyas, when she turned from adultery to prostitution and claimed the right to every kind of licence with unknown partners'. The reference to the statue of Marsyas, however, puts a different complexion on the story, for the image of this swaggering little satyr was the symbol of popular liberty, near the old Comitium. When Pliny echoes this reference (*Natural History* 21.8–9, Appendix II.3b) he attributes it to 'a/the letter of Augustus'. In his earlier comment, (*Natural History* 7.149–50, Appendix II.3a,) in which Julia's sins form the climax of the sorrows of Augustus, Pliny goes further, asserting that Augustus' daughter actually formed an open conspiracy for parricide.[21]

Authors seem to agree that Augustus himself was the source for this horrendous indictment and express shock that in his rage he made no effort to cover up this disgrace, but sent his quaestor to read his words to the Senate – presumably the 'letter' mentioned by Pliny. Yet, although there was a legal procedure to judge accusations of adultery, and modern scholars sometimes speak of Julia's trial, it is clear that there *was* no trial, and therefore no public verification of his charges. Tacitus indignantly denounces the Princeps for going beyond his own laws and the clemency of his ancestors by calling a common offence between men and women 'offences injurious to religion and the violation of his majesty' (*Annals* 3.24.3, Appendix II.4b).[22]

Julia may well have committed adultery with more than one lover during the five years of her husband Tiberius' absence, but was her actual offence the adulteries with which she was charged? The accusation of adultery was used throughout Roman history to discredit women of high rank. Let us start with Lucretia, whom Sextus Tarquinius (in Livy's account) subdued by threatening to kill her, putting a naked and murdered slave in her bed so that she would be charged not just with adultery but with a socially shameful adultery.[23] As we saw in the introductory chapter, Pompey divorced his third wife Mucia for adultery when his marriage became politically inconvenient, as did Caesar at about the same time when the two men wanted to be free to make new alliances – in Pompey's case to marry Caesar's daughter, Julia.

Leaping over our Julia and her daughter, we come to the most explicit case of a 'framed' adultery: poor Octavia, daughter of Claudius and wife of Nero. Although she was eager to cooperate in Nero's desire to divorce her, Nero suborned the freedman Anicetus, who had helped him get rid of his mother, to 'confess' he had committed adultery with Octavia and promised him a comfortable exile in return.[24] We might note the probable complicity of Sempronius Gracchus implied by his lenient treatment (only exiled, not executed) and of the younger Julia's lover Silanus in the crisis of 8 CE (*Annals* 3.24, Appendix II.4b) allowed to take himself out of harm's way before he was denounced as her lover, and to return under Tiberius less than ten years later.

I shall not attempt to claim that Julia was celibate after her third husband left her, nor would I exclude the possibility that she had been the lover of each of these men at one time or another. But the timing of her exposure is too convenient. Either Augustus himself postponed her exposure until he had completed his agenda, or she chose to bring things to a crisis 'by going public' at this time. Had Augustus forced himself to ignore what was going on until he had accomplished his goals of launching Gaius and Lucius, inaugurating his Forum and accepting the grand title of Pater Patriae? Is Lacey right that Augustus had to divert attention from Julia's supposed early affairs in order to protect the legitimacy of her sons, now his heirs, and so invented the moment of discovery as a recent development since Tiberius' absence (1980: 127–40)?

Or are we to believe that Julia would hold a drunken party in the Forum, when she had a choice of houses in which to be debauched in comfort? Was she perhaps what we call a self-destructive personality? Have scholars underestimated the importance of sex, or the human temptation to take ever-increasing risks? Had Julia 'got away with' her love affairs for so long that she became careless and put enemies in the position to force Augustus to act? British scholars since Syme[25] have traditionally discounted the tale of adultery in favour of a political conspiracy to seize control either in the event of her father's death, or even by assassinating him, as Pliny suggests. If this was the case, we have to consider whether Julia would have entered such a conspiracy at the expense of her own sons. Pliny assumes she intended to assassinate Augustus, but although he had become a virtual despot, especially to his family, it is inconceivable that any plot to assassinate him would have opened with a public display of disloyalty. A coup d'état is hardly conceivable, but would Julia, or, as Syme suggests, the ambitious Iullus Antonius, have risked a pointless demonstration instead of awaiting the best political opportunity for action? The gathering apparently took place by night, but if Julia's gesture of crowning the statue of the Satyr Marsyas, Rome's symbol of popular liberty, seems to point to a more overtly political protest or an appeal to the people (with whom she was popular) why not protest by day? Let us suppose that Augustus refused to let Julia divorce and then marry Iullus, that he had also refused to include Iullus as a member of his family council or senatorial advisory committee; then they might well have 'gone public' to appeal to popular support. Would it have been impossible by day? Perhaps, but it is equally likely that such a nocturnal gathering would have been automatically broken up. Since the time of the Twelve Tables, Romans were only supposed to assemble at the summons of a magistrate, and any unauthorized group meeting by night was forbidden.[26] If the nocturnal gathering really happened, did informers alert the Princeps to intercept Iullus and Julia and others seizing them and dragging them to the Palatine for summary condemnation?

Let us change the question: why would Augustus accuse them of debauchery or rioting by night? One advantage of accusing Julia of nocturnal rioting would be that no respectable citizens would have been witnesses to confirm or deny the tale. For we could also base our attempts to understand the story on the hypothesis that it was a slander, that there was no such nocturnal gathering, and no conspiracy. This could have been a false accusation, like the promiscuous adulteries. Then was the story of this affair a plot of Livia's? The timing is against this, for Livia would have wanted her son back in Rome to claim his share of authority before she could entrap Julia and make her *persona non grata*.[27] As it was, Augustus now compelled Tiberius to send Julia a letter of divorce. Tiberius, in turn, supposedly pleaded on her behalf, and asked that she should retain his own gifts. He did not disguise his relief that Julia was removed but asked repeatedly to be allowed to return to see his kinsmen. (We should not forget that he had left in Rome his own son by Vipsania, now reaching puberty.) The reply – Augustus' reply, I presume – was that he should abandon all concern for his dear ones, since he had been so eager to leave them (Suet. *Tiberius* 11).

Had Julia been given any warning? Or did the blow strike her unprepared? Ovid's recall of his own condemnation can help us to envisage her plight:

> When the memory comes to me of that saddest of nights, which was to be my last time in the city, when I recall the night on which I left so much that was dear, a tear falls even now from my eyes. The dawn was approaching when Caesar had ordered me to depart from the shores of furthest Italy. I had neither time nor presence of mind to prepare, and my heart had grown numb with long delay. I felt no concern to choose companions or slaves, or clothing and equipment for an exile. I was numb like one struck by Jupiter's thunderbolt who lives unconscious of his own life.
>
> (*Tristia* 1.3.1–12)

The violence of Augustus' reaction suggests that he was genuinely taken by surprise. Given his uncontrollable rage, we can also assume Julia was sent orders to leave without delay; he may even have forbidden her to attempt to see him. But the suicide of Julia's freedwoman Phoebe (reported by Suetonius

Augustus 65.2, because Augustus praised her for her courage) suggests that there was time for Julia's household to be interrogated. If Phoebe had been a slave, she might have killed herself to avoid torture. (Interrogation of slaves entailed torture, since it was believed they would only tell the truth under duress.) As a freedwoman, she may have been equally exposed to abuse, but determined not to betray her mistress, or she may have feared (or suffered) rape while in custody. Julia herself was so popular with ordinary Romans that it would have been politically dangerous to allow her time to stir up public resentment.[28] We can be sure that the Princeps would have taken care to keep his decision hidden from the people of Rome, who loved their princess as a 'merry widow', to prevent them from gathering in violent protest as they would do over the divorce and relegation of poor pathetic Octavia by Nero sixty years later.[29]

Tiberius and later emperors used squads of the praetorian guard to deliver sentences of death or exile, but in 2 BCE they had not yet been moved into barracks in the city. This is why I assume that a trusted member of the Emperor's household (or even Livia?) came to Julia's home with instructions for her to prepare some possessions and slaves, ready to depart the next day.

***

Suetonius' description of the circumstances in which Julia was isolated on the remote and windy island of Pandateria (now Ventotene) stress their austerity. Only Julia's mother Scribonia went as her companion in exile, and she may have needed time to make her arrangements before joining her daughter. Since Scribonia was not accused of any offence, she could have taken most of her possessions and closest slave attendants with her. Her choice was a declaration of love and affirmation of faith in her daughter's morality. Scribonia may well have felt isolated and at risk in Rome,[30] but she undoubtedly hoped her presence would not only comfort but protect her daughter.

Can we imagine this exile? According to Suetonius, Julia was forbidden all wine (virtually the only drink available to Romans) and fancy food. No free man or slave was allowed contact with her without prior permission from Augustus, who required to know the age, physique and complexion of any man, with any identifying features. But who would risk the Emperor's displeasure by attempting to visit her? No Roman aristocrat like her former youthful caller Vinicius.[31] This can only have referred to the ordinary craftsmen or professionals – doctors, scribes and readers, architects, whether freeborn Greek or slave – who might be summoned to the island. She would not have been allowed the usual entertainers of elite households, nor would she have wanted edifying visits from scholars or philosophers, and it is difficult to imagine how she passed the time. We do not know whether she was allowed to send letters to her children or friends (which would of course be vetted for the Princeps) or to receive them or, perhaps, reading matter.

Maybe Augustus allowed her Homer and a copy of his favourite, the *Aeneid*. He would no doubt have permitted her to weave, like a good Roman matron, and one can only hope she refused to do so. Was there a contingent of soldiers to guard her? Was she allowed to take walks around the bleak and treeless island?

We know more about the second phase of Julia's exile, thanks to the survival of inscriptions from former members of her household and Jerzy Linderski's learned and sympathetic study of Julia 's last years (Linderski 1988). After five years (probably in 4 CE, when Augustus reinstated and adopted Tiberius, after the death of Gaius[32]) Augustus consented for her to be brought to the mainland, to Rhegium, and to live under less austere circumstances. Suetonius' *Life of Tiberius* (50, Appendix 2.5e) reports that by Augustus' decision she was confined to the city, but allowed to leave the house and communicate with people. Rhegium was probably as unattractive then as now, but Augustus had settled veterans from his fleet in the community and may have maintained an active naval station – plenty of supervision available (Linderski 1988: 183–4). The inscription that is the initial topic of Linderski's discussion is a private funerary tablet erected by Julius Gelos, who identifies himself and his father Julius Thiasus as freedmen of Julia, daughter of Augustus. The father had flourished – he became a *sevir Augustalis* (freedman priest of Augustus) at Regium – and the open honorific mention of Julia probably dates the tablet after her official rehabilitation, along with her daughter Agrippina, when her grandson Gaius became Emperor, or possibly after the Emperor Claudius married her granddaughter. But the mother is described as a freedwoman not of Julia but of Livia ' Diva Augusta'.[33] Could she have been planted in Julia's household as a spy? Linderski finds a better explanation based on Julia's extraordinary legal situation. Suetonius' report that Augustus had given her an allowance (*peculium*) and an annual budget corresponds to the way that Roman fathers equipped their legally dependent sons and daughters to live apart. Indeed, Linderski notes that once adopted by Augustus in 4 CE, Tiberius himself was in the same legal position. For Julia, real deprivation came with her father's death and the terms of his will, which left everything to Tiberius and Livia. Roman law required that natural heirs (which included daughters) would have to be expressly disinherited or they would receive their share; *peculium*, on the other hand, would end with the testator's death, unless he expressly included it in the will. There can be no doubt that Augustus had expressly disinherited the daughter he abominated, and Suetonius' evidence shows that her *peculium* too ceased at his death. The possessions and household she enjoyed would become Livia's, and this is the probable explanation for the status of Julius Gelos' mother as freedwoman of Livia *'diva Augusta'*.[34]

Now Livia outlived her husband by fifteen years and could have interceded for Julia, but she did not. Any relaxation in the conditions of Julia's custody ended with the death of Augustus. In a section of the life of Tiberius significantly headed 'His hatred of his kinsmen', Suetonius (*Tiberius* 50) contrasts Tiberius' behaviour with Augustus' concessions: 'he cheated Julia of the *peculium* and annual income, making a pretext of the law'. Now she was confined to the house and denied all contact with others – no doubt including her mother Scribonia. Tacitus notes that Tiberius caused her death: 'exiled, disgraced and deprived of all hope by the murder of her last son Agrippa Postumus, he starved her by cutting off her supplies, sure that her killing would be concealed by the sheer distance of her exile.'[35] It is true that until the murder of Postumus on Planasia, efforts were still being made to raise a rebellion on his and his mother's behalf.[36] Tiberius had grounds to fear the living Julia, as he feared her son, and even Sempronius Gracchus. Once he was Princeps, all three perished within the year.

If Julia had humiliated him during their enforced union, she more than paid for it, but in due course Tiberius would suffer in his turn, assassinated by her grandson after more than a decade of self-imposed exile in his palace on Capri.[37]

8   Julia's boys

It can be disappointing to modern readers that our Roman sources for biography showed so little interest in childhood or most aspects of family life, but it is understandable. The genres of non-fiction reporting that have survived, history, biography, oratory, were primarily concerned with the public careers of the nation's great men as generals or statesmen, while much of the day-to-day detail of their home lives was controlled by members of their slave household. Cicero may mention in a letter to his closest friend that he feels isolated in the political world around him and only finds comfort in his wife and young children,[1] but he would not have found it natural to talk about them. Romans tended to mention their fathers or mothers only in connection with the supervision of their education and encouragement of their careers.

So the first thing we know about Agrippa's and Julia's sons Gaius and Lucius is the fact of their simultaneous adoption by their maternal grandfather Augustus in 17 BCE, when Gaius was in his fourth year and Lucius less than a year old. Adoption of such young children was unusual; most cases attested in the republic were adoptions of boys in their teens or already qualified as adults by the toga of manhood, and most cases were of single adoptions, since the purpose was to provide the childless older man with an heir. We know why Augustus wanted to adopt, and wanted to adopt a child of his own bloodline, but why did he wait until the birth of Julia's second son? And why adopt both boys at once when the younger one was still an infant with a relatively low statistical chance of reaching adulthood? The answer may emerge from his subsequent treatment of other members of his family and potential heirs. In the decade that his stepsons Tiberius and Drusus reached manhood, he put both young men in equal and cooperative commands against the Tyrolean tribes, although Drusus was three years younger.[2] While we will see that Gaius and Lucius were promoted within the Senate and civil offices according to the age of each one, when it came to marking new heirs in 4 CE, he adopted Tiberius simultaneously with the much younger and untested Agrippa Postumus and forced Tiberius himself to adopt Drusus' son Germanicus (aged not quite twenty) as his son alongside his natural son Drusus Gemellus (slightly older). Why the insistence on fraternal pairs?

There was a negative model in Romulus and Remus, of whom only Romulus survived to be founder. Or one might cite the positive model of the Dioscuri, by the elite. According to the myth, when the mortal twin was killed, his brother shared his privilege of immortality with him. Better perhaps to consider the political model of Rome's highest republican office, the consulship: consular colleagues cooperated during their year of office, alternating their months to preside over the Senate, but also jointly proposing legislation on occasions. If one of the two colleagues opposed a decision, this had the effect of veto and the decision was void. The Romans saw this constitutional feature as a way to avoid monarchy (and ensure continuity of authority should one of the Consuls perish). The premature death of Augustus' first chosen heir, Marcellus, may have further provoked him to wait until he could mark two simultaneous heirs. For now, of course, the future princes were infants, and since both Augustus and Agrippa went out to the provinces – to Gaul and the eastern provinces respectively – in the year following the adoption, we can assume that Augustus was willing to wait until his 'sons' were older before beginning to rear them in his own home.

As infants, they nonetheless shared in the honours paid to their parents. When Agrippa and Julia toured Greece and the islands and cities of Asia Minor, as we saw in Chapter 5, many statues were erected, often incorporating honours to the whole family. Although the statues did not survive (were they recycled – bronze statues melted down and marble ground and burned to make lime?) their bases did, and their inscriptions indicate who was honoured, under what form of their name, and even how the family was grouped.

This family presented a problem of etiquette that we left unexplored in the earlier discussion. The Commander's wife was the Emperor's daughter, and their sons were now the Emperor's sons. So the people of Thasos set up two statue bases in the Agora: on one block[3] are inscribed the names of Julia and her daughter Agrippina, and separately of Livia with (and presumably holding) Julia's daughter, Julia the Younger, while a second block (now lost) was reported as inscribed to Gaius and Lucius. Discussing this dynastic group, Rose (1997a, Catalogue 95), suggests that Livia was added so that she could hold the infant Julia who could not have been shown standing. Similarly, the people of Greek Thespiae, not far from Delphi, set up on one base in the precinct of the Muses five statues, with the inscriptions in this order:

> The people (honour) Agrippina daughter of Marcus Agrippa
>
> The people (honour) Marcus Agrippa son of Lucius for the Muses
>
> The people (honour) Lucius Caesar: (honour) Gaius Caesar
>
> The people (honour) Julia, daughter of the Ruler Caesar Augustus, wife of Marcus Agrippa for the muses.[4]

From the inscriptions, Rose (1997a) infers that Agrippa was depicted standing and holding his little daughter Agrippina. Next to him were Lucius and Gaius, each named as Caesar, and at the end Julia, fully styled as daughter of Augustus. There is also an inscription for little Agrippina on the statue base at Delphi along with Julia, Gaius and Lucius and Agrippa.

At Ephesus, the gateway to the Agora shows a different combination of Augustus, Livia, Agrippa and Julia, but the inscription shows that although it was proposed when Agrippa was still in the East in 13, it was not finished until well after his death, in the Greek year corresponding to 4/3 BCE.

Can we assume that a statue implies that the child accompanied its parents on the ceremonial visit? It seems fair for Gaius and Lucius; their sisters offer a different problem. We do not know when the girls were born, and scholars have disputed which girl was the elder. The statue of Livia holding little Julia II at Thasos seems an afterthought, and Livia certainly did not accompany Agrippa's family. Since Julia was already represented as mother holding little Agrippina, the people of Thasos may have added Livia in order to represent the other baby in her arms. This suggests that Agrippina was the younger daughter, but if so, why is there no evidence from Thespiae of any statue of Julia II? This is why some scholars have argued that Agrippina must have been born first, but nothing conclusive can be inferred *ex silentio*. The probable dates of the daughters' marriages are enough to guarantee that, as Syme has shown, the elder daughter was Julia II, born perhaps as early as 18 BCE, and married around 4 BCE to L. Aemilius Paullus (grandson of Scribonia), by whom she soon had a daughter Aemilia. Agrippina must have been born by 14 BCE, but she would not marry Germanicus (born the previous year) until 4 CE.[5]

The boys may have lived with Agrippa until the family returned to Rome in 13, but they were not officially associated with him. As Rose (1997a) points out, the coinage honouring Agrippa, such as the gold and silver issues from Rome in 13 and 12 BCE featuring Augustus and Agrippa on obverse and reverse, is distinct from the more-or-less contemporary coins honouring Agrippa's natural sons. A separate denarius issued by C. Marius Tromentina in 13/12 BCE features a small silhouette of Julia, flanked by male heads, usually construed as Gaius and Lucius,[6] (see Figure 5.1, p. 67)and other coins after this date will honour the young men, but no coinage depicted them with their natural father Agrippa. As we noted in Chapter 5, Agrippa was sent out to Pannonia a few months after the return from the East, and fell ill there, dying in April of 12, soon after his return to Italy. Julia would give birth to his last child later that year.

By 12 BCE, Gaius was entering his ninth year and Lucius his sixth. Suetonius reports that Augustus monitored the boys' behaviour, making them sit at the foot of his couch when he dined, instructing them in swimming and even making them copy his own handwriting.[7] Gaius at least must have learned his letters (this was normally handled at home by a slave *paedagogus*) and was ready for formal education, and this too was taken in hand by his grandfather. We know from Suetonius' *Lives of Grammatici and Rhetors* that Augustus approached the learned freedman *grammaticus* Verrius Flaccus, who was running a flourishing school. Suetonius even describes that Verrius' methods were much more interactive than most teachers, who were content to provide their own interpretations of texts or fair copies of exercises – instead, Verrius assigned the boys exercises in composition matched to their ages and ability, such as writing their own version of a fable, and awarded a valuable prize (a rare book, we are told) to the best performer. Augustus invited him to move to the Palatine, where he set up his school in the house that had once belonged to Catulus.[8] Given the success of his school, Verrius bargained to bring with him those boys already in his programme, who will have provided a necessary stimulus to the young princes.

What was Roman elite schooling like? As part of learning to read around the age of seven, boys (and some girls) learned both Greek and Roman letters, progressing from syllables (ba-be-bi-bo-bu, ca-ce-ci, etc.) to words, and memorizing lines and passages of Homer. Literary education seems to have become much more prestigious in this generation, and Suetonius gives sketches of the careers of *grammatici* who taught Iullus Antonius[9] and the children of Scribonia – perhaps not Julia, who was taken from her mother, but her elder half-siblings. Scribonia bought a learned slave from the renowned teacher Orbilius and freed him, no doubt when her children no longer needed him. In the same decade, Caecilius Epirota, a freedman of Atticus, taught his daughter Caecilia after her teenaged marriage to Agrippa, but was dismissed for what seems to have been an attempted seduction. Epirota is important, however, because he started to teach his students modern Latin poetry, the poems of Catullus' avant garde friends, and the *Eclogues* and *Georgics* of the young Virgil. When Virgil died in 19 BCE, he regarded the *Aeneid* as unfinished and supposedly wanted it burned. It was only published at the instigation of Augustus. Was it already being taught – that is, interpreted – by Verrius a decade later?

Grammatici were not teachers of formal grammar, or grammarians in our modern sense, but as teachers of literature they also explained points of grammar as well as historical or religious details to help understand the epic narratives of Homer or the early Romans Naevius and Ennius. Naevius and Ennius would offer the same kind of difficulties of meaning to young children that we experience with Shakespeare, and *grammatici* would have to give instruction in context as well as language. After all, the Latin of the poets was not how the students themselves were expected to write prose. But Verrius was quite exceptional among his peers. He not only wrote on the principles of correct spelling,[10] he was an antiquarian, writing volumes on Etruscan affairs, on Saturn and the Saturnalia, a volume (of marvels?) and a twenty-two-volume work on the meaning of archaic and rare terms (*De verborum significatu*). This was later excerpted by Pompeius Festus and re-excerpted by Paul the Deacon in the age of Charlemagne, but even twice excerpted (and damaged), his book is central to our knowledge of Roman religion and institutions. Young Gaius and Lucius could hardly have used this kind of expertise, but Augustus wanted his sons to have the most prestigious instruction, and paid Verrius 100,000 sesterces a year – the salary of a top-level administrator. Verrius would be needed by Gaius for about five years, and by Lucius for three more years, by which time their youngest brother would have reached the age for instruction. But although Verrius was still alive and researching for a learned religious calendar when Agrippa Postumus reached the status of an adult, we have no evidence that Postumus was taught by Verrius (or was even teachable).

In this generation, boys normally moved on from the *grammaticus* to the school of the *rhetor*, who taught more advanced exercises in composition and, in particular, the oral skills of 'declamation' or improvised speech. Two types of speech were used as exercises. The pupil might be asked to speak, advising a historical figure faced with a moral crisis; this was supposedly preparation for giving deliberative, advisory speeches in the Senate. More often, perhaps, he was expected to compose a speech defending (or occasionally prosecuting) someone accused of a crime against the family. Typically, the teacher would provide his students with a fictitious situation in which a son (like the pupil in age) offended or disobeyed his father on behalf of some moral principle, such as supporting his impoverished uncle who had quarrelled with the father. The father was now threatening to disown his son; how could he justify himself? The 'kit' would also include some real or imaginary laws that the student had to reconcile with his case. What made this particularly artificial is that all the students in a class might have to speak about the same situation in turn. This was how the elder Seneca was trained, and how Ovid was trained. Augustus himself visited some of the more famous schools, on one occasion indeed with the boys' father Agrippa. But did he put his 'sons' through this type of schooling? Neither Suetonius nor Seneca, in his memoirs of the *rhetors*, mentions any *rhetor* as having taught Gaius and Lucius. But then, Augustus had more reason than most parents to introduce the boys early to their future roles in both civil and military life. Given their position as his heirs, it was more important to introduce them as soon as possible to the *tirocinium fori* (observing the courts as students of a senior orator) and even the Senate, where they could learn by observation their future public roles, and to their first *stipendia* (military campaigns) under the *contubernium* (protection) of a kinsman commander.

Like many rulers and fathers, Augustus found it difficult to strike a balance of authority and indulgence with both his people and his children. In a surprising vignette, Suetonius reports that when the audience at the theatre took up an actor's lines to hail him as 'Dominus', Augustus issued a stern decree forbidding it, and from then on would not let even his children and grandchildren address him by that title as a joke.[11] The most delicate aspect of the boys' upbringing must have been achieving a balance between ensuring their popularity with the people of Rome and preventing Gaius and Lucius from too much self-esteem and self-indulgence. Even before the boys reached puberty and could set aside their purple-bordered boys' togas for the togas of manhood, Augustus made the boys known to the Roman people through carefully controlled festival appearances and familiar to the provinces through their images on coinage. Something of this careful calibration of publicity appears from two notices in Dio, both for 13 BCE or perhaps 12, after their return. There were many festival games each year, which were presided over by different members of the Augustan family. So, for example, Iullus Antonius (as Praetor?) gave one set of games in 13 and entertained the Princeps and the Senate at an official dinner. The ten-year-old Gaius was on show when he took a prominent part in the *lusus Troiae*, a set of figured equestrian manoeuvres we know best from Virgil's imaginative description of young Ascanius leading his squadron in the first display at Aeneas' Sicilian Games.[12] But on another occasion, when Tiberius was presiding (Dio 54.27.1 sets this too in 13 BCE, when Tiberius was Consul for the first time), Augustus scolded him for putting young Gaius at the Emperor's side and rebuked the people for acclaiming Gaius. These festival occasions were not confined to Rome: when Augustus received the news of Agrippa's approaching death, he was exhibiting a contest of armed warriors 'in the name of his sons' at the Athenian festival of the Panathenaia.

The most famous of Augustus' dynastic monuments, and one still almost entirely preserved, was first proposed by the Senate in this year, but not completed until 9 BCE. On what we call the Altar of Peace, erected in the Campus Martius but moved to the banks of the Tiber seventy years ago on the orders of Mussolini, we see the whole Augustan family and the chief priestly officials in procession to dedicate the altar itself, with Augustus, his head covered in his toga, to officiate as Chief Priest at the centre of the south frieze, and Agrippa, similarly veiled, occupying the central position on the north frieze (see the three panels illustrated in Plates 2(a) and 2(b) and 3(a)). By 9 BCE, Agrippa was dead and Julia married to Tiberius, but the original design was retained. The boys are not, however, shown with either their natural or adoptive father. Instead, we can see them with their mother on the north frieze. On the left, next to the damaged female figure which has been interpreted as Julia, there is a handsome and bashful young Gaius, dressed as a *camillus* or altar-boy, with a smaller boy nearby who must be Lucius (see Plate 3(a)).[13] The composition is not only a masterpiece of vivid but idealizing art; it represents a triumph of design within the limits of protocol.

But our sources only develop a real interest in Gaius when he approaches puberty. In 8 BCE he was sent to Tiberius at Lugdunum to take part in exercises with what would become the Rhine army.[14]

Tiberius' Gallic mint at Lugdunum commemorated this with a denarius showing the young prince on horseback (see Figure 8.1, overleaf), but he seems to have returned quickly to Rome, and the following year he presided, standing in for the absent Tiberius, over the games to celebrate Augustus'

Figure 8.1 Denarius from Lugdunum mint, 8 BCE. Obverse: Augustus, laureate;
Reverse: Gaius Caesar shown with military standards as cavalry officer.

return, and combined this with funeral games in honour of his late father
Agrippa. This is the year in which Dio reports that Augustus included Gaius
among the boys of military age (*epheboi*), and it is perhaps because of his
new status that the people, as we noted in the previous chapter, elected the
thirteen-year-old as Consul. During the republic, the presiding officer at
elections could and did reject unwelcome candidates out of hand, so we may
wonder how the Roman electoral *comitia* could have achieved this without
Augustus' approval, yet in 19 BCE, they had actually elected Augustus against
his will. As for young Gaius, the people of Rome may have been confident
that as Consul he would be politically obedient to the Princeps, but Augustus
felt compelled by the situation to make a public statement, and in his speech
reproving the people, he declared that no one should become Consul until
he was old enough to exercise mature judgement and to resist the follies of
the people. In fact, Suetonius reports that whenever Augustus recommended
his sons to the people (presumably for new privileges or future office), he
would add the qualification, 'if they deserve it' (*Life of Augustus* 55).

According to Dio (55.9.2) Augustus was troubled about the growing
wilfulness of the two princes. This was probably little more than normal
teenaged attempts at self-assertion, just as their so-called self-indulgence was
the usual materialism and extravagance of adolescents. The historian reports
that Augustus was alarmed by their arrogance and self-indulgence, but the
only example he provides is that young Lucius (now ten or eleven) went
to the theatre 'on his own'. What does this mean? That he went without
obtaining permission? Or incognito? Otherwise, Lucius would have taken
the usual attendant *paedagogus* as bodyguard and sat in the theatre section
reserved for boys of his age. We can hardly imagine him deliberately
occupying the imperial box. No doubt there were other escapades. It is a pity
that with the spotlight on his elder brother we know so little about Lucius.

Augustus met the popular demand for Gaius' promotion to public office by giving him a priesthood and introducing him to the Senate, designating him to be Consul in five year's time (1 CE), but according to Dio (our only continuous source for these years)[15] this also provoked him into giving Tiberius tribunician power for five years, a position almost equal to his own, which he had formerly used to mark Agrippa as his colleague. But Dio has surely got his priorities wrong. Tiberius had considerable seniority (he had already held two consulships), and it is more likely that Augustus' decision to give him this extended authority (probably tied to a specific assignment in the East to deal with Rome's uneasy alliance with Armenia and still flourishing Parthians) was the motivation, rather than the result, of any action affecting the young princes. It was this 'promotion' of Tiberius that seems to have both offended the young princes and triggered Tiberius' defiant decision to renounce his public duty and take himself to Rhodes.

Augustus himself held a consulship in 5 BCE, to introduce Gaius to the Senate in the year when the prince officially came of age and put on the toga of manhood. News of his coming of age was sent out to the provinces, probably enhanced with details of the Roman ritual for the better understanding by the Greek and Grecizing communities of the East. We can, to some extent, reconstruct the imperial announcement from the inscription surviving at Sardis in Lydia of the congratulatory decree delivered to the Senate at Rome by the city's envoys.

> Whereas Gaius Julius Caesar, the eldest of the sons of Augustus, has – as has been fervently prayed for – assumed in all its splendour the pure-white toga in place of the purple bordered toga, and all men rejoice to see the prayers for[16] his sons rising together to Augustus. And whereas our city in view of so happy an event has decided to keep the day which raised him from a boy to a man as a holy day, on which annually all shall wear wreaths and festal garb, and the annual; strategi shall offer sacrifices to the gods and render prayers through the sacred heralds for his preservation, to unite in consecrating to him an image set up in his Father's temple.
>
> (Ehrenberg/Jones (1955: no. 99),
> Lewis/Reinhold (1990: II, 210)

Loyal subjects of Rome were now expected, whether in Italy or the provinces, to honour imperial birthdays (and days of death) with a communal public sacrifice and ritual supplication, not just every year but each month – the ceremonies and statues too would multiply.

Soon after this, Augustus had reason to renew his anxieties about Rome's eastern boundaries and the disloyal dynastic intrigues of the Parthian and Armenian monarchies (which seem to have been quiet since 19 BCE). Phraates of Parthia had sent his four legitimate sons to Rome as an earnest of his goodwill, but in their absence Phraataces, an illegitimate son by an Italian slave girl, murdered his father[17] and made himself king, either in, or more likely before, 2 BCE. Now Augustus saw the opportunity (or need?) to use his own son to deal with the Parthian usurper. It is most likely that the Princeps knew of this coup well before he felt ready to intervene. For example, Pliny reports that he 'sent ahead Dionysius of Charax to the east to write a full account of that part of the world for his elder son who was about to go and deal with affairs in Armenia, Parthia and Arabia', and Juba also composed several volumes of a study of Arabian geography 'for Gaius Caesar who was consumed with a passion for Arabia'.[18] Augustus knew that Gaius was still too young and inexperienced and sent him first as a legate to the troops of the Danube region, to learn how to command in a pacified region (Dio. 55.10.17). However, he himself had other business to deal with at home that was more important than Phraataces. It was in 2 BCE, twenty-five years after he had 'restored the republic to the Senate and people' in 27, that he finally agreed to accept the title of Pater Patriae (in February)[19] and would preside in August over the inauguration of the new Forum Augustum and the temple of Mars Ultor. With Tiberius self-exiled on Rhodes, it was Gaius who presided over the *ludi circenses* in honour of Mars and, incidentally, saw his youngest brother Agrippa Postumus ride in the *lusus Troiae*. Only after this would Gaius embark on the great expedition to the East.

The expedition was seen as a great adventure, and poets wrote in hyperbolic terms, as if Gaius was setting out to conquer the unconquered and elusive Parthians. The Greek court poet Antipater of Thessalonica turns a neat epigram on the four deities Hercules, Venus, Minerva and Mars painted (or in plastered relief) on the ceiling of Gaius' residence: 'O Gaius, fortress of thy country, may Heracles the ox-eater make you invincible, may Aphrodite Cypris make you happy in marriage, Pallas make you wise in counsel and Ares make you fearless' (*Anthologia Palatina* 9.59)[20] Another epigram is more explicit:

> Depart then to the east, son of Zeus; for already the oriental feet of the Parthians are deserting at your approach. Depart, prince Caesar, and you will find their bows slackened with fear. But always begin from your father's commands. Be first to make Rome, which holds the Ocean as her boundary in every direction, rounded and completed by the rising sun.
>
> (*Anthologia Palatina* 9.297)

Greeks easily adopted the extravagant language of divine birth, but Horace had long since paralleled Augustus with Jupiter in his poetry (cf. *Odes* 1.12 and *Epistles* 2.1, addressed to Augustus at the Princeps' own request). After Horace, Ovid accepted the trope as expected of him. In his first book of *Ars amatoria* (*The Art of Love*), he digresses from outlining the best places to meet accommodating girls, to insert his tribute to the young prince; indeed it is this which dates the poem to 1 BCE.

See! Caesar prepares to add to the conquered world whatever was still missing: now furthest East, you will be ours. Parthian, you will pay your punishment; buried Crassi [father and son] exult now, and those standards which suffered shame in barbarian hands. Your avenger is here, and has demonstrated his leadership from his earliest years, handling as a boy wars not to be waged by mere boys. You fearful men, do not count the birthdays of gods; valour comes to the Caesar's before time. His heaven-sent genius soars swifter than his years and is impatient with the waste of cowardly delay [. . .]

[. . .] You will send your arms into action with the auspices and years of your father, though you are a boy, and conquer by his auspices and years. You owe such a beginning to so great a name, now *prince of young men and destined to be prince of the old*.

(Ovid, The Art of Love 1.177–86, 1.191–4,
emphasis added)

This is skilfully composed, to move from Rome's shame at the defeat of Crassus and his officer son by the Parthians at Carrhae in 53 BCE to the captured standards recovered through the negotiations of Tiberius in 19 BCE and newly installed in the temple of Mars the Avenger, whose title 'Ultor' Ovid now gives to Gaius Caesar. Like Antipater, Ovid diplomatically reminds his readers that it is Augustus' wise judgement and his official auspices as commander-in-chief that guarantee confidence in Gaius' success (and will take credit from it). The apostrophe which ends my quotation touches on a new title that Augustus had awarded to both Gaius and his younger brother as leaders of the knights, Rome's cavalry class. He now called them '*Principes iuventutis*', 'Leaders [or can we say princes, since this is what they were?] of the Youth.' It was to honour this new title that Augustus issued one of his favourite denarii, inscribed '*C. L. CAES. PRINC. IUV.*' depicting the two youths on the reverse with their shields and spear (see Figure 8.2).

This coin issue would be continued by the Princeps until at least 10 CE, long after the death of both his heirs. But his hope was, of course, that Gaius would become his successor, *Princeps* among the Senate and the people of Rome – and Ovid's coinage 'prince of the old' (*senum*) would automatically suggest seniority among the Senate – the preeminence which the republic had given to the *princeps senatus*.

Ovid does not neglect Augustus' new title in his compliments to Gaius: 'the father of your country and yourself dresses you in your armour'. Indeed, he apostrophizes both Augustus and Mars on equal terms: 'Father Mars, and father Caesar, give your divine power to him as he departs, for one of you is already a god and the other will become one.' But he reserves his most exalted tones for the vision of Gaius' future triumph, which the young lover can turn to his advantage.

Figure 8.2 Denarius of Augustus, 2 BCE. Obverse: Augustus laureate;
Reverse: Gaius and Lucius Caesar armed as *Principes Iuventutis*.

So that great day will come when you, most handsome of men, will ride golden with four snow-white horses; enemy leaders will go before you, their necks loaded with chains, to ensure they cannot find safety in flight as before. Young men with girls among them will joyfully watch, and that day will relax all men's hearts. And when one of the girls asks the names of the kings, what places, what mountains and rivers are being paraded past, answer it all, and not only if she asks first, and quote as well-known things you did not know. Here is the Euphrates, his brow encircled with reeds, the river whose blue hair hangs loose will be the Tigris. Make these men Armenians, and this land Persia founded by Danae's son; and identify that city as within the valleys of Achaemenia.

(Ovid, *The Art of Love* 1.213–26)

The poet is a realist and combines the high hopes for victory with the lover's easier conquest of the girl standing nearby as they crowd to watch the triumphal parade with its floats displaying personifications of defeated cities, tribes and rivers, or more explicit maps and panoramas. Only Augustus probably realized the risks of sending a young man on a mission that should have remained diplomatic but offered such temptations to unfamiliar warfare with a treacherous enemy in the hope of popular glory. According to Plutarch, he prayed to the gods to give Gaius 'the popularity of Pompey, the boldness of Alexander and his own good fortune.'[21] An altar erected by the local *vicomagistri* for the Lares of the Vicus Sandaliarius shows young Gaius clad in a military cloak with Augustus as Augur, with an augural hen at his feet, preparing him for departure, while a veiled matron (more likely Livia than Julia by this date) offers a dish for a libation (see Plate 4(b)).[22]

Despite the historians' muttering about the boys' indiscipline, Augustus seems to have been genuinely fond of Gaius. A letter has been preserved by Aulus Gellius (15.7) 'from the volume of Augustus' letters to his grandson Gaius'. It must, then, have been one of many,[23] but this one was special, written by Augustus on his sixty-fourth birthday, so on 23 September, 1 CE. The age of sixty-three was regarded in the ancient world as a man's climacteric, or natural, limit, and Augustus, who had more than once been acutely ill and at risk of death, uses the occasion to express his fond hopes to his son:

> Hello, dear Gaius, my sweetest little donkey, whom I always long for when you are away from me. But especially on days like this one, my eyes look for my Gaius, and hope that wherever you have been today, you will be happy and healthy as you celebrate my sixty fourth birthday. For, as you see, we have escaped the common Climacteric of all old men, the sixty third year. Now I beg the gods that we may be allowed to pass in safety through whatever amount of time is left and with the state in a most fortunate condition, while you boys perform like heroes and take on my watch.
>
> (cited by Gellius 15.7)

What I have translated as 'Hello' is both more solemn and more personal – *Ave* – the greeting Catullus makes at his brother's tomb, and Aeneas uses to salute the dead Pallas. There is no modern equivalent. Augustus cannot know where Gaius is, or when the letter will reach him ('you have been' thinks from the time when Gaius will receive it). Gaius may be in peaceful Syria, the provincial base of Roman imperial commanders, or he may be on an expedition in the dangerous hinterland. But Augustus is thinking into the future, and associates his hopes for the Empire itself with the survival of his sons. The last phrase combines a Greek ideal of heroic and manly success in battle (*andragathein*) with the more prosaic but long-term Roman concept of being assigned a *statio*, a military watch or posting which the good soldier endures with patience and loyalty.

Gaius had been sent with his own household and experienced advisers such as Lollius (currently Governor of Syria) and Censorinus.[24] What Augustus intended was that Gaius should obtain by negotiation the confirmation of a king of Armenia who would acknowledge Roman suzerainty and ensure Parthian acceptance of this situation. And Velleius confirms that this did take place after Gaius had met Tiberius by arrangement and manifested goodwill. This may have been all the harder since he could hardly avoid blaming both his mother's disgrace and his own present onerous tour of duty on Tiberius' desertion of his posting. But Velleius himself was witness when Gaius met with the Parthian King at what we know as Baghdad, on an island in the Euphrates, remembering with justified excitement: 'this spectacle of the Roman army drawn up on one side, and the Parthian army on the other, while the two most important persons not only of their empires but of mankind came together in conference' (Velleius 2.101.1–3). Full diplomatic protocol was observed as, first, Gaius was host to the Parthian 'on the river's Roman bank', then was feasted by the King on Parthian soil. Even so, it is difficult to see how Gaius was occupied for the next two years. Barnes has argued from Pliny's allusions to Arabia and the congratulatory decree inscribed at the behest of Cornelius Scipio, Governor of Achaea that Gaius was intended to conduct an expedition to Arabia, that legendary home of exotic and costly spices, and actually won some kind of victory in this campaign, for which Augustus was awarded his fifteenth salutation as victorious general.[25] This would occupy the summer of 1 CE and perhaps the following campaign season, before Gaius heard of his brother Lucius' death of sickness at Massilia on 20 August, 2 CE.[26] Only after this expedition did Gaius embark on his campaign in Armenia, which is reported as meeting with initial success. Dio (55.10a.4–9) is more helpful than Velleius: Gaius had originally been dealing with Tigranes of Armenia, but on Tigranes' death in battle now confirmed the kingship of Ariobarzanes, known to the Romans from his earlier time in Rome. This was why the Armenians now took up arms against the Romans in support of a rival claimant. Or had Gaius made the situation a pretext for action in hope of a glamorous victory?

It is likely, then, that Gaius did not embark on hostilities against Armenia until 3 CE. Neither Velleius nor the Dio excerpts (55.10a.6–10) indicate the year. Like Crassus before him, he had virtually no experience of dealing with these eastern peoples, and naively made the mistake of trusting a false friend – in his case, Addon, or Adduus, the commander of the garrison at Artageira, who invited Gaius to a parley at which he was treacherously wounded on 9 September.[27] The excerpted narrative of Dio adds that after being wounded, Gaius reduced the town by siege, captured Addon and was hailed by his troops as Imperator. Now the accounts of Velleius and Dio converge: Gaius' wound became infected and he seems to have suffered something of a breakdown. Both historians imply that there had been some mental weakness and that he now begged to lay down his command and live privately in Syria. There was enough time (three to four months?) for Augustus to receive his plea and consult the Senate, sending reply that Gaius should at least come to Italy, and he was presumably hoping to do so when his men set off for the coast. We have to imagine the General suffering agonies from gangrene as he was carried by litter for days on end from the hinterland to reach the small port of Limyra in Lycia (on the south-western coast of Turkey), where he died on 21 February 4 CE.[28] While Artageira is so small that the compilers of the Barrington Atlas have not been able to locate it,[29] both it and Limyra won their moment in history from the death of Augustus' chosen successor.

The death of Lucius from illness had been duly honoured and commemorated, but Gaius' pathetic fate drove Augustus, the Senate and the people to a mass of ceremonies and both visual and verbal monuments.

At Limyra, a team of designers sent from Rome constructed a cenotaph consisting of a square tomb with a Latin inscription. On its side, four reliefs, now only recoverable from fragments, showed the big moments in Gaius' campaigns, such as his presentation to the Armenians of King Ariobarzanes. Above it rose a tower, probably like the tomb still standing at Glanum (St Remy in Provence), supporting a statue of the prince.[30] Augustus himself records the coronation of Ariobarzanes in his *Res gestae* (27).[31]

Many cities must have hastened to pay proper tribute, but Pisa, where a new colony had been added to the community under the patronage of Gaius and Lucius, provides the best documentation of such monuments. The town had been taken by surprise by the death of Lucius, in the absence of the Mayor and councillors, and had evidently acted only when guided by the model of a decree from the Senate, but it was quick to adapt this into an affirmation of loyal mourning. The council was more experienced by the time Gaius died, eighteen months later, and had its own man in Rome, the equestrian Statulenus Iuncus, a priest (*flamen*) of Augustus, and with his advice could determine the proper measures of mourning and commemoration. The great inscription from the Pisan *Augusteum* declares that an arch was to be erected to honour Gaius, decorated with spoils from nations conquered or having surrendered themselves to Roman authority (*fides*) and surmounted by gilded statues of Augustus in triumphal dress flanked by the two princes on horseback.[32] Something of the impact on ordinary citizens (even the women) comes through from the paragraph in the decree of the decurions and colonists which ordains both rules for immediate mourning and for each successive anniversary of the prince's death:

> That from the day on which his death was announced to the day on which his bones are brought back and buried and the due rites are performed to his departed spirit all should wear mourning, keep the temples of the immortal gods, the public baths, and all shops closed, and abstain from festivity, and the matrons of our colony should make public lamentation:
>
> That the day on which Gaius Caesar died, February 21, should go down in history and be observed at the present time by order and wish of all as a day of mourning like that of the Allia, and that it should be expressly forbidden to hold, plan or announce for or on that day, any public sacrifice, thanksgiving, weddings or public banquets, or to hold or view on that day any theatrical performances or circus games.

Instead of all these normal pleasures and activities, solemn public sacrifices were to be offered by the magistrates 'in the same place and in the same manner as the solemn sacrifices established in honour of Lucius Caesar'. Presumably, the proposed arch, like many others throughout the Empire, was erected and stood until dilapidation or a change of dynasty made it appropriate to remove it.

Epilogue

But young Agrippa Postumus still lived, and after the news of Gaius' death, on 26 June, 4 CE, Augustus adopted the fifteen-year-old along with his forty-seven-year-old stepfather Tiberius as his joint heirs and successors. This can hardly have been good news for any of the three. Historical tradition, determined by those who actually succeed to power, has represented Postumus as brutish and violent, and although he still had an official coming of age in 5 CE, he was disinherited within three years of his adoption and relegated first to Sorrento and later to the island of Planasia near Corsica.[33] If he was surly and aggressive, he had good reason: he had never known his father; his mother (who may admittedly never have given him much attention, let alone affection) was exiled when he was ten; his brothers were now dead and his sisters set up in their married households. Even before the marriages and military service took away his siblings, he must have lived alone, apart from his servants, whom he could not trust to take his side.

Dio reports that Agrippa spent his exile fishing, and he may well have been eager to escape his confinement on land, and even hoped for smuggled communications with friends. The Roman plebs still loved his mother Julia and had demonstrated fiercely in 3 CE for her restoration, until Augustus answered them face to face with a refusal.[34] Similarly, Suetonius knows of reports of attempts to rescue Agrippa and Julia [35] and to take them to the armies. But when it came to his end, immediately on the death of Augustus, the historians are full of conflicting accounts of what occurred on that remote island. The elder Pliny hints that Augustus wanted to restore his grandson, and both Tacitus and Dio (56.30.1) quote a rumour[36] that not long before he died Augustus experienced a change of heart and made a secret voyage to Planasia, where he was reconciled with Agrippa. All three associate this tale with Fabius Maximus, supposedly the Princeps' only companion on this trip, who is said to have revealed the secret to his wife, through whom the story got back to Livia. While Levick (1976a: 64–5), accepts the truth of the voyage, Syme (1979: 149) points to the whole tale as gossip to explain the sudden death, perhaps suicide, of Fabius. The story is certainly incompatible with the official version that Augustus had authorized Agrippa's death.

But if Agrippa was never reunited with his grandfather and adoptive father, he may still have been able to communicate with potential supporters. About the time of Augustus' death, a slave, Clemens, had tried to reach Agrippa with a band of fighting men but arrived too late.[37] The most vivid picture of the wretched boy's situation emerges from Tacitus' account of his killing:

> The first crime of the new principate was the murder of Agrippa Postumus. Although he was unwarned and unarmed, the centurion [sent to kill him] only finished him off with great difficulty. Tiberius made no statement about this in the Senate, but pretended his father had sent

orders, writing ahead to the tribune in charge of his custody not to hesitate to kill Agrippa at the time of his own death.

It is true that Augustus had made many savage complaints about the young man's behaviour in order to obtain a decree of the Senate sanctioning his exile, but he had never been harsh enough to execute any of his kin, nor was it easy to believe that he imposed the death of his grandson to protect his stepson. It is more likely that Tiberius and Livia had hurried on the murder of the hated and suspect youth, he from fear and she from the hatred of a stepmother.

(Tac. *Annals* 1.6)

Suetonius attributes his death to the tribune commanding Agrippa's guard, who acted on written instructions, whether from Augustus, or Livia and Tiberius acting in Augustus' name. He adds that when the Tribune reported to Tiberius that his commands had been carried out, the new princeps denied that he had given such orders. Although Tacitus has been accused of malicious misrepresentation of both Livia and her son, it is straining credibility to believe they had not ensured the young man's death. The act was nothing to be proud of, but they may have been justified in believing it was necessary for Tiberius' survival in his new and dangerous position.

9 Julia's girls

I Julia, granddaughter of Augustus: a pattern repeated

We saw in discussing Julia's time as wife of Agrippa and mother of his children that there was no direct evidence for either the naming of her daughters or their relative or absolute ages. The known birth-dates of Gaius and Lucius (and year of Agrippa Postumus' birth) left the years 19 and 18 BCE and again 15 and 14 BCE open for these pregnancies and suggest that one daughter was born before 17 and the other after 16 BCE. In fact, the relative ages of Julia the Younger and Agrippina must be deduced from their marriages, which are themselves a matter of inference. We infer Julia's marriage to Aemilius Paullus from the marriageability of their daughter Aemilia Lepida. If she was betrothed to Germanicus' young brother, the future Emperor Claudius, and expected to marry him in 8 CE,[1] this implies that she was approaching twelve years old and her parents must have been married by 4 or at least 3 BCE. This in turn implies that Julia must have been born before 16 BCE, the year when her parents set out for the Aegean and Asia Minor. She may well have been born the year before Lucius; if so, she would have been fourteen at marriage. Her sister Agrippina was certainly an infant during the eastern tour but did not marry Germanicus (born in 16 or 15 BCE)[2] until 4 CE. Their eldest children Nero and Drusus come of age in 20 CE (Tac. *Annals* 3.29) and 23 CE respectively (Tac. *Annals* 4.4.1). The sisters seem to have been four or five years apart, but although they would both ultimately be victimized by the dominant males of their family, their destinies were radically different and reflect the changing fortunes of the dynasty between 4 BCE when Tiberius, in self-imposed exile, was apparently disgraced, and 4 CE when he was adopted by Augustus, together with the fifteen-year-old Agrippa Postumus.

On the face of it, one daughter was frivolous and inherited the sexual promiscuity attributed to her mother, while the other inherited from her mother only her famous fertility and her assertiveness and relish for power. But the same vested interests that have distorted Julia the Elder's reputation and suppressed a better knowledge of her character and tastes have almost completely succeeded in wiping out any details that would help us to understand Julia the Younger.

For censorious male critics, it was a case of 'like mother, like child'. But I would insist that the pattern so easily observed in the limited data about the younger Julia, whether or not it had a basis in her actual life, is the one deliberately imposed by her enemies, imposed so thoroughly that even Tacitus cannot give a clear picture of her personality or activities.

What do we know of Julia the Younger? That she was married to her not-quite-second cousin, L. Aemilius Paullus, grandson of Scribonia, her own grandmother, and son of Julia's half-sister Cornelia[3] and Aemilius Paullus, a suffect consul of 34 BCE. In turn, the younger Julia's husband Paullus is found as consular colleague of his brother-in-law Gaius in 1 CE. And then what did he do? No proconsular governorship is known, no responsible post as Curator of the Tiber basin or the grain supply of Rome. Nor is he recorded as serving as a legate in any military campaign. True, the years when Gaius was in the East seem to have been empty of serious military engagement in western Europe, but if Augustus had wanted to promote Aemilius without giving him access to provincial wealth or armed force, he could have given him a civilian office. Instead, it seems that with Gaius commanding in the East and Lucius rising to manhood, Augustus felt no need to look after the careers of lesser members of his family. When Lucius died in 2 CE, but not necessarily because of his death, Tiberius was finally allowed to return to private life at Rome. Two years later, when Gaius' death was known, Tiberius was raised from his private status to that of adopted son and heir, along with Agrippa Postumus, young enough to be Tiberius' son. Agrippa's position quickly proved precarious, but it would in any case have done nothing to benefit his brother-in-law. We saw that he was first relegated to Campania and then sent in 7 CE to exile on Planasia.

It seems that a series of natural calamities and provincial uprisings beginning in 5 CE led to political disturbances at Rome. Pliny (*Natural History* 7.149, Appendix II.3b) mentions famine and plague at Rome and uprisings in Pannonia and Illyricum; it looks as though Aemilius Paullus may have taken advantage of public discontent to form a conspiracy against the Princeps – or against his new heir Tiberius. Thus, Suetonius lists the conspiracy of Plautius Rufus and L. Paullus, the husband of Augustus' granddaughter, after the attempted coup of Egnatius Rufus and before the attempts of Audasius and Epicadus 'to carry off Julia, Augustus' daughter and Agrippa his grandson from the islands where they were confined to the armies' (*Augustus* 19).[4] Dio, who mentions the famine and precautionary measures to send gladiators and surplus slaves out of the city in 6 CE, speaks of a Publius Rufus (55.27.2) who spread talk and even written pamphlets fostering revolution, but although he points to suspicion of more influential but unnamed figures working through Rufus, he does not connect Rufus' activities in any way with Aemilius or Julia.[5] Aemilius was condemned, but in which year – 6 or 8 CE? And was his penalty death, or exile? The distinction is important, as Syme (1985) has shown,[6] because the younger Julia was only found guilty of adultery by her grandfather two years later, in 8 CE. Scholars have argued that this must mean her husband was living (and they were not divorced). But the only evidence for Aemilius Paullus' survival after the detection of the conspiracy is the entry of a man with the same name in the list of Arval brethren for 14 CE – best interpreted, as he is by Levick (1976b), as Paullus' young son, replaced in 14 because he had died naturally.

It is strange enough that Paullus was fomenting treason in the year his loyalist brother Aemilius Lepidus was Consul, and his condemnation may not have occurred until early 7 CE. But the events around this year are even more confusing. There was agitation in support of young Agrippa, perhaps even of electing him to the consulship, which can be used to explain both his further removal from Surrentum to Planasia and Augustus' suspension of troubled elections. Either late in 6 or early in 7 CE, the Princeps himself appointed the magistrates for this year. If we follow the notes of an ancient commentator on Juvenal, the younger Julia may have been relegated from Rome and then recalled before further misbehaviour (but what?) led to her final exile to Trimerus in 8 CE.[7]

Again, the nature of Julia's offence is confused by the treatment of her alleged lover D. Iunius Silanus. According to Tacitus, he had taken himself into voluntary exile (presumably before Julia's in-house trial). Here is Tacitus' version:

> Although Augustus' public fortune had remained strong, his family circumstances were unlucky because of the unchastity of his daughter and granddaughter, whom he expelled from Rome, punishing their adulterers with death or exile. For he had exceeded the mildness of his ancestors and his own legislation by giving the dreadful name of injury to religion and violation of the majesty of the state to an offence routinely committed by men and women. Silanus was stigmatized as adulterer of the granddaughter, but suffered no more savage penalty than being banned from Caesar's friendship. Taking this as a hint of exile to come, he had not dared to request forgiveness from the senate and Princeps until Tiberius was emperor.
>
> (Tac. *Annals* 3.24 1–3: Appendix II.4b)

When Silanus' brother petitioned Tiberius in the Senate, the Emperor replied that he was glad Decimus was returning from his long travel abroad, as was quite lawful, since he had not been exiled by a decree of the Senate or any law, but that he personally would maintain his father's attitude of offence with Silanus. This episode, as reported by Tacitus, seems to be an extreme case of hypocrisy in both Principes, father and adopted son, but it also prompts the question: why was Silanus not punished more severely? Did he escape only because he had left Rome before the storm broke and he was implicated by evidence at the senate hearing? Or was he being given generous treatment because he was somehow complicit in Julia's condemnation and exile? Had he actually informed against her? One interpretation is that he and Julia had regarded Aemilius Paullus as divorced and had contracted a marriage unknown to and unauthorized by Augustus. Was he, in fact, the father of the child she gave birth to after her condemnation, the child that Augustus had put to death? Or was the alleged adultery of Julia with Silanus supposedly committed earlier, during her husband's lifetime?[8] The fact that Julia was sent into exile so soon after her brother Agrippa's disgrace makes it very clear that someone – whether Augustus or Tiberius – was suppressing a political thrust by the family of Julia to seize power, and the woman's sexual activities, real or imagined, in or after marriage, were the excuse for her victimization. Dio's excerptors have nothing to say about Julia, but Tacitus gives her a death notice in 28 CE consistent with the earlier report.

> Augustus had convicted her of adultery and cast her away onto the island of Trimerus, not far from the Apulian coast, where she had been supported during twenty years of exile by the generosity of Livia Augusta, who had secretly undermined her stepchildren while they flourished but publicly displayed compassion towards them after their downfall.
>
> (*Annals* 4.71.6–7, Appendix II.4d)

We know so little about her. The only evidence for her luxurious frivolity are scattered incidental comments by Pliny the Elder – that she boasted of owning the smallest 'pet dwarf' in Rome, and that Augustus found her house (or palace) so luxurious that he had it razed to the ground after her disgrace. This may have been a symbolic act, imitating the practice in the early republic of destroying the houses of traitors such as Spurius Maelius or Manlius Capitolinus. Augustus had also razed the house of Vedius Pollio after his death in 15 BCE, but then Pollio had made Augustus his heir. We do not even know where the younger Julia and her husband had lived – on the Palatine, no doubt. It might have been convenient to raze the house so as to have the site free for new building. One thing generally assumed is Julia's association with the poet Ovid, but we 'know' it only from his relegation to Tomis in the same year that she was isolated on Trimerus, 8 CE, and from what he hints about his incrimination in an unnamed offence in his poems from exile, especially the second book of the *Tristia*, his defence before Augustus. In this he claims, and claims repeatedly, that he had been punished by the Emperor for two things: a poem and a blunder (*carmen et error*). The latter implies that he had unwittingly been involved as a witness or accessory in an offence against the Emperor. But even the more specific reference to the *carmen* creates problems.

Guilt by association: did Ovid preach adultery?

We have already had reason to consider Ovid's love poetry as a probable influence on the youth of the first Julia, since he certainly began to publish his 'Love Affairs' (*Amores*) during her impressionable teenaged years. He had edited and reissued the *Amores* before the elder Julia's disgrace, and was bringing out a new set of books about the art of conducting love affairs from 1 BCE. (As we saw in the last chapter, Ovid's first book of *Ars amatoria* (The Art of Love) contains an excursus on Gaius' eastern expedition; the second has no internal evidence of date.) It is thought that he brought out his third book, addressed to women, with a fourth book, *Remedia amoris* or Cures for Love, around 2 CE. This was six years before his relegation, of which he seems to have had no warning. Could the books of instruction in love be the offensive carmen? By 8 CE, Ovid was actually well advanced in composing a respectable epic covering world history from Chaos and the Creation to 'his own times', his fifteen books of *Metamorphoses*, which spoke with ostentatious reverence of Augustus in both its first and last books. And he had probably drafted most of the first six months of his learned poem explaining the Roman ceremonial and religious calendar, the *Fasti*. Recently, a number of scholars have pointed to the potential subversiveness of those ostensibly respectful allusions in Metamorphoses 1 and 15, and similar ambiguities in the poet's honorific treatment of Augustus and his dynasty in the calendar poem. By 4 CE, Augustus was probably increasingly aware of criticism and opposition to his protracted exercise of autocratic power and ready to see veiled insult in, for example, a Jupiter compared to himself who acts as judge and jury and executes the alleged conspirator Lycaon before 'consulting' his senate of gods, or a Great Leader who declares his father a god, because he would not otherwise have been the Son of God.[9] In the *Fasti*, Ovid boldly affirms that Augustus is a far greater leader than Romulus because Romulus actually kidnapped the Sabine women, whereas Augustus ordered women to be chaste (*Fasti* 2.133–44).

It is the timing of Ovid's relegation, most of all, that compels us to associate it with the fall of the younger Julia and the sexual licence that Augustus alleged against her, which Ovid treats as the chief charge against his own work. He is sufficiently explicit in affirming his discretion over the blunder – whatever it was – to make it clear that it was really more politically sensitive than any erotic verse, but also to guarantee to Augustus and all his own readers that he would not let the side down by providing inopportune information. So let us follow the direction of his argument and suppose that his licentious poetry was the issue, that it had so far escaped imperial anger, but only until the Father of his Country was made to feel shame over his own granddaughter's promiscuity.

What was so new and shocking about Ovid's love poetry? Romans and Greeks alike knew and enjoyed two kinds of realistic poetry about love. First, the comic dramas in which young unmarried men loved and made love to non-citizen girls who made a living by their attractions, whether in street prostitution or hired as entertainers, or as up-market 'kept women'. These comedies could be enjoyed without embarrassment, since young men were allowed to have their fun before they grew up and made correct marriages;

besides, this kind of woman was not entitled to protection from sexual activity. She was not their neighbour's daughter, still less a gentleman's wife. Women who were ineligible for marriage had to survive by their physical charms. The other genre, the erotic epigram or extended elegy, was normally written in the first person, describing the poet's pleasures with a girl or boy, again assumed to be from the non-citizen and unprotected class. Ovid was familiar with both the Greek and Roman versions of these provocative poems. And he himself began, like his predecessor Catullus or older contemporaries, by presenting a personal love narrative, articulated discontinuously in a series of shorter vignettes describing situations that could (almost) all have been part of one extended love affair with his girl Corinna. Her Greek name – that of a famous woman poet – would suggest that she was one of these free-loving women, but he never tells who she is; late in the collection of *Amores* (3.12), he simultaneously protests that others have been guessing who she is and have tried to seduce her and that they should not expect her to be real, since poets specialize in lies, fantasy and fiction. But in a number of these poems, his girl belongs to a *vir* and lives and is kept guarded in his home. The word *vir* can be explained away as denoting a 'protector' or sugar daddy, but what else would Ovid have said if she were wife and the *vir* her husband? What we should watch for are words like *maritus* (husband), *uxor* (wife), or *coniunx* (a married partner, male or female). Still, if we single out only the poems which involve a *vir*, we have first *Amores* 1.4 which opens with the words 'Your Man is going to the same banquet as us' (as if she might have gone out without him!). Ovid tells the girl to watch for his signals at the party, to play footsie with him and touch her cheek when she is thinking of their own lovemaking (*Veneris lascivia nostrae*), to brush against him as she passes on her way home, and to contrive a rendezvous. If she must go home with her *vir*, then let her make sure she is unresponsive, or thinks only of the poet while she is being made love to. In the second elegy of *Amores* 2, addressed to his girl's eunuch attendant, he calls her man a fool to spend effort on guarding a woman who loses none of her value if she is seduced while unguarded;[10] he is chiefly concerned with hoodwinking her man by claiming false appointments visiting sick friends or temple ceremonies; he urges her to get round her man. In the paired poems 2.7 and 2.8, he blatantly displays his duplicity: to his girl, he repudiates her accusation that he is sleeping with her maid; to the maid he asks 'how did she find out' and threatens blackmail if the maid accuses him. In the triumph poem of 2.12, his triumph is that Corinna is now his, although her man, her minder and her tightly fastened door were all keeping the girl from him; and in case we should think this is not adultery, he boasts Helen as his model for Corinna's behaviour.

I shall isolate two more poems from the early *Amores*, both addressed to the man, and taking opposite stances to prove the poet's wit and versatility. In 2.19, he mocks the man, telling him to guard his woman better if he wants her to be worth stealing: 'what is allowed goes unappreciated: what is not allowed burns us with a fiercer desire. The man who only loves what another allows must be made of iron. To love the wife of a blind fool (*stulti*) is like stealing sand from an empty beach, and 'if you don't begin to watch our [!] girl she will stop being my beloved.' The word *stulti*, which actually opens the poem, would immediately suggest to Romans the deceived husband in the popular adultery mimes, a fixed and recurring role known either as *stultus* or *stupidus*. But the poem takes its whole essence from the supposition that seducing another man's woman is a game only worth playing if the other man makes it difficult. In the final couplet, 'why do I bother with an easy husband, a married panderer?' (*lenone marito*), Ovid turns another Augustan value upside down. He is openly defying the new Augustan law on its own terms: for the *Lex Iulia de Adulteriis* made a husband who did not divorce and then prosecute his adulterous wife guilty of pandering and liable to the penalties and dishonour of that sleazy profession.[11]

Amores 3.4 reverses this stance by supposing a man cautious and protective of his woman; it also contains the greatest concentration of open references to adultery. 'Harsh man, it is useless to put a guard on your woman: any woman must be protected by her own nature; even if you guard her body, she is my adulteress at heart' (3.4.5–6). Twice he reverts to this antithesis: 'The woman her man/husband guards does not become virtuous, only a costly adulteress, whose body is lent added value by fear [29–30]: in fact the man who is hurt by an adulterous wife [*coniunx*] is just a yokel, ignorant of the ways of the city' (37–8).[12]

You may think, as Ovid himself implies in 3.12, that autobiography and pseudo-confessional poetry has the licence of fiction, which makes it less vicious than Ovid's next project, first instructing lusty and idle young men how to seduce and keep a woman (*Ars amatoria* 1 and 2), then providing women with advice on how to keep their man. Certainly, Ovid begins his third book with a warning to respectable married women to shun his permissive verse (3.58–9) and reiterates the warning at length (*Ars amatoria* 3.601–15), but again his model is Paris: if Menelaus was no fool to demand the return of his wife, 'you too, Trojan seducer, were no fool to keep her' (3.253–4). Compare the opening of his second book: 'just so did the guest, Priam's son, set his white sails with his stolen bride from Amyclae that would rise up in arms' (*Ars amatoria* 2.3–4). In a longer excursus in Book 2, Menelaus is called a fool (*stupor*, 2.359) for leaving Helen with Paris: 'Helen is not doing wrong, nor is her adulterer committing an offence: he is just doing what you or any man would do' (2.371–2).

Book 2, (like the climax of Book 3, addressed to women, 793–804) ends with open instruction in the pleasures of intercourse, and the use of skill in prolonging foreplay:

> When you have found the places where the woman delights to be touched, let no bashfulness prevent you from touching her; you will see her eyes glittering with quivering flashes, as the sun is often reflected

from liquid water: to this she will add cries and a loving murmur and sweet groans and words encouraging your sport.

(2.719–24)

Man and woman must match each other's pace and share their pleasure:

you must not abandon your mistress on swifter sails, nor should she anticipate your pace; hasten together to your destined goal; pleasure is only full when woman and man lie overwhelmed together.

(2.725–8)

What follows confirms once again that the encounter is clandestine (*furtivum opus*),[13] and the poet has default advice when delay is too risky (*cum mora non tuta est*, 2.730–1). But perhaps Ovid offended more by his more general judgements: men can have intercourse with their wives at will, which makes it impossible to love wives (3.585–6); and childbearing ages the body. Even his praise for the elegant modern lifestyle is provocative: he is happy to have been born in this age, because it suits his *mores*. It has sophistication (*Ars amatoria* 3.122–7); for a man to take offence at his wife's adultery is boorish and unsophisticated (*Amores* 3.4.37–8), and shows his ignorance of our city's ways. Having once sown his own wild oats, Augustus did not want his city elite to waste their lives in parties but to be fruitful and rear a new generation of soldiers and statesmen.

To some extent, Ovid must have suffered for his sheer popularity. In a previous generation, such poems would have been enjoyed privately at parties or in recitation and perhaps circulated among a few smart friends, but Ovid's books were now in demand at the booksellers, and he openly courted a wider readership. In his poetic defence before Augustus, he claimed first that every kind of creative writing from Homer onwards involved love affairs, why even Virgil, Augustus' great poet, was most cherished for the fourth book of the *Aeneid*, which brought Aeneas into Dido's bed, and, second, that Rome's temples were full of images, such as the divine patron and origin of the Julian family, Venus Genetrix, goddess of love, and Rome's parks and gardens were full of statuary depicting mythological embraces. Ovid rightly pointed out that Tibullus and Propertius had given advice on winning women and making love to them before him and, less plausibly, that he had always been careful to discourage decent Roman matrons from reading his work or acting on the advice he had intended for a very different clientele.

We can be fairly sure that Augustus had little time for reading love elegies, but if it had been seen as a serious social menace, surely some rival or enemy of Ovid could have warned the poet. Probably the outburst of Augustus' fury was all the more violent because he had been suppressing his desire to silence such a popular and infectious kind of poetry. Then it seems the infection spread too close to home – or he wanted others to believe that Julia's association with Silanus was not political but just the bad heredity of lust from her mother, that she was an irrational creature dominated by her body and beneath contempt. If Augustus could not entirely control what people did, he could control what was said. He was successful not only in ensuring that Julia, like her mother, died in exile, but also in obliterating any memory of her except of her disgrace.

He could not do this to Ovid – the poet was too vocal and too popular to be eliminated from history – but he could deprive Ovid of his public and put an end to poetry, whether about a single and passionate Catullan love or about the games of love and chance that were Ovid's contribution to the genre of love elegy. From now on there would be plenty of shallow erotic epigrams in Latin (and Greek), but complex psychological analyses of love between man and woman would have to wait until the coming of the novel.

II Agrippina: matrimonial virtue and political ambition

It is likely that Agrippina grew up under the supervision of Livia and Augustus, either from her mother's remarriage when she was about three years old or in the five years from her mother's disgrace in 2 BCE until her marriage in her late teens.[14] This union was probably part of Augustus' planning for the career of young Germanicus which culminated in the young prince's adoption by Tiberius in 4 CE. As eldest child of Livia's younger son Drusus and Antonia, child of Octavia, Germanicus had the blood of both Julian and Claudian families, and his union with Agrippina would also unite the two clans. Drusus had been a military hero, commanding in Germany beyond the Rhine and even conducting the first Roman naval expedition eastwards along the north coast of Germany. When he died young in his consulship, this increased his glory and he was posthumously honoured as Germanicus, conqueror of Germany.[15] This honorific title became the name of his sons, and when Augustus had Tiberius adopt Germanicus as co-heir with his natural son Drusus and then adopted Tiberius himself, all three men became members of Augustus' Julian family. Tiberius was already over forty-five and the eighteen-year-old Germanicus Caesar would be next in line, in hoped-for partnership with his cousin, the slightly younger Drusus Caesar. It seems that both under Augustus and after Tiberius' accession, Germanicus was given the usual princely advancement through the ranks. According to Dio (55.31.1), he was sent to Illyria with reinforcements for Pannonia in 7 CE, although he was holding the quaestorship (and so would have been expected to have duties at Rome). If the year is correct, Germanicus may have been given less than the full five years advancement, but after the victory in Illyricum of 9 CE, Dio's language (56.17.2) suggests he was exempted from holding the praetorship. Instead, he was given the dress and honours of a praetor and the first rank among ex-praetors in senatorial debate and advanced towards the consulship, which he in fact held in 12 CE. But during this time, while Germanicus was constantly on campaign, serving under Tiberius, he and Agrippina were creating an unusually large family. Of the nine children she bore, three boys and three girls reached adulthood – and all would at different times suffer exile, imprisonment or unnatural death.[16] Suetonius (*Aug.* 39) tells us that Augustus was so proud of this fertility that he exhibited Germanicus' children as a model when he harangued the Roman knights in 9 CE in support of the *Lex Papia Poppaea*, by which he had diluted some penalties of celibacy and had increased the financial incentives to marry. This was the year of Varus' disastrous loss of three legions to the ambush of Arminius (Hermann), a Roman-trained rebel chieftain, in the Teutoburgerwald, and Augustus had to divert Tiberius and Germanicus to restore Roman control in Germany. One of Tacitus' most graphic descriptions is of the scene at the site of this ambush found six years later by Germanicus and his men, with the gruesome clearing in the dark forest covered with whitened and exposed bones – but this was still to come.

Our focus will remain on Agrippina, but her close partnership with Germanicus and commitment to her sons means that we must follow their lives and premature deaths in order to understand hers. Her two eldest boys were already infants when Agrippina accompanied her husband to Gaul, where two of her daughters were born.[17] Our sources suggest that the couple were seldom parted, and she accompanied him throughout his mission to the more urbanized East starting from 17, giving birth to her last child, Julia Livilla at Mytilene.[18] Only Gaius was born in Italy; the location is disputed, but the date is beyond doubt: it was the 31 August 12 CE, the year of Germanicus' first consulship. Although young Gaius notoriously grew up in the camp wearing miniature army boots (hence his nickname Caligula), authorities disagreed about his birthplace. Some said it was among the Treveri of northern Germany, others said Tibur, but Suetonius determined that he was born at Antium and did not join his parents until he was almost two, as is attested by Augustus' letter to Agrippina in May 14 CE:

> I arranged with Talarius and Asillius yesterday to take your boy Gaius with them on May 18, if the gods are willing. I am also sending a doctor from my slave household with him, and wrote to Germanicus that he should keep the doctor if he wished. Keep well, dear Agrippina, and see to it that you reach your Germanicus in good health.
>
> (Suet. *Gaius* 8.4)

The letter shows that while Agrippina was in the province, she was not with Germanicus at the front, but waiting, probably at Lugdunum, the capital city of the three Gallic provinces, to be reunited with her child. This would be an autumn fraught with anxiety and military disturbances caused by Augustus' death in August. Tacitus gives a rather theatrical picture of Germanicus' style as a commander when he had to face protests and even mutinies in the different army camps along the Rhine. As Governor and Legate of Tiberius, it was his role to obtain oaths of loyalty from both provincials and the legions. Confronted by veterans angry because they had been kept in service long after the expected term, he also had to resist a thrust to set him up as princeps instead. This he countered by threatening to kill himself rather than be disloyal to the Princeps (*Annals* 1.35). Then to assuage their complaints, he produced a forged letter from Tiberius promising them bounties (*Annals* 1.37). There followed another melodramatic scene after he met the Senate's envoys at Cologne, come to report the death of Augustus and confer *proconsular imperium* upon him. He was now commander-in-chief on the Rhine in lieu of Tiberius, but still had to deal with the 1st and 20th Legions, who were on the point of murdering their commanding officer. The chief mutineers had been lynched by the time of his arrival, but given the soldiers' unstable mood, Germanicus' council of war urged him to send away his little son and pregnant wife. Tacitus exploits the dramatic scene to convey something of Agrippina's pride in reporting her reaction: 'she was a descendant of the divine Augustus, and no unworthy coward in face of danger', and portraying the emotional impact of her departure, which shamed the disloyal troops:

> they pitied her, remembering her father Agrippa and grandfather Augustus, and Drusus, her father-in-law: they revered her conspicuous fertility and exceptional chastity, and were touched that her little boy had been born (*sic*) in camp and grown up under canvas.
>
> (*Annals* 1.41)

The historian is a creative writer who invents or suppresses circumstantial detail to maximize effect, but he seems to imply criticism of Germanicus' handling of this crisis through his pointed contrast with the preceding account of the orderly restoration of control in the Pannonian army under young Drusus (*Annals* 1.16–29).

After allowing the repentant soldiers a bloody reprisal on the ringleaders, Germanicus led his force against the Germans and shamed the 20th Legion into atoning for their mutiny by a victory, which was duly, if insincerely, honoured by Tiberius before the Senate (*Annals* 1.52). But the young general was eager to repeat his father's achievements and to push the frontier as far as the Elbe. Tacitus' source for Germanicus' campaigns is the 'German Wars' of the Elder Pliny, who served under him. The victory in 15 CE, for which Germanicus was awarded a salutation and triumph, was only short term, and further exploration almost brought disaster. Tacitus credits Pliny's lost history for his account of Agrippina's unprecedented behaviour in forestalling a rout that would have breached the Rhine frontier.

> The rumour spread that the army had been surrounded and the Germans were marching against the Gauls under arms. If Agrippina had not forbidden them to demolish the bridge over the Rhine, some would have committed this outrage out of terror. But this mighty spirited

woman took on the role of a leader during these days and distributed clothing and comforts to the soldiers who were wounded or had lost their equipment. Pliny reports that she stood at the approach to the bridge thanking and praising the returning legions.

(Tac. *Annals* 1.69)

But with his attention focused on political repercussion at Rome, Tacitus gives as much space to Tiberius' imagined disgust at a woman meddling with the army. 'Why, Agrippina was more powerful over the armies than their officers and commanders: the mutiny which could not be stemmed by the name of the Princeps had actually been quenched by a woman'. He adds that already Sejanus, the evil genius, was at Tiberius' side fostering the new emperor's resentment. Germanicus would stay two more years in Germany attempting new initiatives before Tiberius, perhaps wisely, recalled the prince and sent him out on a diplomatic mission to Syria.

The visit to the eastern provinces was to some extent a grand ceremonial tour in which Germanicus held a wide overall command but was based at Antioch in Roman Syria, where Tiberius had sent his old friend Gnaeus Piso as governor.[19] After some preliminary settlements of the Armenian hinterland, Germanicus alarmed Tiberius by visiting Alexandria, although Augustus had forbidden anyone of senatorial status to visit Egypt without his authorization. Inscriptions from Alexandria record popular enthusiasm for the Prince and his royal wife Agrippina, but although Germanicus claimed he had gone there to deal with an emergency in the grain supply, Tacitus presents this as virtually a tourist visit, including a Nile voyage to Elephantine and Syene. In his absence, the story darkened, as Piso ignored or overthrew Germanicus' measures to deal with Vonones of Armenia and relations with Parthia, criticizing him publicly and denouncing him in messages to Tiberius. On his return, Germanicus protested at Piso's disobedience and there was a bitter quarrel. Next, Germanicus fell ill, leading to accusations of poisoning. Where a modern traitor would have fitted the Governor's residence with clandestine microphones, Roman houses were full of eager slave informants. Instead of microphones, Germanicus found spells and curses and sinister animal body parts hidden in the walls of his house. Whatever he was suffering proved fatal, and the dying Germanicus formally wrote a renunciation of friendship with Piso and ordered him to leave the province. On his deathbed he begged his friends to secure vengeance for him, but he had also a warning for Agrippina: 'she must subdue her fierce temper and yield to the cruelty of fortune, for fear that when she returned to Rome she should enrage those with the strength to harm her by her own competition for power' (*Annals* 2.71). I have tried to reproduce Tacitus' words exactly, not because he was reporting exactly what Germanicus was heard to say, but because Tacitus knew what would happen – what had happened – on the widow's return. And her return to Rome, after processing through Italy from Brundisium clutching her husband's ashes, brought on a real public crisis whose extent we have only recently been able to appreciate to the full.

The popular reaction at Rome to the news of the Prince's death had been exceptionally violent. People closed their shops and taverns, attacked the temples and altars of the gods and supposedly even exposed their newborn children, while showing that they acted from grief rather than anger – at this stage Piso's behaviour was still unreported. Inscribed decrees of both senate and people have survived, decreeing public mourning and honours for the dead prince in terms that repeated but also exceeded the honours for the dead Gaius and Lucius. The popular decree (*Tabula Hebana*) added five voting units named after Germanicus to combine with the ten units named for Gaius and Lucius to vote at elections ahead of (and virtually instead of) the centuriate assembly. But the real emotional crisis only came with the return of Agrippina, when Tiberius and Livia avoided the crowd welcoming Germanicus' ashes. British readers will immediately recall the violent popular grief over the accidental death of the divorced Princess Diana and the resentment against the Queen and royal family for their abstention from public mourning. (They may also remember that the father of Diana's lover continued to claim the car crash was a conspiracy to murder organized by the palace.) With Agrippina's return, if not before, came denunciations of Piso that forced the Senate's hand and a show trial that was only deprived of its full impact by Piso's suicide after the first hearing.

The elaborate decree of the Senate recording the charges against Piso and the verdict was officially issued for publication throughout the Empire, and two copies from Spain have now been transcribed, edited, translated and analysed.[20] The decree is too long to reproduce more than excerpts. Piso was condemned because:

> when he should have remembered that he had been given as a special assistant to Germanicus Caesar (who had been sent by our Princeps in accordance with the authority of this order to settle overseas affairs that required the presence of either Ti. Caesar Augustus himself or one of the other of his two sons) ignoring the majesty of the imperial house [. . .] conducted himself when he was in the province of Syria as if everything ought to be subject to his decision and control – insofar as it lay in him, stirred up both an Armenian and a Parthian war [. . .]
> (*Senatus consultum de Cnaeo Pisone patre*, 29–32, 37–8)

> [he] also tried to stir up civil war (though all the evils of civil war have long since been laid to rest by the divine will of the deified Augustus and the virtues of Ti. Caesar Augustus, by trying to return to the province of Syria after the death of Germanicus Caesar [. . .] because of this Roman soldiers were forced to fight with Roman soldiers
> (*Senatus consultum de Cnaeo Pisone patre*, 46–9)

A number of details that I have omitted here were clearly designed to affirm the harmony of purpose between Tiberius and Germanicus. After the narrative of his suicide and the completion of the trial follow the decisions, including the forgiveness of his wife Plancina as a favour to Julia Augusta (Livia's new name), the restoration of his confiscated fortune to his innocent sons and the prohibitions of any act of mourning or memorial to the guilty man. But some fifty lines are taken up by recording affirmations of Tiberius' grief and the wish that he might now give to his one surviving son the care he had previously divided between his two sons. After Tiberius, thanks were given for their restraint to Livia and Drusus Caesar and to others connected with Germanicus Caesar, beginning with

> [the moderation of] Agrippina, who was greatly commended to the Senate[21] by the memory of the deified Augustus, by whom she had been greatly esteemed, and of her husband Germanicus, with whom she had lived in unique harmony, and the numerous children born by a birth most fortunate for those who survived.
>
> (*Senatus consultum de Cnaeo Pisone patre*, 137–9)

There follow Germanicus' mother Antonia, his sister Livia, his children and his brother Claudius. This elaborate document (some eight pages of modern print) is dated to 10 December, 20 CE.

For three years, Tiberius treated Agrippina's sons Nero and Drusus as princes of the family, marking their coming of age (*Annals* 3.29 and 4.4) and introducing them to the Senate.[22] Nero was given the daughter of Drusus Caesar in marriage, and the princes were included in the prayers of the pontiffs, albeit to Tiberius' displeasure (*Annals* 4.17). But when Drusus Caesar died in 23, a death taken as natural but later attributed to poisoning by his wife Livia under the influence of Sejanus, the difficult relationship between Tiberius and his former stepchild and daughter-in-law Agrippina became incurably bitter. Sejanus was working through hidden slander and open prosecutions of Agrippina's friends and she recognized the nature of his attacks.

Tacitus concentrates their enmity in three vignettes included in the narrative of 26 CE.[23] First, he describes how Agrippina went to see Tiberius when he was sacrificing to his deified father and commented that it was incompatible to worship Augustus and persecute his descendants – she was the true blood of Augustus, and her friend Claudia Pulchra was being prosecuted only because she was her friend. Tiberius replied with a Greek tragic quotation, saying she was not being injured just because she did not rule.

On another occasion, according to the memoirs of her daughter Agrippina, Tiberius had been to visit her and she provoked ill will against him by asking for permission to marry; there were many who would want to take Germanicus' widow and children into their family. Aware of the political risk, Tiberius simply left her without a reply.

In the third story, Sejanus arranged for Agrippina to be warned to fear poison from Tiberius, and when the Princeps offered her an apple from his hand, she took it and passed it on uneaten to her servants. Afterwards, Tiberius drew his mother's attention to Agrippina's mistrust, saying it was not surprising if he made negative decisions about a woman who suspected him of poisoning. But with Livia's death, Agrippina had no refuge from the designs of Sejanus, and under his influence Tiberius, now secluded on Capri, sent a letter denouncing her to the Senate (*Annals* 5.3).

Suetonius (*Tiberius* 53.2) says he accused her of wanting to take refuge at the statue of Augustus or with the armies (the latter of course was both more likely and more threatening). Tacitus, who at first (*Annals* 4.67) speaks only of those whom Sejanus suborned to accuse Agrippina to Tiberius, notes that this fatal letter did not speak of either young Nero or his mother as fostering revolution but accused the boy of sexual perversion ('love of young men and depravity': *Annals* 5.3) and his mother Agrippina of intransigence of speech and attitude. No matter, a motion for senatorial discussion was frustrated by the ambiguously diplomatic speech of Iunius Rusticus. After further delay and increased popular agitation, Tiberius sent a second, more impatient, letter treating the Senate's hesitation as an insult to his own majesty.

Only the interruption of Tacitus' text curtails this hideous story. Readers of the surviving narrative learn the fate of Agrippina and her adult sons in retrospect after her death (*Annals* 6.25) two whole years after the too-long-delayed disgrace of Sejanus. Nero's accusation and death are attested by Suetonius, along with that of his younger brother Drusus (*Tiberius* 54.2). Through Sejanus' scheming, the young men were treacherously provoked into abuse of Tiberius and then betrayed to him. The Emperor, now self-exiled on Capri, accused them by letter, bitterly heaping up insults, had them judged public enemies, and then starved to death. Nero died exiled on Pontia; Drusus, kept imprisoned in the Palatine precinct itself, died of starvation in 33 CE, driven, so Tacitus reports in *Annals* 6.24, to chew even his bedding. Predictably, there were rumours of secret instructions to Macro to rescue the boy, if Sejanus should take to arms. A more credible report by those spying upon Drusus said that he had cursed Tiberius, that just as Tiberius had killed his daughter-in-law and his brother's son and his grandsons and had filled the whole house with bloodshed, so he should pay the penalty to his (Drusus Caesar's) name (which Tiberius had only obtained by adoption) and to the ancestors and descendants of his family.

As for Agrippina, she met her death just after Drusus, banished, but we do not know in what year, and kept in harsh circumstances, living on only in hope of outlasting Sejanus. Tacitus does not know whether she in fact starved herself or was starved. When the enraged Tiberius sends the report of her death to the Senate, he uses it to heap absurd accusations upon her of adultery with the dead Asinius Gallus. The historian offers his own ambiguous obituary: 'she had been intolerant of equity and hungry for dominance, discarding the vices of women for the preoccupations of a man'(*Annals* 4.71).[24] She died two years to the day after Sejanus had been executed, and the Senate duly gave thanks to Tiberius and declared that on that day, 17 October, there should be an annual sacrifice to Jupiter.

At this point, four of Agrippina's children still lived. Writing under Nero, Seneca had referred to Julia's fertility as a curse on Rome. Her children hardly deserved this slur, but Agrippina's son Gaius was certainly a disastrous ruler, vindictive against his sisters as well as Rome's senatorial elite; and her daughter, the younger Agrippina, born late enough to escape Tiberius' suspicions, would give birth to the wanton and monstrous emperor who brought his mother and the Julio-Claudian dynasty itself to an end.

10 Julia in the judgement of posterity

'Hide my features, so they may not behold the abominable face of my daughter!'

(Ovid *Fasti* 6.615–16)[1]

These words may be the earliest allusion to Julia and the disgrace imposed upon her by her angry father. Here Ovid is actually retelling Livy's story of the wicked daughter of a much earlier ruler, Rome's second king, Servius Tullius. Livy reports in his extended narrative of the conspiracy against Servius (1.46–8), and Ovid implies that this Tullia was originally married to the more virtuous son of Tarquinius Priscus, whereas her virtuous sister was wife of the wicked son, Lucius Tarquinius. Livy's wicked Tullia takes the initiative in instigating the murders of her husband and sister so that she can marry Lucius, and Ovid begins his account after the murders, quoting Tullia's words as she drives him to seize power by murdering Servius: 'Crime is royal business. Seize power by killing your father-in-law and dip our hands in my father's blood' (*Fasti* 6.595–6).

In both narratives, Servius Tullius dies as he struggles to reach his palace, and his daughter forces her charioteer to drive over her father's body as it lies in the street. Indeed, this gruesome tale is the supposed origin of the name given to the *Vicus Sceleratus* ('Abominable Street': Livy 1.48, Ovid *Fasti* 6.609–10). This was an ancient legend, narrated by Livy when Julia was still a child, but when Ovid retells it, more than twenty years have passed – he is probably writing well after 2 BCE. How could he have written these words without thinking of Augustus' disgraced daughter and expecting his readers to do the same? But if he has Julia in mind, he may be closer to the political nature of her offence than the Princeps' official version.

Julia's disgrace and exile may well have silenced members of the political and literary elite who had previously supported her. We saw that the earliest account to survive was that of Tiberius' supporter Velleius. Seneca was himself accused of adultery with a princess (whether the younger Agrippina or her sister Livilla) and should have known better than to believe a version that ultimately derived from Augustus' furious report to the Senate.[2] For

Pliny the Elder, she was simply one of the troubles Augustus had to suffer – a motif going back to the Princeps' own comment on his two difficult daughters, Julia and the *Res Publica*. Even Macrobius' source, obviously enjoying if not admiring Julia's witticisms, saw her in the context of Augustus' forbearance – the behaviour of a *civilis princeps* (we might almost translate *civilis* as 'democratic'). But after Tacitus, who betrays some sympathy, if it is only prompted by antipathy to Julia's chief tormentor Tiberius, there is a long silence.

Two stories, almost 1,000 years apart, associate Julia or her daughter with poets. The Gallic bishop Sidonius Apollinaris, writing in the fifth century, addresses Ovid, 'you too, known for your lecherous songs, delicate Naso, and sent to Tomi, once too much associated with a girl of [the house of?] Caesar, [*Caesarea puella*] under the false name of Corinna'(*Poem 23*, 158–61).[3] While authorities have read this as referring to our Julia, the words *Caesarea puella* could be construed to mean the younger Julia, given her disgrace and exile in the same year as the poet. But was she even remembered? Her mother Julia's memory must have been stronger, as is suggested by another story, a medieval tale of magic. This is both more fantastic and more Protean. In the version that concerns Julia, the poet Virgil fell in love with the Emperor's daughter, who pretended to reciprocate his passion and arranged a rendezvous that depended on Virgil ascending to her tower in a basket drawn up on a rope, since normal access to her was carefully guarded. But she only drew him halfway up, then left him suspended all the next day, to great public amusement. When he was released after this humiliation, Virgil devised his revenge. He extinguished all the fires in Rome, and when the Emperor approached him after three days asking how the fires could be restored, Virgil told him that relief could only be obtained by humiliating the Emperor's daughter. She must come naked into the public square and let the people kindle their torches at her person (a sort of ritual rape?). What is more, the spell would continue until everyone in Rome had visited the lady.

This is the version offered by Spargo (1934) at the beginning of his exploration of two legends that proliferated and blended in the Middle Ages. The basket story often appears (and is illustrated in, for example the great tapestries of the Wicked Tricks of Wily Women in the Augustiner-Kloster at Freiburg) without the sequel of the poet's revenge. It appears in an oriental version and is told separately in Spanish, Dutch and Italian versions, notably Boccaccio's *Il Filocolo* and Aenea Silvio Piccolomini's fifteenth-century 'Tale of Two Lovers'. (This man, who became Pope Pius II, was a considerable humanist scholar.) Between Boccaccio and Aenea Silvio, Bonamente Aliprande, from Virgil's city Mantua, offered a version in his *Chronicles of Mantua* (1414) in which the woman went unnamed, but the Emperor Octavian/Augustus took Virgil down from mid-air and scolded him. The sheer variety of both male suitors and females pursued in variants of this tale (the woman was often a respectable merchant's respectable wife, who suspended the unwanted suitor to teach him a lesson), shows that it is pure coincidence that one version should settle on Virgil (revered as a great magician) and an anonymous emperor's daughter. Julia was the only emperor's daughter in Virgil's lifetime (he died when she was twenty), but the shy poet avoided women; his tastes ran in other directions. By 1506, the English version of Stephen Hawes in the *Pastime of Pleasures* combined the basket story with the fantastic revenge, and made the lady Nero's beautiful daughter (Nero's only daughter died as an infant).

Rather than see in this tale a remote echo of Julia's bad reputation, we must, I suspect, see the emperor himself as a transmogrification of some appropriate prince or caliph. 'The Poet and the Princess' is an attractive theme for a romance and has recently been adapted to involve the younger Julia in the tale of Ovid's exile, but as his patroness, not his mistress (Allison 2001).

A current web site refers to Julia as 'the Emperor's nymphomaniac daughter', perhaps only to attract readers, but so long as ancient history and Latin literature were chiefly studied by men, the worst slanders against Julia, like Juvenal's scandalous tales of Claudius' first empress, Messalina,[4] have been smugly accepted. Some men find it gratifying to think that women can be so animal and uncontrolled. Julia's reinstatement may have begun towards the end of the eighteenth century, with the scholar and critic C. M. Wieland, a contemporary of the poets of the German Romantic movement and a poet himself. An enormously prolific author, both as scholar and original playwright, Wieland published an essay 'Towards Rescuing the Honour of Three Famous Women of Antiquity' (1796, repr. 1984, pp. 303–87). The women were Aspasia (also the subject of a biography in our series), Julia (338–77) and the younger Faustina, wife of Marcus Aurelius, like Julia a mother of many children and a princess accused of promiscuity.

Wieland is tenderhearted: 'poor Julia', he writes,

> wasn't it enough that you wasted so great a part of your best years on the rock of that hateful island Pandateria? Not enough to be made a sacrifice to the politics and weakness of an irascible father, anxious for his usurped absolute power, to the secret persecutions of a stepmother seeking unlimited domination, and to the slow and cold-blooded revenge of an inhuman monster (*Unmensch*) like Tiberius? To make the full measure of your doom, did you have to be treated by writers of history and romance as a creature that brought disgrace on the name of woman, branded with the most disfiguring abuse, to be condemned by the contempt and loathing of all ages?[5]

Far from being the product of her own debauches, Wieland sees Julia as victim of a loathsome cabal, as maligned as Mary Queen of Scots (heroine of his contemporary Schiller's *Maria Stuart*). The comparison is certainly apt, for Mary was a king's daughter, marked from infancy to rule Scotland and married early to the Dauphin of France in a political alliance. Like Marcellus, her husband Francis died early, and she returned to Scotland when she was not yet eighteen, to be treated as a mere instrument of power both by the men who wanted to control her and by those such as Darnley and Bothwell whom she naively loved. But Mary suffered two further disadvantages: she was a loyal Catholic, when Scotland was undergoing an impassioned Protestant revolution, and she was seen as a potential rival of Elizabeth for the English throne. Like Julia, Mary was confined in more than one prison, first briefly in Scotland, then for the remaining nineteen years of her life at Fotheringay in England, until she was executed on the orders of her kinswoman, Elizabeth, Queen of England.

Wieland's image of Livia and Tiberius is that of Tacitus and, more recently, of Robert Graves,[6] but, unlike them, he puts the blame for Julia's unhappy life squarely on her father Augustus. Thus, he even makes a reproach of her marriage to Agrippa (which I see as the least frustrating period of her life) on the grounds that the older man was not one to satisfy her young blood, and Augustus was merely following Maecenas' advice, that Agrippa was now so powerful and indispensable that he must either be eliminated or made the Emperor's son-in-law. 'Augustus treated his daughter as a commodity to be sold to the best advantage and Agrippa took her as the best available bargain' [*Handel*].

Wieland makes some points not found in later critics: Augustus loved only himself in his daughter, bringing her (and her sons) up severely so as to present his family as impeccable models of virtue reflecting credit on himself. So long as Agrippa lived, Wieland suggests, Augustus may have listened to him rather than to Livia. But from Agrippa's death onwards, he interprets the marriage to Tiberius and all that followed as part of Livia's plan to bring her son to power. He does not believe that Julia could ever have been attracted to 'this false and treacherous man', only that they at first maintained a public semblance of harmony. In an original interpretation, he suggests that Livia and Tiberius already knew by 6 BCE that Julia's affair with Iullus would soon become public knowledge, and Tiberius left Rome so as not to incur blame (or prosecution for pandering under Augustus' new adultery law) for tolerating his wife's infidelity. Instead, Livia bided her time, and at her chosen moment confronted Augustus with all the affairs Julia had (or even was said to have) enjoyed over the previous twenty years, converting them into a political conspiracy against Augustus himself and making this a motive for instant action, so that the offenders would have no time to take over power. The great French historian Gaston Boissier too suggests in his pioneering study *L'Opposition sous les Césars* (1875/1900) that Livia encouraged Julia's moral lapses 'in order to get rid of her rival in Augustus' heart'.

As I have claimed (in Chapter 7), the Emperor's haste and omission of due process confirmed, in Wieland's judgement, the absence of firm proof of Julia's disloyalty. No argument can restore what has been suppressed, but it

is not unlikely that Livia also acted to forestall any softening of Augustus'
anger when the people of Rome repeatedly demanded Julia's restoration. The
chief weakness in Wieland's interpretation, it seems to me, is his failure to
incorporate into his reading the roles played by Gaius and Lucius, and the
separate reactions of Tiberius and Julia to the boys' promotion towards
higher office. Nor can we be sure, given Tiberius' absence in 2 BCE, that Livia
contrived and timed Julia's exposure, though the timing is itself suspect.

The nineteenth and twentieth centuries have devoted abundant, precise
and careful scholarship to the house of Augustus, but my concern here is
to single out critics of wider appeal, or those writing for a more general
audience. Thus, in the late nineteenth century the humane Boissier – a student
of both republican and early imperial Rome – included Julia in the first
generation of resistance to imperial autocracy and renewed Wieland's
championship. Julia, like her daughter, features in his book as a leader
of this internal opposition, and an anterior cause of Augustus' delayed exile
of Ovid (Boissier 1875: 133–6). How, Boissier asks, could a woman married
off successively to all the candidates for empire distinguish her husbands
from her lovers? This was a strange way to teach a young girl to value
marriage and protect her modesty. Julia's marriage to Tiberius was a deadly
mistake, given his longing for his former wife, and her lover Iullus had
every reason to hate Augustus as his father's enemy and murderer of
his brother Antyllus. While she loved to flout public opinion (but, as we
know, only the public opinion of the old and self-righteous), Augustus
hated elegant society. He saw Ovid as the main reason that smart young
people now thought it fashionable to be promiscuous. To quote Tacitus,
'they called it modern to corrupt and be corrupted' (*corrumpere et corrumpi
saeculum vocant*, Tacitus *Germania* 18). With slightly more hesitation,
Boissier goes on to suggest that Augustus established a link in his mind
between the shame he suffered over Julia and Ovid's work. By a distressing
coincidence, Ovid's *Art of Love* was published within a year of Julia's fall.
While this does not argue Ovid's responsibility for Julia's supposed
promiscuity, the closeness in time would inevitably provoke an association
in the angry father's mind. Why then did Augustus not exile Ovid until 8 CE?
Because the adultery of the younger Julia and perhaps Ovid's involvement
in her affairs as an accessory renewed Augustus' resentment to the point
where he took revenge on Ovid himself for the corrupting effect of his verse
(Boissier 1875: 141–4).

We should perhaps deal summarily here as does Boissier (1875: 138) with
one accusation against Julia that no modern has believed. According to
Suetonius,[7] the Emperor Gaius (Caligula) wanted to be descended from the
blood of Augustus on both sides and so spread it about that his mother
Agrippina had been conceived by Julia after incest with her own father. The
man was mad, and probably no contemporary believed him. I do not think
that even with the growing fashion for child molestation and incest as a
literary and theatrical theme, our own age will find this plausible.

One aspect goes untreated by Boissier: the political. It is also disregarded by the author of a three-volume history of Augustus, V. Gardthausen, in his discussion of Julia (1904: 1095–105). Believing the worst of the sexual accusations cited by Seneca and Pliny, Gardthausen takes the line that 'anyone who conducts orgies in the street has no scope for political conspiracies' (1904: 1101). Certainly, open promiscuity and political ambition seem incompatible, but this is surely a better reason for rejecting the tales of public prostitution that seem to have been swallowed whole by respectable historians like Gardthausen. Not that he is indifferent or unsympathetic to Julia. Indeed, he makes the most of the small coin portraits from 13–12 BCE to describe her and infer her personality:

> Her smooth brow forms a line with her straight nose. Her eyes are large and wide open, and combined with her firmly closed mouth give a strong proud expression to the face. Her sleek hair lies flat on the crown of her head, while the edges of her forehead are framed by bouffant waves of hair which ends over the brow with a *nodus* and with a chignon in the nape of her neck. Her attributes are those of a goddess, most often Diana, but the coin portraits are either small, like those which show Julia with her two eldest sons, or strongly idealized, like those from the cities of Asia Minor which venerate her as Aphrodite or Diana, so that they are a poor substitute for what was lost.
>
> (1904: 1096)

Gardthausen pays due respect to the evidence for Julia's education and literary interests, her family pride and difficult relationship with her father, and comments realistically that though he found her a difficult daughter, she suffered far more from their relationship than he did. (He does add one warm touch from Suetonius [*Augustus* 71], which I have passed over: when Julia could not attend her father's gaming table, he sent her a sum of money to gamble with.) But in this German historian's eyes, Augustus was as gullible as some ancient sources suggest, and it was again Livia who exploited Julia's weaknesses, using the marriage to Tiberius to make Julia (again called her opponent) the tool of her own plans for Tiberius.

Gardthausen suggests that when Tiberius could no longer endure her adulteries and left for Rhodes, Julia saw this as release and relied on her father's trust, forgetting that Livia was shrewd and could be monitoring her behaviour until it was opportune. Then Livia waited until she had enough evidence to persuade Augustus that Julia was conspiring against him and that both his life and power were in danger (1904: 1101). It is at this point in his argument that Gardthausen privileges the tales of public scandal and promiscuity over the possibility that Julia had serious political ambitions.

Regretfully, he concludes that Julia deserved her punishment (although he notes that its summary nature violated Augustus' own legislation) but points to the double standard for men and women in her time, which required fidelity from wives (who might otherwise conceive children not of their husband's blood) but not from husbands. Augustus himself

> had set an example of adultery; he had legislated principles which he did not observe in practice. He expected his daughter and other family members to make and break marriages as they would discard their clothes for richer garments.

There are, as he notes, more general factors. Morality itself had been shaken by civil war and the transition to monarchy, and it was natural for the victims of Augustus' statecraft to separate public life from private inclinations.

Despite his generous attempts to understand behaviour which he finds it difficult to excuse, Gardthausen reflects a very different morality from that of the present day, one in which the act of sexual intercourse was seen as uniquely sinful – at least for women – and of a different order from other forms of marital betrayal. But he also belongs to an age in which public and official falsehood was not expected, in pronounced contrast to our own disillusioned age of the cover-up. We were taught in the 1930s by European politics and shrewd historians[8] to disentangle Antony's actual policies and behaviour from the misrepresentations of Octavian's propaganda. If Octavian could falsify the relatively known record of his political rival, how much easier it would be to falsify the more private activities of a mere woman. It took the greatest Roman historian of the last generation some years to turn from 'real' political and military history to the domestic aspects of the Julio-Claudians, but when he did, he judged the reports about women with equal scepticism and objectivity.

For we must come to Ronald Syme, the Syme who had observed Hitler and Mussolini gathering autocratic power before 1939 and rounded out his portrayal of this Augustan era as a phase in which the Princeps mastered the art of manipulating public opinion and suppressing free expression, while gradually turning autocrat. Augustus took increasing control of the existing media, taming aristocrats into self-interested collaborators and excluding the unruly people of Rome. Syme's paper 'The Crisis of 2 BC' reprinted in *Roman Papers* III (1984) from 1974 is still the definitive analysis of the lacunose and one-sided tradition about Julia's fall which remains after Augustan manipulation.

But while Syme offers a political explanation of Julia's behaviour in 2 BCE, he transfers the emphasis from Julia to her unsanctioned partner Iullus Antonius. How, in fact, can we tell which of these proud members of the palace community was using the other, or whether indeed they actually felt strong mutual loyalty or passion? Syme's explanation of their 'going public', that they wanted to stir up popular support to obtain a position of authority for Iullus on the Emperor's Council, possibly a sort of unidentified regency, does not exclude the worst options, but allows for milder and non-violent intentions, not to hasten the death of Julia's father or to dispossess her sons, but to be in a position of advantage in face of Livia (and the absent Tiberius) should Augustus be incapacitated by illness (this would not be the first time) or actually die. After all, Julia's elder son was far away in the East and his younger brother was still only sixteen.

Both Julia and her sons had much to fear from Livia if Augustus should be incapacitated. Even so, Syme's position, which is probably the one still accepted by most students of the period, takes a step back from the extreme hypothesis of Jerome Carcopino (1958)[9] who makes Julia into a replica of King Servius Tullius' murderous daughter Tullia. According to Carcopino, who feels no need for any ancient evidence, Julia had already tried on her marriage to Tiberius to persuade her new husband to eliminate Augustus, and only turned to Iullus when Tiberius refused and left her and Rome in disgust. On his theories, she would have planned to murder her father and her young sons, and no doubt have Tiberius assassinated on Rhodes. (She would surely have needed to dispose of Livia too.)

We should not pass over the portrait of Julia offered by J. V. P. D. Balsdon (1962), whose study of Roman women was influential fifty years ago. In a few vivid pages (1962: 80–7) Balsdon follows an essentially sympathetic portrait of Julia's earlier life with a vivid description of the austere isolation of Pandateria (Ventotene), which he apparently visited. He discriminates between the credible infidelities and drunken celebrations and the allegations that she openly played prostitute and 'used the uncomfortable public platform of the Rostra for a brothel', recognizing this as sheer journalistic colour.

Balsdon is the first critic to suggest that 'we have no conception of Julia as a person' (1962: 84), but quickly remedies the Augustan silence with the anecdotes of Macrobius.[10] Unwilling to accept the absurd products of Carcopino's imagination, he turns to a much better known character – Augustus himself. Why did he react so precipitately? Surely the Princeps' utter fury and lurid public denunciation did not just spring from naivety, sexual revulsion or even paternal self-love. It can only be explained if Julia had shown herself to be a serious political threat – 'a dangerous adventuress' (1962: 86). Here Balsdon's language speaks for his generation. If the Emperor's only child had been a son, would he have been called a dangerous adventurer for acting to take over power before a later and younger wife could divert it to his stepbrother? Perhaps Julia's worst offence from her birth to her virtual death was to have been a woman.

It is difficult not to see Julia's behaviour after her marriage to Tiberius as some sort of poetic justice on her autocratic father, and now Peter Wiseman's radical study *The Myths of Rome* (2004) has followed this line of thought. In his eyes, many episodes that we think historical rapidly acquired the status and function of myths at Rome. With the coming of the principate's overwhelming autocracy, Augustus (who called it by the respectable name of 'authority') both imposed intrusive moral legislation and practised the fostering and renewal of approved religious cults while neglecting others. Thus, when the temple of Ceres, Liber and Libera burned down, along with its neighbour, the temple of Flora, he left them unrestored. Wiseman suggests that his disregard for the gods of pleasure and indulgence may have contributed to an inevitable rebellion. This manifested itself not in the rioting of the largely acquiescent city populace but in the rebellion of the one person who shared Augustus' pride and spirit – Julia, his daughter, now the vehicle of 'Liber's revenge' as Wiseman has titled the chapter (IX) dealing with her fall.

Those who have read my book will feel no surprise that Wiseman's short chapter is illustrated not by a portrait of Julia herself, but official portraits of Livia and Octavia, a family tree and a brief account of Julia's successive marriages. It is here that Wiseman introduces an inset account of Ovid's teaching before the sad outcome of Tiberius' 'impossible' marriage and withdrawal to Rhodes. In keeping with his earlier chapters, Wiseman stresses the foolish indulgence of Julia's nocturnal parties in the forum and her garlanding of Marsyas, spirit of liberty, and cautiously confines the implication of conspiracy to 'some people . . . working out contingency plans. Or even planning the contingency'. But he sees it as part of the struggle for succession: 'Augustus had discovered the iron law of autocracy: once your succession is known not everyone wants to keep you alive' (2004: 235). While this carefully stops short of naming names, he is more explicit on the role of Livia and her long and privileged access to Augustus, contriving the fate of Julia and soon that of her daughter and of Ovid. For Wiseman, as for us, these successive tales of ruined lives are more emblematic of the price of autocracy than of the individual destinies of the princesses and the poet. They should not be forgotten when historians celebrate the Emperor's glorious and self-glorifying record of his own achievements.

It would be foolish for me to represent Julia as an injured innocent, but I am not willing to accept the distorted picture given by Augustus' denunciation of a self-destructive 'party animal' and nymphomaniac. No doubt, Julia's position as Augustus' only child had made her arrogant, but it is not until her enforced marriage to Tiberius, and not even immediately after that union, that she shows signs of self-assertion. We are told she despised him as her inferior (*impar*), and this has been plausibly interpreted by Herbert-Brown (1998) as telling him that he owed the commands bestowed upon him in 6 BCE to his position as her consort. This interpretation of Tacitus' comment has the advantage of explaining why he then refused the eastern commands and withdrew to private status at Rhodes. But it is also quite likely that her contempt was provoked by his personality (or even sexual habits).

Prevented by Augustus' veto on divorce from making the disastrous marriages that Mary Stuart, Queen of Scotland, made with her cousin Darnley (a man with a dynastic claim to the throne) and the outsider

Bothwell, whom some think Mary herself suborned to kill Darnley, Julia survived twenty years as an endangered adult in a conspiratorial court. She may still have sought out Iullus Antonius (or others) as her lover during the five years of her grass-widowhood, to protect herself politically. It is possible that Mary initiated the murder of her second husband. So, too, Julia may also have gratuitously planned a murderous coup against her own father, but she may only have tried to appeal to the people of Rome to bring pressure upon the Princeps – whether to allow her divorce and remarriage or to promote the career of Iullus. It is equally possible that she was driven to take precipitate action by a warning or by her own anticipation of the disgrace and exile which were actually imposed on her, once her natural sons whom her father had appropriated, reached manhood. It might seem that she was now superfluous, just as the birth of Mary Stuart's son James removed the Queen's last usefulness to the Scottish lords.[11] As I have admitted, we cannot turn Julia into an innocent, but we can acquit her of unprovoked folly, if we see her actions after 6 BCE as taken in self-defence, the desperate miscalculation of one more unsuccessful conspirator during the more than fifty years of Octavian/Augustus' uninterrupted power that stretched from 43 BCE to 14 CE. Given the imposition of Augustus' official version, let us at least offer the Scottish verdict of *not-proven*.

Appendix I
Material sources

Few material commemorations of Julia seem to have survived her disgrace. Portrait statues and busts could easily be removed from the public eye or recut to represent later members of the dynasty. Unlike Livia, whose official portraits were promulgated in plaster models or copies distributed to the provinces, going through several sequences as they aged with her, Julia only earned official prominence during her tour of duty in the East with Agrippa. The habit of honouring members of imperial dynasties and even designating female as well as male members as deities was observed freely with the Seleucids in Syria and Ptolemaic successions well before Cleopatra VII. Thus, it was natural for Greek cities of the mainland, islands and Asia Minor, to erect statues and honorific inscriptions for the mother of the Emperor's adoptive children and expected successors. Items listed here include those footnoted in Reinhold's *Marcus Agrippa*, and documented in *PIR* IV, 298 s.v. Iulia. I have also relied heavily on the chapter 'Octavia Minor and Julia f. Augusti' in Susan Wood *Imperial Women* (1997: 35–74).

As Wood demonstrates, a fair estimate of the reverence offered to Julia in the East can be formed by comparing the busts and coins featuring her aunt Octavia during Octavia's marriage to Antony. These seem all to be datable before his death by suicide in 30 BCE.

Public monuments: temples, and inscribed statue bases

Lesbos: temple, erected to Julia as a girl, as a new Venus Genetrix, *Bil.* III 7156, 7157 = *IGR* 4.9 + *IG* XII 2.537; it may have been dedicated later.

Ephesus: gates of forum, dedicated to Julia and Agrippa, after his death, in 4 BCE. Presumably vowed during his tour of Asia Minor and delayed.

Inscribed statue bases

Mainland Greece

Delphi: Dittenberger *Sylloge Inscriptionum Graecarum*, ed. 3, 3.779 (Julia,
with Gaius, Lucius and Agrippina.) No base for Julia II has been found
here or at Thespiae; she may not have accompanied her family on this
visit.

Thespiae: with Agrippa, Lucius, Gaius, Agrippina: see p. 140 and n. 3
Bull. Corr. Hell. 50 (1926) 448 n89; *Ann. Epigr.*1928, 50.

Megara: *IG* VII 65.

Sestos: *Bull. Corr. Hell.* 4 (1880) 517, with Agrippa.

Islands

Mytilene, Lesbos: *IG* XII 2.204 (*IGR* IV 64) and 482 (*IGR* IV 114)
'Nea Aphrodite'.

Andros: *IG* XII 5, 740.

Thasos: *IG* XII 8, 381 = D 8784 (to Julia with Livia and Julia II) see p. 140
and on Paphos, Cyprus: *IGR* 3.940 (cf. *JHS* 9 (1888) 243).

Samos: *IGR* IV 1717, (*Athen. Mitteilungen* 44 (1919) 35 and 75 (1960) 106
and n. 119.

Cos: Reinhold cites R. Herzog, *Koische Forschungen und Funde* 229,
no. 223, Leipzig 1899.

Delos: Dittenberger *Sylloge* 3.777 (*Bull. Corr. Hell.* (1878) 399, no. 7).

Asia Minor: Priene n. 225 'Kalliteknos'.

Ceramos: *JHS* 11 (1890) 128 n. 15 'Agrippa kai Ioulias.'

Egypt: Pelusium, *IGR* I 1109: honoured with Augustus, Livia and her sons,
(no reference to Tiberius); 4 BCE.

Possible portrait busts

Five otherwise unidentified busts are still canvassed by various scholars as
likenesses of either Octavia or Julia. See Wood (1999: 69–74).

(1) Portrait bust from Béziers (Roman Baeterrae) in Musée de Saint
Raymond, Toulouse, Cat. 30.004, Wood figs 18, 19. Found with a group
including Augustus, Agrippa, Livia, Tiberius, Germanicus, Drusus II, and a
male child, this bust could, by elimination, be Julia, but it could also be
Octavia the Younger (whose other busts it does not resemble). Again, given
that three of the busts date from Tiberius' principate, this is more likely to
be Vipsania Agrippina, Tiberius' first wife, the mother of Drusus II, just
as the child might be Gaius, but could also be either a son of Germanicus or
Drusus II's son Gemellus. After Vipsania's death in 20 CE, there would be
no embarrassment in giving her prominence as mother of the Emperor's

future heir. According to Wood's description, the bust has 'a rather broad squarish and large boned face, slightly hooded eyes and a wide full-lipped mouth' (Wood 1999: 70), which could represent assimilation of the wife to her husband Agrippa (see also Rose 1997: 126–8, cat. no. 52).

(2) Bust now in Ny Carlsberg Glyptotek Copenhagen, apparently found at Caere with portraits of Livia and Tiberius, and featured on the cover of this volume. Wood (1999) allows the possibility that it could be Julia; the Glyptotek catalogue is more confident.

(3) Portrait bust from Glanum, found with a bust of Livia, but different in form and dimensions. See Rose 1997a: 128–9, cat. 53. pl. 166) on this head, favoured by Carcopino (1957) as Julia. The hairstyle is distinctive: behind the nodus the hair is 'divided into two plaits that circle the head like a diadem', while hair on the crown of the head is divided into melon-shaped segments, and the chignon is worn low in the neck. This can be compared for hairstyle with similar head from Velia (Rose 1997a, see (5) below, with the same braids and long thick lock of hair falling on neck. Some of Julia's coins (see below) appear to have braids around head, but lack the trailing lock of hair. Winkes (1995) is prepared to accept this as possibly Julia. Wood (1999: 60) notes 'the proud lift and turn of the head and the upward direction of the gaze [suggest] that the intention of the artist in this public work is to characterize the woman as a figure of formidable character and dignity.'

(4) Fragmentary marble head from Corinth: coiffure resembles that of Octavia, but the features are different: 'long thin nose . . . hooded eyelids, long fleshy oval face, pouting lips'. K. de Grazia Vanderpool argues from its findspot near the Julian basilica that this could be Julia (*Corinth: the Centenary, 1896–1996*, Fig. 22.12, p. 378). It is an arresting face, almost too expressionless to be a human portrait.

(5) The Velia head (Rose 1997a); 120–1, cat. no. 49, plates 125–6).

Wood, who offers the most recent detailed discussion, tends to regard difference of coiffure as marking different women, despite a lapse of some twenty years in which surely any fashionable woman would have changed her hairstyle. But she rightly allows for the possibility that these unidentified busts may not be women of the imperial family but members of prominent local families (especially if they financed the imperial busts with which they were found).

Coins

The only undeniable likenesses of Julia are to be found on two coin types from Asia Minor, one minted in Pergamum during Agrippa's Asian tour, the other from Ephesus, and on a denarius from the revived Roman mint which shows Julia between her sons.

Pergamum: Bronze coin with portraits of Livia and Julia: Inscribed Livia Hera on obverse, Julia Aphrodite on reverse. Brit. Mus., Mysia 249 (Wood 1999: fig. 21).

Ephesus: bronze coin with portraits of Agrippa and Julia (Cohen 1.180).

Rome: Coin of C. Marius (Tromentina) IIIvir 13 BCE, showing Augustus on obverse, with unlabelled profiles (R) of Julia between Gaius and Lucius on reverse. Wood (1999: fig. 20) reproduced from Berlin Staatliche Museum.

What is the significance of Julia's depiction? In the case of Pergamum the city also issued another coin with Augustus (obverse) and Agrippa (reverse), which suggests that Livia and Julia were featured to honour the Princeps through his family. Seleucid coins had previously represented rulers with their wives (on the reverse): this is probably a better precedent than Cleopatra's presence (as rightful ruler of Egypt) with Antony on reverse, or Antony's representation of Fulvia on earlier coinage. But an unavoidable precedent had been set by coinage of Antony with Octavia (Wood 1999: figs 4 and 5): aurei produced by an unknown city, from 40 BCE, or the bronzes from 37–35 BCE whose obverses depict portraits of Antony and Octavia, facing each other, or Antony and Octavian conjoined facing Octavia (Wood 1999: figs 9 and 10). The Roman coin surely features Julia to demonstrate the origin of Augustus' heirs and adoptive sons – she is significant as their mother born of his blood.

Theatre and gaming tokens

Lead tokens have been found at Rome showing a woman with the nodus coiffure and central braid, and inscribed (IU)LIA AUGUSTI. The bone gaming token found at Oxyrrhyncus also shows the profile of a woman with nodus coiffure and has IOULIA scratched on the reverse, but could refer to Livia after her adoption as Iulia Augusta in 14 CE.

Appendix II

Testimonia (in chronological order) for Julia's disgrace, exile and death

1abc Velleius 2.93, 96, 100
1a 2.93

Post cuius (Marcelli) obitum Agrippa, qui sub specie ministeriorum principalium profectus in Asiam, ut fama loquitur, ob tacitas cum Marcello offensiones praesenti se subduxerat tempori, reversus inde filiam Caesaris Iuliam, quam in matrimonio Marcellus habuerat, duxit uxorem, feminam neque sibi neque rei publicae felicis uteri.

After Marcellus' death, Agrippa, who had departed for Asia in the pretence of imperial service, but as rumour has it, had withdrawn from the immediate circumstances because of unspoken hostility with Marcellus, came back. Then he married Caesar's daughter Julia, whom Marcellus had held in marriage, a woman whose fertility was good neither for herself or for the state.

1b 2.96

Mors deinde Agrippae qui novitatem suam multis rebus nobilitaverat atque in hoc perduxerat, ut et Neronis esset socer, cuiusque liberos nepotes suos divus Augustus praepositis Gai et Lucii nominibus adoptaverat, admovit propius Neronem Caesari quippe filia Iulia eius, quae fuerat Agrippae nupta, Neroni nupsit.

Then followed the death of Agrippa who had ennobled his lack of birth by many achievements, and had even become the father-in-law of Tiberius Nero: indeed the deified Augustus had adopted Agrippa's sons, his own grandchildren, naming them Gaius and Lucius. This death brought Tiberius Nero closer to Caesar, because he married Caesar's daughter Julia who had been the wife of Agrippa.

1c 2.100

At in urbe eo ipso anno . . . foeda dictu memoriaque horrenda in ipsius domo tempestas erupit. Quippe filia eius Iulia, per omnia tanti parentis ac viri immemor, nihil quod facere aut pati turpiter posset femina, luxuria libidineque infectum reliquit magnitudinemque fortunae suae peccandi licentia metiebatur, quicquid liberet quo licito vindicans. Tum Iullus Antonius, singulare exemplum clementiae Caesaris, violator eius domus, ipse sceleris a se commissi ultor fuit (quem victo eius patre non tantum incolumitate donaverat sed sacerdotio, praetura, consolatu, provinciiis honoratum, etiam matrimonio sororis suae filiae in artissimus adfinitatem receperat), Quinctiusque Crispinus, singularem nequitiam supercilio truci protegens, et Appius Claudius et Sempronius Gracchus ac Scipio aliique minoris nominis utriusque ordinis viri, quas cuiuslibet uxore violata poenas pependissent, pependere, cum Caesaris filiam et Neronis violassent coniugem, Iulia relegata in insulam patriae parentumque subducta oculis, quam tamen comitata mater Scribonia voluntaria exilii permansit comes.

But that very year at Rome a calamity occurred in Caesar's household loathsome to report and dreadful to recall. His daughter Julia, utterly indifferent to her great father and to her husband, left no wanton or lustful disgrace undone that any woman could inflict or suffer, and measured the greatness of her fortune by her licence in sinning, claiming whatever she fancied as permissible. Then Iullus Antonius, a unique proof of Caesar's clemency and now the violator of his household, avenged on himself the crime he had committed. (After his father's defeat, Caesar had not only granted him survival but honoured him with a priesthood, praetorship, consulship and provinces, and even brought him into close relationship by marriage with the daughter of his sister.) Besides Quinctius Crispinus, a man who disguised his exceptional wickedness with a grim frown, and Appius Claudius and Sempronius Gracchus and Scipio and other less prominent men of both orders, paid the penalty that men would pay for violating anyone's wife, although they had violated Caesar's daughter and Tiberius Nero's wife. Julia herself was relegated to an island, removed from the sight of her country and family: but Scribonia accompanied her there as a willing companion in her exile.

2a Seneca *Brev. Vitae,* 4.6 (On the sorrows of Augustus)
Nondum horum effugerat insidias: filia et tot nobiles iuvenes adulterio velut sacrmento adacti iam infractam aetatem territabant Iullusque et iterum timenda cum Antonio mulier. haec ulcera cum ipsis membris absciderat; alia subnascebantur . . .

He had not yet escaped from treachery: his daughter and so many noblemen bound by adultery as if by an oath terrified his declining years, Iullus and once again the dread threat of a woman allied with an Antonius. In cutting out these sores, he cut off his own limbs, and yet others were forming after them.

2b Seneca *De Beneficiis* 6.32

Divus Augustus filiam ultra impudicitiae maledictum inpudicam relegavit et flagitia principalis domus in publicum emisit; admissos gregatim adulteros, pererratam nocturnis comissationibus civitatem, forum ipsum ac rostra, ex quibus pater legem de adulteriis tulerat, filiae in stupra placuisse, [ad] cotidianum ad Marsyam concursum, cum ex adultera in quaestuariam versa ius omnis licentiae sub ignoto adultero peteret. (2) Haec tam vindicanda principi quam tacenda, quia quarumdam rerum turpitudo etiam ad vindicantem redit, parum potens irae publicaverat. Deinde cum interposito tempore in locum irae subisset verecundia, ingemens, quod non illa silentio pressisset, quae tam diu nescierat, donec loqui turpe esset, saepe exclamavit 'horum mihi nihil accidisset, si aut Agrippa aut Maecenas vixissent'.

The deified Augustus relegated his daughter, unchaste beyond the curse of unchastity, and made public the scandals of the imperial household: that she had invited adulterers in crowds and scoured the city in nightly escapades; that his daughter had chosen the forum itself and the platform from which her father had carried his law against adultery for her fornications; that there had been a daily gathering by the statue of Marsyas, when she turned from adultery to prostitution and claimed the right to every kind of licence with any unknown adulterer. (2) Lacking control over his rage, he had made public these scandals, which had to be punished by the Emperor, but should equally have been suppressed, since the disgrace of some behaviour also affects whoever punishes it. Later, when embarrassment had replaced rage, groaning that he had not concealed in silence the events of which he had so long been unaware, until it had become shameful to speak out, he often cried out 'none of this would have happened to me, if either Agrippa or Maecenas had been living'.

3a Pliny *Natural History* 7.45 On Agrippa

Quanquam is quoque adversa pedum valitudine misera iuventa, exercito aevo inter arma mortisque adeo obnoxio accessu, infelici terris stirpe omni sed per utrasque Agrippinas maxime, quae Gaium, quae Domitium Neronem genuere totidem faces generis humani, praeterea brevitate aevi quinquagesimo uno raptus anno in tormentis adulteriorum coniugis socerique praegravi servitio, luisse augurium praeposteri natalis existimabatur.

And yet Agrippa was thought to have expiated the augury of his inverted birth, with a youth made wretched by his foot ailment and his prime consumed in warfare and exposed to sudden death: all of his descent brought the world bad fortune, worst of all the two Agrippinas, who gave birth to Gaius (Caligula) and Domitius Nero, two firebrands to destroy the human race: in addition he was unlucky in the shortness of his life, dying in his fifty-first year and suffering torture from his wife's adulteries and the burdensome service to his father-in-law.

3b Pliny *Natural History* 7.149

Tot seditiones militum, tot ancipites morbi corporis, suspecta Marcelli vota, pudenda Agrippae ablegatio, totiens petita insidiis vita, incusatae liberorum mortes; luctusque non tantum orbitate tristis, adulterium filiae et consilia parricidae palam facta, contumeliosus privigni Neronis secessus, aliud in nepte adulterium, iuncta deinde tot mala . . .

Augustus suffered so many mutinies of his armies, so many dangerous diseases, the dubious intentions of Marcellus, the shameful dismissal of Agrippa, a life so repeatedly threatened by assassinations, the suspicious losses of his sons, mourning that was grievous for more than childlessness, the adulterous behaviour of his daughter and her acknowledged plots of parricide, the insulting withdrawal of his son-in-law Tiberius Nero, another pattern of adultery in his granddaughter, with so many other misfortunes accompanying it.

3c *Natural History* 21.8–9 on Marsyas

P. Munatius cum demptam Marsuae coronam e floribus capiti suo imposuisset atque ob id duci eum in vincula triumviri iussissent, appellavit Tr. Pl. nec intercessere illi. Aliter quam Athenis, ubi commissabundi iuvenes ante meridiem conventus sapientium quoque doctrinae frequentabant. apud nos exemplum licentiae huius non est aliud quam filia Divi Augusti, cuius luxuria noctibus coronatum Marsuam litterae illius dei gemunt.

When P. Munatius took the garland of flowers from the head of Marsyas and put it on his own head, and the triumvirs ordered him taken off for punishment, he appealed to the tribunes, but they would not intervene. It was different at Athens where partying young men would even attend the meetings of philosophers before noon. There is no better proof of this licence in our society than the daughter of the deified Augustus: his letters groan with the shame that Marsyas was nightly garlanded by her wantonness.

4a Tacitus *Annals* 1.53

Eodem anno Julia supremum diem obiit ob impudicitiam olim a patre Augusto Pandateria insula, mox oppido Reginorum qui Siculum fretum accolunt, clausa, fuerat in matrimonio Tiberii, florentibus Gaio et Lucio Caesaribus spreveratque ut imparem: nec alia tam intima Tiberio causa cum Rhodum abscederet. Imperium adeptus extorrem, infamem et post interfectum Postumum Agrippam omnis spei egenam inopia ac tabe longa peremit, obscuram fore necem longinquitate exilii ratus, par causa saevitiae in Sempronium Gracchum, qui familia nobili, sollers ingenio et prave facundus eandem Iuliam in matrimonio Marci Agrippae temeraverat, nec is libidini finis: traditam Tiberio pervicax adulter contumacia et odiis in maritum accendebat; litteraeque quas Iulia patri Augusto cum insectatione Tiberii scripsit a Graccho compositae credebantur.

In the same year [14 CE] Julia left this life: she had long before been imprisoned for her immorality on the island of Pandateria, then in the town of the Regini on the Sicilian strait. She had been married to Tiberius when her sons Gaius and Lucius Caesar were flourishing, and despised him as socially inferior; nor was there any other motive so strong for Tiberius to withdraw to Rhodes. When he came to imperial power, he caused her death through loss of support and a slow wasting away, exiled, disgraced and bereft of all hope after the murder of Agrippa Postumus. He thought the murder would go unnoticed because of the distance of her exile. He felt an equal motive for cruel punishment of Sempronius Gracchus: this man of noble descent, talent and perverted eloquence, had seduced the same Julia during her marriage with Marcus Agrippa, nor was this the end of his lust; when she passed on to Tiberius, this persistent adulterer continued to inflame her with insults and hatred against her husband; indeed the letters which Julia wrote to her father with accusations against Tiberius were believed to have been composed by Gracchus.

4b *Annals* 3.24.3, 5–7 (Restoration of D. Silanus)
(3) Ut valida Divo Augusto in rem publicam fortuna, ita domi improspera fuit ob impudicitiam filiae ac neptis, quas urbe depulit adulterosque earum morte aut fuga punivit. Nam culpam inter viros ac feminas vulgatam gravi nomine laesarum religionum ac violatae maiestatis appellando clementiam maiorum suasque ipse leges egrediebatur . . . (5) D. Silanus in nepti Augusti adulter, quanquam non ultra foret saevitum quam ut amicitia Caesaris prohiberetur, exilium sibi demonstrari intellexit, nec nisi Tiberio imperitante deprecari senatum ac principem ausus est M. Silani fratris potentia. [When Marcus thanks the senate for his permission to return, Tiberius replies:] (6) Idque iure licitum, quia non senatus consulto neque lege pulsus foret; (7) Sibi tamen adversus eum integras parentis sui offensiones, neque reditu Silani dissoluta quae Augustus voluisset.

(3) As Augustus' public fortune had been successful, so that of his household was unfortunate because of the immorality of his daughter and grand-daughter, whom he expelled from Rome, punishing their adulterers with death or exile. For by calling an offence common between men and women by the solemn name of pollution of religion and violation of his majesty he went far beyond the clemency of our ancestors and his own legislation. . . . (5) D. Silanus, the adulterer of Augustus' granddaughter, had understood that he was being marked for exile, although no worse penalty had been imposed than exclusion from Caesar's friendship. In fact his brother M. Silanus, though powerful, did not dare to ask for mercy from the Senate until Tiberius was emperor. [When Marcus thanks the Senate for his permission to return, Tiberius replies:] (6) This was legitimate, because he had not been exiled by a senate decree or a law. (7) But in his eyes the

offences against his father were undiminished, and Augustus' will had not been cancelled by the return of Silanus.

4c *Annals* 4.44 (Death of Iullus Antonius' son)
Obiit et L. Antonius, multa claritudine generis, sed improspera; nam patre eius Iullo Antonio ob adulterium Iuliae morte punito hunc admodum adulescentem, sororis nepotem, seposuit Augustus in civitatem Massiliam, ubi specie studiorum nomen exilii tegeretur. Habitus tamen supremis honor, ossaque tumulis Octaviorum inlata per decretum senatus.

L. Antonius also died, a man of a most glorious but unfortunate family; for when his father Iullus Antonius had been punished with death for his adultery with Julia, Augustus had sent away this very young man, his own sister's grandson, to the state of Massilia, where the name of exile was covered with the pretence of his studies. But honour was paid to his last rites and his bones conveyed to the tomb of the Octavii by decree of the Senate.

4d *Annals,* 4.71
Per idem tempus Iulia mortem obiit. Quam neptem Augustus convictam adulterii damnavit, proieceratque in insulam Trimerum, haud procul Apulis litoribus. Illic viginti annis exilium toleravit Augustae ope sustentata, quae florentes privignos cum per occultum subvertisset, misericordiam erga adflictos palam ostentabat.

About the same time Julia Augustus' granddaughter died. Augustus had convicted her of adultery and cast her away onto the island of Trimerus, not far from the Apulian coast, where she had been supported during twenty years of exile by the generosity of Livia Augusta, who had secretly undermined her stepchildren while they flourished, but publicly displayed compassion towards them after their downfall.

5a Suetonius *Augustus* 64–5
Iulias, filiam et neptem, omnibus probris contaminatas relegavit; . . . nepotes C. et L. in duodeviginti mensium spatio amisit ambos (etc) . . . aliquanto autem patientius mortem quam dedecora suorum tulit. Nam C. Lucique casu non adeo fractus, de filia absens ac libello per quaestorem recitato notum senatui fecit abstinuitque congressu hominum diu prae pudore, etiam de necanda deliberavit. Certe cum sub idem tempus una ex consciis liberta Phoebe suspendio vitam finisset, maluisse se Phoebes patrem fuisse. Relegatae usum vini omnemque delicatiorem cultum ademit neque adiri a quoquam libero servoque nisi se consulto permisit, et ita ut certior fieret, qua is aetate, qua statura, quo colore esset, etim quibus corporis notis vel cicatricibus. Post quinquennium demum ex insula in continentem lenioribusque paulo condicionibus transtulit eam. Nam ut omnino revocaret exorari nullo modo

potuit, deprecanti saepe p.R et pertinacius instanti tales filiae talesque coniuges pro contione imprecatus. Et nepte Julia post damnationem editum infantum adgnosci alique vetuit.

Augustus relegated the Julias, his daughter and granddaughter, polluted by every kind of shame. He lost both grandsons within twenty-two months, but he bore the death of his dear ones rather more patiently than their disgrace. For although he was not so shattered by the losses of Gaius and Lucius, he made his daughter's offences known to the Senate in his absence, having them read out by a quaestor, and he shunned men's company for a long time out of shame, and even contemplated killing her. At any rate when one of Julia's accomplices, the freedwoman Phoebe hanged herself about this time, he said he would have preferred to be Phoebe's father. When Julia was relegated, he deprived her of all wine and more choice food, and forbade her to be approached by any freeman or slave unless he had been consulted, on these terms; he was to know what age, physique and complexion this person was, and even any bodily marks or scars. Finally after five years he transferred her from the island to the mainland with slightly milder circumstances. For he could absolutely not be persuaded to recall her: when the Roman people repeatedly begged for mercy and persisted more urgently, he wished them in a public assembly the curse of daughters and wives like these women. He also forbade the acknowledgment and rearing of the child his granddaughter gave birth to after her condemnation.

5b Suetonius *Tiberius* 7

Agrippinam . . . duxit uxorem; sublatoque ex ea filio Druso, quanquam bene convenientem rursusque gravidam dimittere ac Iuliam Augusti filiam confestim coactus est ducere non sine magno angore animi, cum et Agrippinae consuetudine teneretur et Iuliae mores improbaret, ut quam sensisset sui quoque sub priore marito appetentem, quod sane etiam vulgo existimabatur . . . cum Iulia primo concorditer et amore mutuo vixit, mox dissedit et aliquanto gravius, ut etiam perpetuo secubaret, intercepto communis filii pignore, qui Aquileiae natus infans exstinctus est.

[Tiberius] married Vipsania Agrippina, and had reared a son Drusus by her, but was forced to divorce her although she was well suited to him and pregnant for a second time. This caused him great emotional distress because he was attached to Agrippa's companionship and disapproved of Julia's morals, having felt that she had wanted to attract him even while married to her former husband, a matter of general belief . . . at first he lived on good terms and in mutual affection with Julia but soon quarrelled with her quite seriously, so that he always slept apart after the common bond was destroyed of their son, who died still an infant after being born at Aquileia.

5c Suetonius *Tiberius* 10

Statuit repente secedere seque e medio quam longissime amovere; dubium
uxorisne taedio, quam neque criminari aut dimittere auderet neque ultra
perferre posset, an ut vitato assiduitatis fastidio auctoritatem absentis
tueretur . . . quasi possessione usurpati a se diu secundi gradus sponte cessisse
exemplo M. Agrippae, qui M. Marcello ad munera publica admoto
Mytilenas abierit.

He decided to go into sudden retreat and take himself as far away from
public life as possible; it is not clear whether this was from distaste for his
wife, whom he dared neither to accuse nor divorce, but could no longer
endure, or in order to protect his authority in absence by avoiding wearying
men with his constant service. . . . He seems to have withdrawn voluntarily
from position of second in command which he had long held, on the
precedent of M. Agrippa, who went away to Mytilene when Marcellus was
promoted to public service.

5d Suetonius *Tiberius* 11.4

Comperit deinde Iuliam uxorem ob libidines atque adulteria damnatam
repudiumque ei suo nomine ex auctoritate Augusti remissum; et quamquam
laetus nuntio, tamen officii duxit, quantum in se esset, exorare filiae patrem
frequentibus litteris et vel utcumque meritae, quidquid unquam dono dedisset
concedere.

Then he discovered that his wife Julia had been condemned for promiscuity
and adultery and notice of divorce had been served on Augustus' authority
in his name. Although he was relieved at the news, he thought it a matter of
duty as far as he could, to persuade the father in many letters to relent
towards his daughter, and to grant her any gifts he had ever made, despite
what she deserved.

5e Suetonius *Tiberius* 50

Iuliae uxori tantum afuit ut relegatae, quod minimum est, offici aut
humanitatis alquid impertiret, ut ex constitutione patris uno oppido clausam
domo quoque egredi et commercio hominum frui vetuerit; sed et peculio
concesso a patre praebitisque annuis fraudavit, per speciem publici iuris,
quod nihil de his Augustus testamento cavisset.

He was so far from affording any service or generosity (the least he could
have done) to his wife Julia when she was relegated, that although her father
had only decreed that she should be confined to one town, he now forbade
her to leave the house or enjoy human contact. Indeed he cheated her of the
allowance and annual revenue granted by her father, making a pretext of
civil law, because Augustus had made no provision for these in his will.

6 Dio 55.9.11–16

The Praetor Quinctius Crispinus also gave a gladiatorial show. I mention this only because on this occasion knights and women of distinction were brought upon the stage. Augustus however took no notice of this, but when he at length discovered that his daughter Julia was so wanton that she actually took part in revels (*komazein*) and drinking bouts at night in the forum and on the very rostra, he became exceedingly angry. He had surmised even before this that she was not leading a proper life but refused to believe it. For those who hold authority, it appears, know everything else better than their own affairs; and although their own deeds do not pass unnoticed by their associates, they have no precise knowledge of how their associates behave. On this occasion when Augustus learned what was going on he gave way to a rage so violent that he could not keep the matter to himself but went so far as to communicate it to the Senate. As a result Julia was banished to the island of Pandateria, off the coast of Campania and her mother Scribonia voluntarily accompanied her. Of the men who had enjoyed her favours Iullus Antonius was put to death on the grounds that he had done this to obtain the monarchy, along with other prominent men, while the rest were banished to islands. And since one of them was a tribune, he was not tried until he had completed his term of office.

As a result of this many other women were accused of similar behaviour, but the Emperor would not accept all the suits, but set a time limit before which events were not to be investigated.

Notes

1 Introduction: daughters and wives in Roman society of the late republic

1 On the age of elite Roman men at marriage, see Saller (1987); of elite young women, Shaw (1987). For a comprehensive and accessible study of every aspect of Roman marriage, see Treggiari (1991a), also the collections of essays by Rawson (1991), and on social legislation in the age of Augustus, Treggiari (1996: 873–904).

2 His sister Octavia, six years older, would always be of great importance to him, and for lack of sons he would treat her child Marcellus as his natural heir. He also had an older half-sister by a different mother, Octavia the Elder, wife of Sextus Appuleius, but they were not particularly close.

3 Cicero, for example, was Aedile in 70 BCE. Although curule (patrician) and plebeian aediles had different functions, both groups won their popularity by acting as impresarios for public games.

4 Since the tribunate was most often held by sons of senators, many or more tribunes were orthodox supporters of the status quo than idealists or radicals basing their career hopes on popular favour.

5 If he married around twenty-five, the young aristocrat would have completed the years of military service required for a political career, but that career itself would probably send him abroad as Quaestor, and certainly as praetorian or consular governor of a province, where money was to be made, and even glory, if the man had military talent and a good (but not too good) local enemy to defeat.

6 See Corbier (1991: 59), Treggiari (1991a: 480).

7 Cic. *Letters to Atticus* 1.12.3: 'Pompey's divorce is generally approved.' Cicero is clearly replying to Atticus' comments on the scandal.

8 For the political implications of this restrictive priesthood and the motives for Caesar's nomination and subsequent exclusion, see Gelzer (1948, trans. Needham, 1968 19–21) and Weinstock (1971: 30–1).

9 Priesthoods at Rome were highly politicized, and Caesar, already a pontifex, had won this extraordinary position in electoral contest with the senior ex-consul Catulus by extravagant, even ruinous bribery.

10 Boy: Livy *Epit.* 106, Vell. 2.47, Suet. *Caesar* 26.2. Girl: Plut. *Pompey* 53.4, Dio 39.64.

11 In view of the special treatment that Caesar as a young man had given to the funerals of his aunt Julia and his wife Cornelia, we might expect that Caesar himself would take the initiative in obtaining a public funeral and the typical burial of a Roman war hero on the Campus Martius for his daughter. On the other hand, as Plutarch (*Caesar* 26) shows, he was in Gaul and might not have

heard of Julia's death in time to affect her burial. Gladiatorial games, too, were normally offered in honour and memory of a distinguished man, such as a deceased father or brother. The rioting on the death of Clodius two years later (and again on the assassination of Caesar himself ten years later) shows how passionately the Roman plebs participated in the fate of their popular leaders.

12 For Caesar's daughter Julia, in Lucan, cf. (besides 1.111–14), 3.10–35 and 8.102–05.
13 Plut. *Cato minor* 52, Lucan 2.326–80.
14 Cf. Treggiari (1991a: 145, 164 and 216–17).
15 The age differential seems to have averaged about nine years. See references cited in Note 1 above.
16 Cf. Treggiari (1991a: 210, 269).
17 On divorce, see Treggiari (1991a: 435–82) and Corbier (1991).
18 On divorce initiated by women, see McDonnell (1983).
19 Cf. Treggiari (1991a: 350–7).
20 See Kuttner (1995).
21 Supposedly held every 110 years. Augustus' experts contrived the due date of the next games for 17 BCE. These will be discussed below.
22 Cf. Wallace-Hadrill (1996).

2 Julia's parents and childhood

1 Syme 1939: 229, based on her ex-husband Octavian's later report in Suet. *Aug.* 62, quoted note 3 below.
2 Scheid (1976: 185–201) cites an inscription from Rome (*CIL* [*Corpus Inscriptionum Latinorum*] 6.26033) erected by the freedmen of Scribonia, wife of Caesar, 'and of her son Cornelius Marcellinus'. For the Quaestor Marcellinus at Dyrrhachium, cf. Caesar *Bellum Civile*, 62.4, 64–5.
3 Suetonius *Aug.* 62: 'Presently he took Scribonia in marriage; she had previously been married to two men of consular rank, and was even a mother by the second one '(or possibly 'one of the two' *ex altero*). He divorced her also, 'weary', as he writes 'of her unreasonable temper.' See also Barrett (2003) Appendix 6.
4 R. Billows, *American Journal of Ancient History* identifies this Scipio with the Cornelius Scipio derisively called Salvitto, whom Caesar took to Africa and advertised in response to a prophecy that the war in Africa would be won by a descendant of Cornelius Scipio Aemilianus. In fact Salvitto was not a direct descendant of Aemilianus, as was the republican commander Metellus Scipio (cf. Cic. *Brutus* 212). But Syme (1985: 247) identifies this P. Cornelius Scipio, Suffect Consul of 35, as the son of Metellus Scipio, whether by blood or adoption.
5 For a fuller version of events in the so-called triumviral period between 43 and 31, see Pelling *CAH* X (1996) 1–66.
6 Compare Suetonius' comment (*Aug.* 17) on alliance with Antony as 'always dubious and unreliable, and unsuccessfully revived by a series of assorted reconciliations.'
7 According to republican practice, only men who had held the praetorship were eligible to be elected Consul, and the regular rules and sequence of office prevented men from achieving this office before the age of forty-two. Octavian was appointed Consul at the age of nineteen, without holding any previous office, apart from the praetorian standing voted to him by the Senate. To some extent, Pompey offered a precedent, since he was elected Consul in 70 BCE at the age of thirty-six, without having held any regular magistracies.
8 This Antonia would be known after her younger sister's birth as Antonia the Elder.

9 For a (somewhat unsympathetic) account of the careers of Livius Drusus Claudianus and his son-in-law Tiberius Claudius Nero, see Barrett (2003: Chapter 1).

10 He had probably been married before. Certainly Tiberius Nero was already looking for a wife when he approached Cicero as a potential suitor of Cicero's widowed daughter Tullia in 50 BCE.

11 On the vexed chronology of the marriage and Drusus' birth see Barrett (2003: 23–6 and Appendix 7).

12 The affair is described as a virtual rape (*abducta Neroni uxor*) by the critics cited in Tacitus *Annals* 1.10.5; cf. Dio 48.44.1–2. See Flory (1988) who distinguishes the hostile version promulgated by Antony from a more apologetic account in e.g. Velleius Paterculus 2.71 and 94, and Suetonius *Tiberius*.

13 Suet. *On Grammarians* 19, on which see Kaster's commentary. Note too that in this text Scribonia is called daughter, not sister, of Libo Drusus. This might refer to the father of the Consul of 35, rather than to the Consul himself, but it does lend some support to Scheid's arguments against the traditional identification.

14 Fulvia married C. Scribonius Curio after the murder of her first husband, P. Clodius Pulcher, in 52; after Curio's defeat and suicide in Africa in 48 she married Antony.

15 Marriage was a private matter, valid in any state between citizens of that state or those recognized as eligible according to its laws. Thus a marriage could be recognized in Egypt which Cleopatra's foreign status rendered invalid in Rome. Octavian and other Romans could ignore this relationship as long as it was convenient to them.

16 Appian *Civil War* 5.69 and 72. It is worth noting that Appian reports as part of this settlement yet another betrothal, that of Sextus' daughter to Octavia's son (and Antony's stepson), Marcellus.

17 According to Plutarch *Antony* 35, she was pregnant with a third child, but if so, it either miscarried or was stillborn.

18 Cf. Pelling (1988) on *Antony* 54.1–5; 57.4.

19 Antony would later claim (Suet. *Aug.* 63) that Octavian had even promised his daughter to the son of Cotison, King of the Getae, but one can assess the truth of this allegation from its companion claim that Octavian was at that time seeking the hand of the King's daughter. See Treggiari (1991a: 156–7). There was no time after Julia's birth when this would have been conceivable.

20 Cf. Pelling (1988) on *Antony* 35.2 and 8 and 87.1.

21 On the triumph, compare Augustus *Res gestae* 4.1 listing his two ovations of 40 and 35 and his three curule triumphs, with the details in Dio 51.19.1 (the triumph over Cleopatra) and Dio 51.21.4–9.

22 Augustus reports in his *Res gestae* that he was twenty-one times saluted as Imperator, but this salutation of a general by his soldiers for a victory was republican practice, attested for, for example, by Pompey and Caesar. What was distinctive was that Octavian was awarded this title as a permanent part of his name. (See Syme 1984).

23 We will compare in the next chapter the exceptional career of Agrippa, Praetor in 40 BCE, but of his own choice Aedile seven years later. See however Gruen (1992: 288–95) for a considered argument that the popularity won by aediles from their sponsorship of the public games has been systematically exaggerated.

24 On the Theatre of Marcellus, see Richardson (1992) and *LTUR*, s.v.

25 Because Horace published his three books of *Odes* in 23, apparently before Marcellus' illness, there is only a laudatory and confident allusion to Marcellus in *Odes* 1.12.45–6: 'the glory of Marcellus is growing like a tree, with the unnoticed lapse of years.' His language permits this to be read either of the

young man or of his distinguished ancestor, but its position, just before the poet's own salute to Octavian, makes it clear that Horace has the young prince in mind.

26 This and other translations are my own, except where another translator is specified.

27 Seneca *Ad Marciam* 2–3.

3 Tensions of Julia's youth: the poetry of pleasure and the legislation of morality

1 The name *domina*, with much the same resonance of a unique and powerful relationship as the now archaic term 'mistress', had previously been used by Catullus (*et domus et domina*, 68.156), but the text is ambiguous, and has been taken to mean either Catullus' mistress Lesbia or the wife/partner of his addressee Allius, seen as mistress of their house.

2 These are references to *Elegy* 2.7 and 2.14 respectively. He will later describe the muse of his poetry as triumphing over his rivals. For the controversial issue of the legislation mentioned in 2.7, see note 13 below.

3 On Sulpicia, see Snyder (1989), and Treggiari (1991a: 121–2, 302–3).

4 The pun would play on Greek *keras* and Roman *cornu*, both meaning horn.

5 Propertius 4.3: this fictitious letter from Arethusa to Lycotas fits the chronology of the Roman expedition to Syria to deal with Parthia, starting in 21 and resolved by Tiberius' diplomacy in 19 BCE.

6 Compare Gallus' lament to his beloved, quoted by Virgil *Eclogue* 10. We do not know when Gallus wrote his love elegies, which are almost entirely lost, but by 25 BCE he was already dead, disgraced by Octavian for offending him by writing boastful inscriptions about his achievements as Octavian's military governor of Egypt.

7 The text has been disputed; these triumphs are either ancestral (*patriis*), or Parthian (*Parthis*): with Goold, Propertius, Camb. MA, 1990. I retain the manuscript reading with its stress on tradition and ancestral custom. If Propertius actually wrote Parthian he would be protesting specifically against distant eastern campaigns – and ones with ominous precedents in previous defeats and casualties.

8 Compare the young man's serenade in Plautus *Curculio* Act 1 Scene 1, *Mercator* 408–11, and Catullus 67, in which a married woman's door denounces her promiscuity and incest.

9 Propertius' first book was regularly referred to as the *Monobiblos*, or *Single Book*, suggesting that it was published by itself, perhaps as early as 29 BCE. Book 2 opens with a dedication to his new patron Maecenas (cf. also 3.9) and there are other shifts of orientation. He no longer addresses his circle of friends, but begins to react to poems in Tibullus' first collection, and in Book 3 (1–3) takes up motifs from Horace's *Odes*, which seems to date these two books closer to 25 and 23 BCE, when *Odes* 1–3 were published. But poems were undoubtedly recited long before their collective publication. The poet's allusion to his work in 2.13.25 as comprising three *libelli* has been seen as evidence for the joint publication of Books 2, 3 and 4, which would date the publication of Book 2 up to ten years later. But it is important to understand that new poems were most often made known through recitation, before they were collected in a *libellus*.

10 Compare 3.2.15 'my poems are dear to the reader' and 3.19–20 'so that your book is often displayed on a bench for a young girl alone and awaiting her beau.' The opening poem of book three certainly speaks with a new pride and confidence of the poet's fame.

11 Cf. 2.6.25–26 'what is the point of founding a temple of chastity if any bride can do as she chooses?' and Horace *Odes* 3.6, discussed below.

12 Suet. *Aug.* 69. Antony was of course the most biased of sources. He also alleges that Octavian used his friends to negotiate assignations with *matres familias*: Antony names Tertulla, Terentilla (Maecenas' wife), Rufilla and Salvia Titisenia. Flory (1988) has argued that Antony's allegation about the Consul's wife and perhaps even the dinner of the twelve gods, merely misrepresented Octavian's behaviour at his betrothal party to Livia – held with her previous husband's consent.

13 The purge was no doubt chiefly political (of former supporters of Antony) and economic (of bankrupts) but may have expelled individuals for sexual offences. Certainly the censors of 50 BCE had removed senators for adultery and the sodomy of citizen boys.

14 Badian (1985: 82–98). But Badian has not entirely answered the arguments advanced by Brunt (1982: Appendix 9, 558–66).

15 Not just to obtain or retain the soldiers' goodwill, but as a discreet means of maintaining order, which often broke down into near riots (especially at performances by the idolized pantomime dancers) even under Augustus.

16 Ovid *Art of Love* 1.89–100.

17 On this see Dio 54.30.4, apparently dated in or soon after 12 BCE, in which a concession allowed the holdouts against marriage (or remarriage) to attend spectacles and the feasts on Augustus' birthday.

18 *Res gestae* 6 states that Augustus refused this power when it was first offered to him in 28 and again in 19, but he certainly exercised its equivalent.

19 On the marriage laws, see Suet. *Claudius* 23.1, with Brunt (1971) Appendix 8, Treggiari (1991a: 277–98) and (1996: 887–9). For the age limits, cf. *Digest* 23.2.44.

20 Widows had always been expected to stay unmarried for ten months to protect the deceased husband's paternal rights over any child born after his death.

21 This also applied to freedmen and freedwomen: parenthood released the fathers from certain obligations to former patrons, while the freedwoman mother of four children gained the equivalent of the *ius trium liberorum*.

22 Pliny's *Letters* show that he himself had this status, and requested it for Suetonius as a favour from Trajan.

23 Cf. Suet. *Aug.* 63.1 and Pliny *Natural History* 7.57.

24 In the *Lex Papia Poppaea* passed by the bachelor Suffect Consuls of 9 CE; see Crook (1996: 134–5).

25 See Treggiari (1996: 890–2). The husband had to produce seven citizens as witness to the affair (*Digest* 24.2.9). After the divorce, her father also had the option of prosecuting his daughter.

26 The only instance known to me is the prosecution of an unidentified adulterer reported by Dio 54.30.4 in which Maecenas and Augustus' cousin Sex. Apuleius were witnesses for the defence, and Augustus intervened when the prosecutor abused them, by taking the seat of the presiding magistrate and forbidding any insults to his kinsmen or friends. It seems likely in the circumstances that the prosecutor lost his case. Were there other sympathetic acquittals?

27 Treggiari (1996: 890) begins her appendix of recorded adultery charges with that of Julia in 2 BCE, and notes that no instances of such killings are recorded in the legal literature of the second–third centuries.

28 Julia herself, according to Macrobius (*Sat.* 2.5), left an ironic comment on this proud claim. Asked how she ensured that her children all resembled her husband Agrippa despite alleged infidelities, she replied that she never took on passengers until her cargo was already loaded – that is, she was only unfaithful during pregnancy: a smart retort for the occasion, which I would suggest may simply have been adjusted to her interlocutor's cynical attitude, or a pre-existing witticism fathered on her after her disgrace became known.

29 These two otherwise undistinguished men were the (unmarried) consuls who gave their names to the law of 9 CE.

4 The rise of Marcus Agrippa

1 In Tacitus *Annals* 4.40.3, Tiberius is made to report that:

> when Augustus was distracted by every kind of concern, and it seemed that whoever would marry his daughter would be exalted by such a union to a vast degree above all others, he considered in his discussions C. Proculeius and others of conspicuously peaceful private life, and not involved with any political affairs.

2 Nepos, *Life of Atticus* 12.1 records this marriage as if it were 'beneath' the popular friend of Caesar to marry the daughter of a mere *eques* from a non-senatorial family, but adds that Agrippa's marriage was arranged by Mark Antony – clearly a political act. The daughter of this marriage was betrothed as an infant to Tiberius, and became his first, much loved, wife (Nepos 19.4).

3 Since Caesar was 'father of his country', this law defined the murder of Caesar as equal to killing one's own father.

4 Cf. Reinhold (1933), Roddaz (1984).

5 His loyalty to Octavian is reflected by the coinage he issued in 38, which featured Octavian on the obverse, and the simple legend M. AGRIPPA COS DESIGN on the reverse (Crawford 1974: 543).

6 Velleius 2.79, his first reference to Agrippa, which notes the contradiction between Agrippa's loyalty to Octavian and his unwillingness to accept any other command.

7 With Velleius' account compare the geographer Strabo's description of the area in 5.4.5–6. The earliest poetic reference is Virgil *Georgics* 2.161–4:

> or shall I mention the harbours and barriers applied to the Lucrine lake, and the sea protesting with mighty din where the Julian waves resound afar, as the sea is driven back and the Tyrrhenian tide is let into the waters of Avernus?

Propertius alludes to Agrippa's hydraulics not only in 3.18, the elegy for Marcellus quoted in the previous chapter, but in his first book, 'where the causeway stretches by the shores of Hercules, and the waters just recently submerged beneath the land of Thesprotus are now brought close to noble Misenum' (1.11.2–4). Only Horace declines to celebrate any of Agrippa's military and naval exploits in *Odes* 1.6, ostensibly from an aversion to the grandeur required by epic, but perhaps also because these victories were won in the civil war over the republican side which he had supported. But he is happy to compliment Agrippa on his civic benefactions (see note 28 below).

8 The best example is probably the posthumous commemorative issue of his grandson Caligula, which shows Agrippa wearing his naval crown on the obverse, and a standing Neptune with a dolphin (closely resembling the statue of Agrippa as Neptune now in the Museum of Venice) on the reverse. But although this honour is treated as unique, Pliny 16.7–8 reports that it was also conferred on Varro by Pompey for service as admiral during his eastern campaigns against the pirates in 67 BCE.

9 Compare Horace's irony in *Satires* 2.3.185–6 at the expense of a local bigwig who wants to use his office to emulate the popularity of Agrippa as Aedile, 'that wellborn lion.' In contrast with the sneers of the nobility at the unknown family of the magistrate, Horace's epithet *ingenuum* reflects the point of view of a freedman's son, for whom citizen parentage is a privilege.

10 Pliny refers to Agrippa's memoirs of his aedileship in *Natural History* 36.121 (and 104) but he must be quoting Agrippa through a later source, as he does not name him among the *auctores* for 35 and 36. (In contrast Pliny cites Agrippa for geographical material in *Natural History* 3–6.)

11 Pliny *Natural History* 36.104 reports that in Agrippa's aedileship inspectors navigated the Cloaca Maxima and its seven tributary drains in boats.

12 Cf. Dio 54.11.7, which Roddaz (1984) prefers to Pliny's claim (*Natural History* 36. 21) that the Aqua Virgo also belonged to the year 33. On the Aqua Virgo, carrying by far the largest volume of Rome's aqueducts, see now *MAR* 49, and for the system of aqueducts *MAR* 49–51.

13 Pliny *Natural History* 36.21 quotes these statistics as part of Agrippa's record of his benefactions as Aedile.

14 In *Res gestae* 25.2, Augustus moves immediately from his defeat of the pirates and slaves (Sextus Pompeius' forces) to the oath of loyalty yet without naming the enemy against whom it was directed: 'the whole of Italy of its own free will swore allegiance to me and demanded me as the leader in the war in which I was victorious at Actium. The Gallic and Spanish provinces, Africa, Sicily and Sardinia swore the same oath of allegiance'.

15 Compare Dio 50.11 and 13.

16 *Aeneid* 8.676–84:

> Actia bella/ cernere erat, totumque instructo Marte videres/ fervere Leucaten auroque effulgere fluctus./ hinc Augustus agens Italos in proelia Caesar/ cum patribus populoque penatibus et magnis dis,/ stans celsa in puppi, geminas cui tempora flammas/ laeta vomunt patriumque aperitur vertice sidus./ parte alia ventis et dis Agrippa secundis/ arduus agmens agens; cui belli insigne superbum,/ tempora navali fulgent rostrata corona.

17 Prop. 4.6.55–8 and 63: 'dixerat et pharetrae pondus consumit in arcus/ proxima post arcus Caesaris hasta fuit./ vincit Roma fide phoebi, dat femina poenas:/ sceptra per ionias fracta vehuntur aquas . . . illa petit Nilum cumba male nixa fugaci'.

18 Dio 51.3.1–2. Talking of gemstones and Octavian's successive signet rings, Pliny *Natural History* 37.10 reports that Octavian passed his signet ring on to them so that they could exercise private communications with him (cf. Dio 51.3.5–7).

19 On this house, see Richardson (1992: 114), and *MAR* 112–13, s.v. *domus: Palatium* (3). Antony's house has been identified with the residence visible beneath the basilica of the Flavian palace containing a large rectangular hall, the Aula Isiaca, with remarkable decorations. But when Augustus invited Agrippa to move into his own home, he occupied the part of Octavius' property which had formerly been the house of Lutatius Catulus.

20 Dio 53.27.5. There is no Latin equivalent closer than *contubernalis*, not usually applied to this (rather rare) situation. Messala, on the other hand was merely given financial compensation by Augustus.

21 This was perhaps the most conspicuous and famous of Octavian's monuments. See Richardson (1992) s.v. Apollo Palatinus, Aedes 14, *MAR* 46–7, *LTUR* I: 54–7.

22 *Res gestae* 8.1–3: 'Patriciorum numerum auxi consul quintum iussu populi et senatus. 2 Senatum ter legi et in consulato sexto censum populi conlega M. Agrippa egi. Lustrum post annum alterum et quadragensimum feci'. The only other reference to Agrippa in the *Res gestae* is as Augustus' priestly colleague in presiding over the secular games (*Res gestae* 22.2).

23 On the Forum Iulium and temple of Venus Genetrix, see Richardson (1992) 165–7, *MAR* 134–5 and *LTUR* 2.299–306. Dio reports its progress in 43.22.2

and 45.6.4; see *Res gestae* 20. For the temple of Divus Iulius, compare Dio 47.18.4, and see *MAR* 214 under Iulius, Divus, Aedes.

24 On the Saepta Iulia, see Dio 53.23.2 and Richardson (1992: 340–10), *MAR* 219. For the Diribitorium which was still unfinished at Agrippa's death and dedicated by Augustus in 7 BCE, see Dio 55.8.3 and Richardson (1992: 109–10).

25 On the Stagnum Agrippae, see Richardson (1992: 367), *MAR* 235, and *LTUR* IV 344–5, based on the article of Lloyd (1979: 83).

26 On Agrippa's baths, see Dio 53.27.1 and Richardson (1992: 386–7), *MAR* 244–5, *LTUR* 5.40–42.

27 Ovid *Ex ponto* 1.8.35–6: 'nunc fora, nunc aedes, nunc marmore tecta theatra,/ nunc subit aequata porticus omnis humo./ Gramina nunc Campi pulchros spectantis in hortos,/ stagnaque et Euripi virgineusque liquor.'

28 This portico (Richardson [1992: 312, *MAR* 236–7, *LTUR* IV, 54–61) on the long west side of the Saepta was adorned with a painting of the Argonauts; Horace *Epistles* 1.6.26 shows that it was a place to be seen when taking the air.

29 On the Basilica and its probable connection with the Thermae, see Richardson (1992: 54), *MAR* (s.v. Stoa of Poseidon), 236–7.

30 On the Agrippan Pantheon, see Richardson (1992: 282–3), *MAR* s.v. Pantheum, 188–9, *LTUR* V 280–83. Although the inscription dates the building to his sixth consulship in 27, Dio 53.27.2–4, dates its dedication to 25 BCE. The details of the caryatids and bronze capitals are given separately by Pliny in *Natural History* 36.38–9 and 34.13.

31 Pliny *Natural History* 35.26. But Pliny makes a contrast between this severity and Agrippa's own extravagance in paying the people of Cyzicus (presumably during his time in Asia) over 1 million sesterces for paintings of Ajax and Aphrodite and installing two more paintings in the hot room of his new baths.

32 Dio 53.31.2–32.1.

33 Magie (1950).

5 Old enough to be her father: marriage to Agrippa

1 Since 27, only the provinces requiring a military presence had been retained under the direct control of the emperor, but he also practised intervention in the commands of Asia and Africa the which the senate normally appointed governors.

2 They tried more than once to offer Augustus the dictatorship or again the consulship for life, and refused to elect consuls for 19 BCE (Dio 54.10).

3 Tac. *Annals* 3.34–35. The occasion was a motion of Caecina Severus that no governor was to be accompanied by his wife, which was answered first by Messalinus, son of Valerius Messala, then by the prince Drusus opposing the motion because 'imperial leaders (*principibus*) more often had to travel to the remote parts of empire.' 'How often', he added, 'the deified Augustus had travelled to the east and west with Livia as his companion!' Yet if Tacitus had not invented this speech we should not have known from historians that Livia accompanied Augustus. Wives were a private matter, not a public concern.

4 Although Dio reports that a public celebration was decreed for his birthday we do not know the calendar date.

5 See Rose (1997a: 158–9). The possible identification of the two little girls on the *Ara pacis* as Julia's daughters does not help to decide the name of the elder.

6 See note 11 below, and Appendix I Public monuments: temples and inscribed statue bases.

7 These careful terms are the language used by Augustus himself in the surviving papyrus fragment of his funeral *laudatio* for Agrippa.

8 The Etruscan time unit known in Latin as *saeculum* was not, like its modern equivalent (secolo, siècle, etc.) 100 years but 110 years. Calculation of this infrequent ritual had apparently settled on 16 BCE, but Augustus could not wait. Was this because he would himself become forty-six, *senior*, in 17 and wanted a compensatory sense of renewal?

9 ILS 5050, CIL VI, 32323. This is most easily accessible in Beard *et al.* (2000: II, 140–4, or Reinhold and Lewis, 1990, 2nd edn.

10 This monument has to be inferred from its huge surviving base. Of course, it would be some years before the decree of such a monument was implemented.

11 See Reinhold (1933: 107–8) with notes. The Agrippeion is mentioned by Philostratus *Lives of the Sophists* 2.5.3 and 8.2. Reinhold (1933: note 21) reports inscribed statue bases for Agrippa in the cities mentioned above and Argos, Megara and Delos.

12 See Appendix I, and cf. Rose (1997b: 109) on the informative value of these hard stone bases, which outlived their statues of bronze or precious metals. The Thespiae inscriptions are discussed in Chapter 8.

13 For the historical details, see Rowe (2002: 131–5).

14 For a translation of the Greek text (*OGIS* [*Orientis Graecae Inscriptiones Selectae*] 456) see Rowe (2002: 133–4).

15 The purpose of this vague undertaking was to give a guarantee that Mytilene would keep up with any new forms of imperial tribute devised by other eastern cities. Cities competed to show their loyalty and to outdo each other in homage.

16 Rowe distinguished between statues inscribed in the dative 'to' a deified member of the imperial family, and those honouring them as mortals (in the accusative). Note, however, that the other inscription reported by Reinhold (1939: 117 n. 66) may have been erected for a later imperial Julia, (for example, the daughter of Titus) not Julia Augusti.

17 For Asia Minor and Syria under Augustus see Magie (1950); for the most recent discussion of Rome's government in the east and relationship with Armenia and Parthia during Augustus' principate, see Gruen (1996).

18 Pliny *Natural History* 34.62 quotes a price of 1.2 million sesterces – equal to the property qualification required of a senator. Agrippa was an enthusiast for the works of Lysippus and also put the sculptor's famous *Apoxyomenos* (an athlete scraping off oil with a *strigil* after a contest) on display in his thermae at Rome (*Natural History* 35.26).

19 Strabo 13.1.19.

20 The relevant fragment of Nicolaus (Jacoby *FGH* [*Fragmenta der Griechischen Historiker*] 2 A: 421–2) is confirmed by a brief notice in Josephus *Antiquities* 16.2.2 that Herod obtained pardon for the Ilians. The base survives of the statue erected by the grateful citizens of Ilium to Agrippa as patron and benefactor and kinsman (through his marriage with a Julian) of the city (*OGIS*: 776).

21 Since Reinhold treats Julia as the elder daughter, he dates the Thespiae inscriptions, which include Julia, to the family's return journey in 13.

22 Reinhold (1933: 117, note 70) cites Fitzler, s.v. Julia, *RE* XI.998, for these dedications, and argues for a visit to Ephesus (117, note 74); this is supported by the bronze coinage with portraits of Agrippa and Julia (same chapter, note 22).

23 Livia and Julia, BMC (British Museum Catalogue) Mysia 139. Nos 248–9; see Appendix I.

24 Wood (1999: 64, note 118) mentions coinage apparently from Africa featuring confronting male and female heads, possibly Marcellus and Julia.

6 Julia's homes

1 Wallace-Hadrill (1994: Part I, 3–64). Compare Vitruvius 6.5 on the kind of house needed by nobly born holders of high office, with royal (*regales*) vestibules, lofty reception halls (*atria*) and very spacious peristyles.

2 Cf. *Att.* 2.15.3 written from Formiae.

3 Suet. *Aug.* 72: 'postea in Palatio, sed nihilominus in aedibus modicis Hortensianis, et neque laxitate neque cultu conspicuis': subsequently he lived on the Palatine, but still in the moderate sized house of Hortensius, not conspicuous either in spaciousness or in decoration.

4 On Hortensius, cf. Cicero's witticism reported by Quintilian, *I O* 6.3.98, and Plut. *Cicero* 7.8, also Gellius 1.5.3 on his nickname 'Dionysia'.

5 For a helpful plan of the house's situation, see Wiseman (1994: 105), for plans of the house itself Coarelli (1974: 138 and 142).

6 I have used as resources for the following account Coarelli (1974: 141–4), and Richardson (1992: 73), under Casa di Livia, and (1992: 117–18) under Domus, Augustus. Readers should consult Galinsky (1996), which offers a rich chapter on wall painting and exceptionally fine coloured illustrations (Plates 1–5, a–b) of the Sala delle Maschere, Room M in the Casa di Livia, and Augustus' secret study.

7 The fire in the Circus Maximus: Dio 50.10.3–4; Antony's house, Dio 53.27.5 (see Richardson 1992: 114 for the hypothesis that this house could be the Casa di Livia adjacent to the house of Augustus). For the fire of 3 CE, which also damaged the temple of Magna Mater, cf. Suet. *Aug.* 57.2 (undated), and Dio 55.12.4–5.

8 Figures 98 and 105.

9 Figures 109 and 110.

10 Compare Coarelli's coloured illustration of a short wall of this room (1974: 143) not year given above], and Galinsky (1996: Plate 2) which shows in colour two adjacent walls with their central mythical pictures framed in *aediculae*.

11 See the four illustrations of detail reproduced (courtesy of *DAIR*) in Galinsky (1996: Plate 4).

12 Dio 49.15.5.

13 Ovid, *Tristia* 3.1.61.

14 Cf. Galinsky (1996: 220–1).

15 Cf. Pliny *Natural History* 36.23–4, on the Latona by Cephisodotus, son of Praxiteles, and the Apollo by Scopas (*Natural History* 36.32), for the Diana by Timotheus, whose (damaged?) head had been replaced by Pliny's time with a new head by Avianus Evander.

16 Galinsky (1996: 213–24), Zanker (1988). The terracottas are illustrated in Galinsky (1996: Figs 104 and 125).

17 On Platorinus and Caepio, see Lloyd (1979: 193–204), and Leach (1982) in Gold (1982). C. Platorinus honoured Agrippa on the coins he issued in 12 BCE.

18 For the plan see De Mino (1998: 11).

19 Pliny *Natural History* 35.116 attributes this kind of wall painting 'of villas and porticoes, and landscapes of groves, woods and hills, fishponds, channels, rivers and shores . . . together with various sketches of people strolling or sailing, or approaching villas by land on donkeys or in carts, fishing and fowling, hunting or even gathering the vintage' to a certain S. Tadius or perhaps Studius.

20 *Pinakes* is the Greek name for paintings on boards, which could be displayed on easels. The term is transferred to the images painted on walls to appear as separate framed paintings, often propped up on a (painted) easel or by a supporting figure.

21 Sanzi Di Mino (1998: Figs. 78, 79 and 80).

22 For a plan see Anderson (1987a: 36)
23 The New York Metropolitan Museum has closed its Roman rooms in order to remodel the space; the Museo Nazionale of Naples is simply short staffed and short funded as usual.
24 This is illustrated in black and white in Leach (1982).
25 Illustrated on the back cover of Anderson (1987a).

7 The fatal marriage

1 On this see Syme (1939) citing Tac. *Annals* 4.40.
2 See Chapter 4 above. Their child may not have lived.
3 Suet. *Tib.* 8, confirmed by the detailed account of Velleius Paterculus 2.95.3.
4 Vell. 2.94.2–3: 'nutritus caelestium praeceptorum disciplinis, iuvenis genere, forma, celsitudine corporis, optimis studiis maximoque ingenio instructissimus, qui protinus quantus est, sperari potuerat, visuque praetulerat principem'.
5 Horace speaks of these young men in civilian terms, calls them *studiosa cohors* and asking what poems they are composing. Titius and Munatius bear the family names of former consuls (C. Titius, Munatius Plancus) and were probably kinsmen.
6 It scans as u- u x, impossible in hexameter verse and difficult in Alcaics or Sapphics.
7 Velleius was Tiberius' prefect of cavalry from 4 CE. His testimonial to Tiberius as commander (2.104) recalls Tiberius' previous commands in Armenia, against the Raeti annd Vindelici, in Pannonia and Germany: compare also 2.113, on his combination of his own forces with newcomers to deal with the Pannonian revolt of 6 CE.
8 Indulgentia tam Fortunae quam patris abutebatur, cum alioquin litterarum amor multaque eruditio, quod in illa domo facile erat, praeterea mitis humanitas minimeque saevus animus ingentem feminae gratiam conciliarent, mirantibus qui vitia noscebant tantam pariter diversitatem.
9 See Chapter 5 above. Literal-minded scholars have made too much of this witty piece of bravado, itself almost certainly adapted from Greek comedy or epigram. Julia was fitting her reply to the values of her interlocutor.
10 She was probably wearing a Coan silk dress, the 'see-through' costume favoured by courtesans, but also, according to Seneca (*Helv.* 16.4) by many married women in his day.
11 On the heavy implications of this word, compare the careful analysis of Herbert-Brown (1998: 347–53).
12 On Agrippa's apparent withdrawal from Rome in 23 BCE see Chapter 4. Only Dio (55.10.5) claims Tiberius was sent to Rhodes for further education, rather than choosing to go there: Dio writes that he took no retinue or personal friends with him.
13 Cornelia, mother of the Gracchi, may seem to demonstrate a different attitude in the century before the rise of Octavian, since she was honoured for remaining a widow and refusing offers even, it was said, from King Ptolemy of Egypt. But she was exceptional both in the almost royal prestige of her family, and her relative age: she had borne twelve children by the time her husband died.
14 For Agrippina's widowhood and bad relationship with Tiberius, see Chapter 9.
15 Sancte pater patriae, tibi plebs, tibi curia nomen/ hoc dedit, hoc dedimus nos tibi nomen, eques./ res tamen ante dedit. Sero quoque vera tulisti/ nomina iam pridem tu pater orbis eras./ hoc tu per terras, quod quod in aethere Iuppiter alto,/ nomen habes; hominum tu pater, ille deum (Ovid *Fasti* 2.127–32).
16 'Hic castas duce se iubet esse maritas/ . . . reppulit ille nefas/ . . . florent sub Caesare leges' (*Fasti* 2.139, 140, 141).

17 See Appendix II.

18 Dio 55.10.15, Tac. *Annals* 1.10; 4.44. Velleius 2.100.4 says he committed suicide (which is quite compatible with condemnation to death).

19 In *Odes* 4.2, Iullus is composing a Pindaric ode for Augustus' forthcoming triumph.

20 Tac. *Annals* 1.53 on the death of Julia in 14 CE speaks of Tiberius' motives for savage treatment of Gracchus, who had corrupted Julia during her marriage to Agrippa and persisted as her adulterer when she was handed on to Tiberius, and inflamed her hatred for Tiberius. He adds that Gracchus was said to have composed the letter attacking Tiberius which she wrote to Augustus. Gracchus was relegated to Cercina off the coast of Africa and murdered when Tiberius took over from Augustus, fourteen years later.

21 *Natural History* 7.149, 'consilia parricidae palam facta'.

22 On Augustus' perception of female sexual transgression within the imperial house as impugning his own control as Paterfamilias and political power, see Ginsberg (2006) 123–30.

23 Livy 1.58.4, 'addit ad metum dedecus; cum mortua iugulatum servum nudum positurum ait, ut in sordido adulterio necata esse dicatur'.

24 The shameful tale is told circumstantially in Tac. *Annals* 14.60–64.

25 Levick (1972a: 779–813), and Syme (1984a: 912–36).

26 On the prohibition of night meetings and official perception of such gatherings, including religious celebrations, as a hostile body within the State, see the evidence gathered by O'Neill (2003: 135–65).

27 On this see Syme (1984a: 925 and 934).

28 Cf. Dio 55.13.1 for the popular demonstrations, and their later success in persuading Augustus to bring Julia back to mainland Italy.

29 See Tac. *Annals* 14.59–61.

30 Scribonia was long-lived, and seems to have returned to Rome on her daughter's death. Certainly she gave spirited counsel to her young kinsman Scribonius Libo, when he was accused by Tiberius of conspiracy in 16 CE (Sen. *Epistulae Morales* 70, 12; cf. Tac. *Annals* 2.27–32).

31 According to Suetonius (*Augustus* 64.2), L. Vinicius (Cos. 2 CE) once called on young Julia when she was staying at Baiae and received a letter from Augustus rebuking him for acting 'with too little modesty'.

32 Cf. Linderski (1988: 183) and Levick (1976a: 47–50). On the death of Gaius see the next chapter.

33 As Linderski (1988: 187–8) points out, Livia became Julia Augusta in 14 CE, but was not deified until Claudius gave her the status of diva in 42 CE.

34 Linderski consider that Julia, who would have needed Augustus' permission to free the father and son, may have been unwilling to free the mother. Is it not possible that the father bought his own freedom, then that of his son, so that they could enjoy citizenship, but left the mother's status until later?

35 With Suet. *Tiberius* 50, compare Tac *Annals* 1.53: 'Imperium adeptus extorrem, infamem et post interfectum Postumum Agrippam omnis spei egenam inopia ac tabe longa peremit, obscura fore necem longinquitate exilii ratus'. Cf. Dio 57.18, reporting that Tiberius actually locked her up, so that she died of weakness and starvation.

36 There had been another attempt around the time of the exile of Julia the younger in 8 CE (cf. Suet. *Augustus* 19); for the action of Agrippa's slave Clemens to rescue his master on the death of Augustus and his later insurrection see Levick (1976a: 150–2), and Tac. *Annals* 2.39–40; Suet. *Tib.* 25; Dio. 57.16.3.

37 Tacitus and Suetonius associate his retirement there with a variety of sexual perversions, which it would be foolish to swallow whole. There is now a twentieth-century Latin inscription composed by the American scholar Thomas

Spencer Jerome, and erected in the square of the village of Capri by the Senate and People of Capri, honouring Tiberius for the eleven years in which he lived a virtuous and studious life on the island.

8 Julia's boys

1 *Ad Att.* 1.17: ' I am so neglected by everyone that I only have as much repose as is spent with my wife and my dear girl and honeysweet Cicero.' (This is in 60 BCE, when Tullia would be a teenager and little Quintus only about six.)

2 This system of paired successors was identified by Kornemann (1930). I owe this reference to Rowe (2002: 17), a study that has proved most helpful for the understanding of the aborted careers of all three of Julia's sons.

3 Rose (1997a: 13–14 and notes. See Catalogue 95, 96 and notes.

4 For Thespiae and Delphi, see Reinhold (1933: 123 and note 95). For Thespiae see Rose (1997a: 14), and Cat. 82.

5 See Syme (1979: 140 and 206–10); on Aemilius Paullus see Syme (1985).

6 For the denarius of C. Marius Trom. from 13/12 BCE, see Fig. 5.1, p. 67 For other issues see: Augustus/Agrippa, *Roman Provincial Coinage* 522–6 (Nemausus), 533 (Arausio), 942 (Cyrenaica); others listed in Rose (1997a: note 64). Rose (1997a: note 65) disputes that the denarius of C. Marius Trom. showing Julia represents her sons, and endorses Lanfranchi's proposal that the male heads are Augustus and Agrippa.

7 Suet. *Augustus* 64.3. According to Suet. *Claudius* 23, Claudius too made his children sit at the ends of their parent's couch 'in the ancient manner' when dining.

8 Q. Lutatius Catulus (Consul in 78 BCE) was brother-in-law of Hortensius, whose house Augustus had purchased, and lived near the imperial compound on the north-western corner of the Palatine (Pliny *Natural History* 17.2).

9 This must have been after Octavia brought him back with her to Rome in 33 BCE; he would have been ten years old. Similarly, Scribonia's children by Marcellinus and Cornelius Scipio would have been ready for teaching during the 30s.

10 The best account of Verrius is now Kaster (1992) on Suet. *De grammaticis* 17, to which I owe most of these details.

11 Suet. *Augustus.* 53. The title Dominus would have seemed all the more autocratic to Suetonius who had lived under Domitian, an emperor who expected to be called Dominus et Deus. But the title was used for heads of household in daily life and it might be fairer to translate it 'Sir' (used until quite recently by English schoolboys to address their fathers and teachers), than 'Lord' or 'Master.'

12 Dio 54.26.1–2; (cf. Suet. *Augustus* 43 on Augustus' revival of this ceremony) and Virgil, *Aeneid*, 5.553–603. Virgil describes the boys wearing garlands on their heads and twisted golden torques around their necks. Each rides carrying two javelins and quivers. The three squadrons of twelve boys, led by Priam's grandson Polites, by Iulus-Ascanius and by his friend Atys, ride in increasingly complex interlacing circles. With his contemporaries in mind, Virgil describes the enthusiasm of the spectators as they see boys in their fathers' likenesses, and ends with an account of how Ascanius introduced the game to Alba from which it reached Rome as the *Troianum agmen* (*Aeneid* 5.602).

13 See also Simon (1967: Plates 16a and 23), Pollini (1987: Figs 3, 4). The 'Louvre panel' of the north frieze was separated from the rest of the frieze and supposedly damaged in storage. Thus the 'Julia' is now faceless, but has been identified by her widow's fringed *ricinium*. While earlier scholars identified two small chubby children wearing torques as Gaius and Lucius (they are so

identified in Zanker 1988: Figs 169 and 170). I follow Simon and Rose (1990: 453–68) in identifying these as barbarian princes brought to Rome as hostages by Agrippa, while the older children are Gaius and Lucius, depicted at their actual ages in 9 BCE.

14 For the young Gaius, see Plate 5(a) and Kuttner (1995: 179). Kuttner rightly argues for the importance of Tiberius both commanding with Drusus from 16–13 BCE and after Drusus' death, and claims that scholars have underestimated the prominence Augustus freely gave him even before 6 BCE. But she is surely mistaken in interpreting Gaius' equestrian exercises under Tiberius' command in 8 BCE as the Troy Game, which was only presented at Rome, and in which any youth would only be initiated once.

15 While Dio (55.9.5) or his epitomator seems to have misunderstood the situation in suggesting that Tiberius was sent to Rhodes against his will, he is probably right that Augustus' actions offended both Tiberius and his sons. On the other hand, Tiberius may have been revolting against the Princeps' intention to send him back to the East to repeat the pattern of largely ineffectual diplomacy with Armenia and Parthia.

16 I have changed the reading of Lewis and Reinhold from 'to' to 'for', since provincials were in fact expected to pray to the gods for the princes (cf. Price 1980: 28–43).

17 This is much clearer in Josephus (*Antiquities* 18.42) than in the allusive summary of Dio's epitomator.

18 Pliny *Natural History* 6.141 cf. 160 on Dionysius; 12.56 on Juba. I owe these references to Hollis (1977). Both notices suggest that Augustus was preparing the way for his son.

19 Suet. *Aug.* 58, *Res gestae* 34. The new title of Pater Patriae and the opening of the Forum Augustum are lost from the surviving excerpts of Dio (55.10), but he gives a full account of the dedication of the temple of Mars and the role of Gaius in presiding over the games.

20 Antipater's epigram is evidence for Gaius' recent marriage to Drusus' daughter Livia Julia (who would later marry Tiberius' son Drusus). Unless Gaius' bride accompanied him to the east, the marriage would be almost as brief as that of Protesilaus.

21 Plut. 'The Sayings of Romans' *Moralia* 207e, which he no doubt also included in his lost life of Augustus.

22 See Plate 4(b). There is some dispute about the figure I have identified as Livia. Zanker (1988: Fig. 101) suggests that the *matrona* is depicted as Venus (genetrix).

23 Like any provincial commander, Gaius will have sent dispatches to the Senate, but he must have sent them directly to Augustus, for Dio (55.10.10) reports that Augustus made it his custom to read them to the Senate himself.

24 The Consuls of 21 and 8 BCE. But Lollius worked to alienate Gaius from Tiberius (Suet. *Tib.* 12) and Gaius was only reconciled to him after quarrelling with Lollius. Later Lollius was denounced by the Parthian King, and may have committed suicide. Censorinus also died, but naturally.

25 See Barnes (1974: 22–3). The decree, which was previously assumed to refer to the subsequent Armenian campaign, reports that 'Gaius, the son of Augustus, who was fighting the barbarians for the safety of all mankind, has escaped dangers and avenged himself on the enemy' (*SEG* 23, 206 translated and discussed by Zetzel 1970: 259–60).

26 Barnes points to Seneca's *Consolation to Polybius*, 15.4 in which Seneca reports that Gaius heard of Lucius' death 'while he was still preparing for war and some time before he was wounded'. The death dates of both princes are preserved in the commemorative decrees of Pisa, the *municipium* which honoured them as its patrons. See notes 27 and 32

27 The date of his wound is known not from the Pisa inscription (below) but from *CIL* IX 5290 = *Inscriptiones Italiae* XIII 1, 245.

28 The date was expressed as so many days before the Kalends of March. If this was a leap year, it would have been 22 February.

29 It is mentioned by the geographer Strabo 11.14.6 (p. 529).

30 See Kuttner (1995: 195–6 and notes 65, 66) and Pollini (1986: 134–6) reviewing Ganzert *Das Kenotaph für Gaius Caesar in Limyra* (Tübingen 1984).

31 *Res gestae* 27 'When the same people [Armenians] later rebelled and went to war, I subdued them through the agency of my son Gaius and handed them over to be ruled by King Ariobarzanes son of Artabazus, king of the Medes, and after his death to his son Artavasdes.'

32 On the reactions of ancient Pisae to the deaths of the princes see now Rowe (2002: Chapter 5). Rowe (2002) prints translations (for Lucius, 2002: 107–8; for Gaius 2002: 111–13) of both inscriptions: *CIL* XI 1421, *ILS* 139 (Lucius), 140 (Gaius), (also in Ehrenberg and Jones 1955: 69 and Lewis and Reinhold 1990: II, 212) and discusses the differences of formulation between the earlier Lucius decree and that honouring Gaius. The Latin texts are provided at the end of Rowe's chapter.

33 See Suet. *Augustus* 65, for Postumus' alleged *ingenium sordidum ac ferox*, and relegation. Tac. *Annals* 1.4.3 attributes to gossip the verdict that Agrippa Postumus was 'violent and enraged by disgrace, and not fitted to the responsibility of ruling by age or experience.' For his coming of age, see Dio 55.22.4.

34 See Dio 55.13.1 for the popular protests, but Dio seems to have confused Julia's change of exile to Rhegium with an actual restoration.

35 Suet. *Augustus* 19.2. Was this an attempt to restore his mother Julia, or her daughter, exiled by 8 CE?

36 Tac. *Annals* 1.5, Dio 56.30.1; Pliny *Natural History* 7.150, 'Augustus' disowning of Agrippa, then regret for him after his relegation, which caused suspicion against Fabius, and the betrayal of secrets.' See Levick (1976a: 64–5), Syme (1979: 149).

37 Cf. Tac. *Annals* 2.39–40 for Clemens' plan to rescue Agrippa from Planasia by deceit or force and take him to the armies in Germany. The merchant ship he travelled in arrived too late, after the murder, and he supposedly first stole Agrippa's ashes but then changed his plans, and impersonated the dead prince, spreading the rumour that Agrippa himself still lived and visiting Italian towns surreptitiously. When Clemens came to Ostia a large crowd gathered, but Tiberius sent secret agents to seize him and bring him to the Palatine, where the Emperor and Pretender confronted each other (an anecdote Tacitus shares with Dio). Tacitus claims Clemens-Agrippa had many supporters even in the senate and imperial household, but Tiberius had him executed without repercussions.

9 Julia's girls

1 Suet. *Claudius* 26 notes that Claudius was betrothed twice as a young man; the first time to Aemilia Lepida, great-granddaughter of Augustus 'whom he sent back still a virgin, because her parents had offended Augustus.' (His second bride died on the intended wedding day.) Perhaps the oddest aspect of this report is that Julia and her husband are spoken of as jointly offending against Augustus, although our other fragmentary records suggest that Aemilius' conspiracy occurred two years before Julia's alleged adultery. On the inconsistencies of the record, see Syme (1985: Chapter 10), and Levick (1976b: 303–39). Aemilia Lepida was subsequently married to M. Iunius Silanus Torquatus, cos. 19 (cf. Pliny *Natural History* 7.58).

2 Perhaps in 16 BCE, as argued by Levick (1976b: 315), but if Germanicus were born in 15 BCE, as many scholars believe, it would not affect this argument.

3 This is the same Cornelia honoured by Propertius in the biographical elegy quoted in Chapters 1 and 2.

4 Compare Pliny *Natural History* 7.149–50 cited in Appendix II, 3b. Note that events listed which we can date are not in chronological order; e.g. Agrippa was disowned before Varus' defeat in 9 CE.

5 For bibliography on the political events of 6–8 CE, see Swan (2004: 183). On Dio. 55.27.2, Swan argues (2004: 184) that there is no clear link between this Rufus and L. Paulus. I would add that this Rufus may have existed separately from Plautius Rufus. Neither the common *praenomen* Publius nor the equally common *cognomen* Rufus indicate the man's family name.

6 Syme (1985), especially p. 121.

7 On the events of 7 CE, see Levick (1976b: 326–33). Suet. *Aug.* 51.1 reports that a Iunius Novatus published attacks on Augustus in the name of Agrippa Postumus. The scholiast on Juvenal 6.158 claims Julia was relegated after Paullus' condemnation for treason, then recalled, but having lapsed into immorality, was sent into permanent exile.

8 Although the Julian law on adultery imposed a time limit for the husband to divorce his wife and denounce her adultery, there was probably no time limit on outside prosecution. Anyone could find retrospective evidence (in the form of letters between the supposed lovers, or the testimony of slaves given under torture) that adultery had been committed a year or two earlier.

9 *Met.* 1.168–76 and 200–5 (indirect comparisons), 197–210, Lycaon's punishment imposed by Jupiter before his report to the divine senate. *Met.* 15.760–1, 818–21 for the Augustus' deification of Julius.

10 Cf. *Ars amatoria* 3.89–90, urging women to yield: what have they to lose? For millennia the answer was their (or their family's) honour. It is only very recently that female chastity has been seen (and not by everyone) as pointless in this way.

11 Ovid only adapts the vocabulary of prostitution and pandering to his inverted moral code in the later poems of the collection: in 3.12.11 he reproaches himself with being a pander, for drawing his readers' attention to Corinna; he has prostituted her (3.12.8); in the last poem in the narrative sequence, 3.14, he acts as if he had sole rights over his beloved, and applies the notion of prostitution to her association with any other man.

12 This poem actually uses *maritus* (3.4.27), *coniunx* (3.4.37) and *uxor* (45) – the last in the shocking claim that the sensible man will enjoy the friends his free-living wife has provided for him.

13 *Furtum*, stealthy or stolen love, was the recognized term for adulterous liaisons.

14 The letter of Augustus quoted by Suetonius *Aug.* 86.3 sounds as though she was still a young girl. He praises Agrippina's smartness (*ingenium*) but adds 'you must take care not to write and speak with affectation.'

15 The chief source for his career is Suet. *Claudius* 1–3.

16 One child, who died, was called Gaius. He was particularly dear to Augustus who kept a bust of the little boy by his bedside. The name was reused for Gaius, the emperor-to-be.

17 On the birthplace of her daughter Agrippina, actually in a small German village but reported as occurring in the main tribal centre of the Ubii, site of the future Colonia Agrippinensia Ubiorum of which she was patron, see now Hurley, *American Journal of Ancient History* 17 (2003).

18 See Tac. *Annals* 2.54.1.

19 'Old' is quite literal. Gnaeus Calpurnius Piso had been Consul with Tiberius more than twenty years before, in 7 BCE. We know from the text of the *Senatus*

consultum condemning Piso (see below) that Germanicus had been given *imperium superior* to everyone except Tiberius from whom all authority flowed, and Piso, whatever his private instructions from Tiberius, was officially bound to obey Germanicus.

20 See now Damon and Takács (1999), with the review-discussion of Griffin (1997). For a comparative treatment of the measures recorded in the *Tabula Siarensis* and *Tabula Hebana*, honouring Germanicus, with those honouring Gaius and Lucius Caesar, consult Rowe (2002).

21 I have modified the translation given in Damon and Takács (1999: 34), which I believe should be construed <*moderationem*> *Agrippinae, quam* (object) *senatui memoriam* (subject of acc. and inf.) *divi Augusti commendare.* (We would expect a subordinate subjunctive.)

22 Tac. *Annals* 4.8.5 with a speech attributed to Tiberius:

> Senators, I entrusted these boys, bereft of their father, to their uncle and begged him although he had his own children, to cherish them as if they were his own blood, to rear them and mould them for himself and his descendants. Now Drusus has been snatched from me I redirect my prayers to you, and invoke you before the gods and our country. Take up Augustus' great-grandchildren and direct them; fill both your role and mine. These senators, Nero and Drusus, take the place of your parents. Such is your birth that your good and ill fortune are our country's business.

23 After a summary of Tiberius' resentment of Germanicus (*Tiberius* 52.2–3), Suetonius is clearly following the same source as Tacitus for the vignettes, but cites more details of the brutal treatment of Agrippina in exile on Pandateria.

24 'Aequi impatiens, dominandi avida, virilibus curis feminarum vitia exuerat.' What does Tacitus means by *aequi*? I take the word in its legal sense of what was reasonable, impartial or fair.

10 Julia in the judgement of posterity

1 'Voltus abscondite nostros/ ne natae videant ora nefanda meae.' See Herbert-Brown (1992: 149–55, esp. 155) and the forthcoming commentary of Littlewood (*Ovid: Fasti; Book 6*, Oxford 2006, ad loc).

2 For full texts of the evidence see Appendix II.

3 Sidonius Apollinaris, *Carmina* 23, 158–61, 'Et te carmina per libidinosa/ notum, Naso tener, Tomosque missum, /quondam Caesareae nimis puellae/ ficto nomine subditum Corinnae'. Syme (1979: 215), reads this as identifying Corinna with the daughter of Augustus, both the mistress of the poet, and cause of his exile.

4 Juvenal's imagining of Messalina in the sweaty quarters of the gladiatorial schools or reluctantly leaving the brothel, panting for more, go way beyond Tacitus' account of her foolish public liaison and marriage to Silanus. Surely this man has sexual problems of his own.

5 This and subsequent translations from German and French scholars are my own.

6 In *I Claudius* and *Claudius the God,* both first published in 1934.

7 Suet. *Gaius* 23, gives the motive as a snobbish refusal to believe himself grandson of Agrippa.

8 Compare M. P. Charlesworth's Chapters 3 and 4 in the previous edition of *CAH* X (Cambridge 1952).

9 Carcopino (1958: 114–15 and 120) assumes that Julia first proposed a conspiracy to Tiberius in order to seize power with him at the expense of her own sons, then turned to Iullus Antonius (p. 129) after Iullus' return from Asia and the proclamation of Gaius in 5 BCE as *princeps iuventutis* and Consul

designate for 1 CE, an event that threatened her own prospects of wielding power.

10 These were discussed in Chapter 7.

11 James VI of Scotland was born in 1566, and succeeded his mother the following year when Mary fled Scotland, leaving it again under a regency. It was not Mary Stuart, but her son James who would become Sovereign of England on Elizabeth's natural death in 1603.

Bibliography

Alcock, S. E. (ed.) (1997) *The Early Roman Empire in the East*, Oxford.

Allison, J. (2001) *The Love Artist*, New York.

Anderson, M. L. (1987a) *Pompeian Frescoes in the Metropolitan Museum of Art*, New York.

—— (1987b) 'The Portrait Medallions of the Imperial Villa at Boscotrecase', *American Journal of Archeology* 91: 127–35.

Badian, E. (1985) 'A Phantom Roman Marriage Law', *Philologus* 129: 82–98.

Balsdon, J. V. P. D. (1962) *Roman Women*, London.

Barnes, T. D. (1974) 'The Victories of Augustus', *Journal of Roman Studies* 64: 21–39.

—— (1981) 'Julia's Child', *Phoenix* 35: 362–3 (on Julia II).

Barrett, A. A. (1996) *Agrippina: Sex, Power and Politics in the Early Empire*, New Haven, Conn.

—— (2003) *Livia: First Woman of Rome*, New Haven, Conn.

Bauman, R. (1992) *Women and Politics in Ancient Rome*, London.

Bigwood, J. M. (2004) 'Queen Mousa: Mother and Wife of King Phraataces of Parthia: A Reevaluation of the Evidence', *Mouseion* 4: 35–70.

Boissier, G. (1875/1905) *L'Opposition sous les Césars*, Paris.

Brunt, P. A. (1971) *Italian Manpower*, Oxford.

—— (1982) *The Fall of the Roman Republic*, Oxford.

Butrica, J. (1996) 'The *Amores* of Propertius', *Illinois Classical Studies* 21: 87–158.

Carcopino, J. (1958) *Passion et politique chez les Césars*, Paris.

Champlin, E. (1989) 'The Testament of Augustus', *Rheinisches Museum* 132: 154–65.

Coarelli, F. (1974) *Guida Archeologica di Roma*, Turin. Repr. 1981, Milan.

Corbier, M. (1991) 'Divorce and Adoption as Roman Familial Strategies', in B. Rawson (ed.) *Marriage, Divorce and Children in Ancient Rome*, Oxford, pp. 47–76.

Crook, J. A. (1996) 'Augustus, Power, Authority, Achievement', *Cambridge Ancient History* Vol. X, Cambridge, pp. 115–46.

Damon, C. and S. Takács (1999) 'The Senatus consultum de Cn. Pisone Patre: Text, Translation, Discussion', *American Journal of Philology* 120.1.

Dettenhofer, M. H. (1994) *Reine Männersache: Frauen im Männerdomänen der antiken Welt*, Cologne.

Ehrenberg, V. and Jones, A. H. M. (1955) *Documents Illustrating the Reigns of Augustus and Tiberius*, 2nd edn, Oxford.

Ferrero, G. (1911) *The Women of the Caesars*, London.

Ferrill, A. (1980) 'Augustus and his Daughter: A Modern Myth', *Studies in Latin Literature and Roman History*, Collection Latomus 168: 332–66.

Flory, M. (1988) 'Abducta Neroni Uxor', *Transactions of the American Philological Association*, 118: 343–59.

—— (1993) 'Livia and the History of Public Honorific Statues for Women in Rome', *Transactions of the American Philological Association*, 123: 287–308.

—— (1996) 'Dynastic Ideology, the *Domus Augusta* and Imperial Women: A Lost Statuary Group in the Circus Flaminius', *Transactions of the American Philological Association*, 126: 287–306.

Fullerton, Mark D. (1985) 'The *Domus Augusti* in Imperial Iconography of 13–12 BC', *American Journal of Archeology*, 89: 55–7.

Galinsky, G. K. (1996) *Augustan Culture: An Interpretative Introduction*, Princeton, NJ.

Gardner, J. F. (1988) 'Julia's Freedmen: A Question of Law and Status', *Bulletin of the Institute of Classical Studies*, 35: 94–100.

Gardthausen, V. (1904) *Augustus und seine Zeit*, 3 vols., Leipzig.

Gelzer, M. (1948) *Julius Caesar: Politician and Statesman*, trans. Needham 1968, Oxford.

Ginsberg, J. (2006) *Representing Agrippina: Constructions of Female Power in the Early Roman Empire*, Oxford.

Griffin, J. (1980) *Latin Poets and Roman Life*, London.

Griffin, M. T. (1997) 'The Senate's Story', *Journal of Roman Studies*, 87: 249–63.

Grimm, G. (1973) '*Zum Bildnis der Iulia Augusti*', *Mitteilungen des Deutschen Archaeologischen Instituts*, Rome, 80: 279–82.

Graves, R. (1934) *I Claudius* and *Claudius the God*, London.

Gruen, E. S. (1992) *Roman Culture and National Identity*, Ithaca, NY.

—— (1996) 'The Expansion of the Empire under Augustus, IV, Armenia and Parthia', *Cambridge Ancient History*, Vol. X, Cambridge, pp. 158–63.

Hallett, J. (1984) *Fathers and Daughters in Roman Society*, Princeton, NJ.

Herbert-Brown, G. (1992) *Ovid and the Fasti*, Oxford.

—— (1998) 'Decoding Tacitus (*Ann.* 1.53): The Role of Julia in Tiberius' Retirement to Rhodes', *Studies in Latin Literature and Roman History*, Vol. IX, Collection Latomus, Brussels.

Hollis, A. F. (ed.) (1977) *Ovid: Ars amatoria, Book 1*, Oxford.

Kleiner, D. (1978) 'The Great Friezes of the *Ara Pacis Augustae*: Greek Sources, Roman Derivatives and Augustan Social Policy', *Mémoires de l'École francaise de Rome et Athènes*, 90: 753–85.

—— (1992) 'Politics and Gender in the Pictorial Propaganda of Antony and Octavian', *Echos du Monde Classique*, 36: 357–67.

Kleiner, D. and S. B. Matheson (2000) *I Claudia: Women in Ancient Rome*, New Haven, Conn.

Kornemann, E. (1930) *Doppelprinzipat und Reichsteilung*, Leipzig.

Kuttner, A. (1995) *Dynasty and Empire in the Age of Augustus*, Berkeley, Calif.

Lacey, W. K. (1980) '2 BC and Julia's Adultery', *Antichthon*, 14: 127–42.

Leach, E. W. (1982) 'Patrons, Painters and Patterns', in Barbara K. Gold (ed.) *Literary and Artistic Patronage in Ancient Rome*, Austin, Tex., pp. 135–73.

Leon, E. F. (1951) 'Scribonia and her Daughters', *Transactions of the American Philological Association*, 82: 168–75.

Levick, B. M. (1966) 'Drusus Caesar and the Adoptions of 4 AD', *Latomus*, 25: 227–44.

—— (1972a) 'Tiberius' Retirement to Rhodes in 6 BC', *Latomus*, 31: 779–813.

—— (1972b) 'Abdication and Agrippa Postumus', *Historia* 21: 674–97.

—— (1975) 'Julians and Claudians', *Greece and Rome*, 22: 29–38.

—— (1976a) *Tiberius the Politician*, London.

—— (1976b) 'The Fall of Julia the Younger', *Latomus*, 35: 301–39.

Lewis, N. and Reinhold, M., (1990) *Roman Civilization: Selected Readings*, vols. I and II, New York.

Linderski, J. (1988) 'Julia in Regium', *Zeitschrift für Papyrologie und Epigraphie*, 72: 181–200.

Lloyd, R. B. (1979) 'The Aqua Virgo, Euripus and Pons Agrippae', *American Journal of Archeology* 83: 193–204.

Magie, D. (1950) *Roman Rule in Asia Minor to the End of the Third Century after Christ*, Princeton, NJ.

Meise, E. (1969) *Untersuchungen zur Geschichte der Julisch-Claudischen Dynastie*, Munich.

Millar, F. and E. Segal (eds) (1984) *Caesar Augustus: Seven Aspects*, Oxford.

Norwood, F. (1963) 'The Riddle of Ovid's *Relegatio*', *Classical Philology*, 58: 150–65.

O'Neill, P. (2003) 'Going Round in Circles: Popular Speech in Ancient Rome', *Classical Antiquity* 22: 135–65.

Pappano, A. E. (1941) 'Agrippa Postumus', *Classical Philology*, 36: 30–45.

Pollini, J. (1987) *The Portraiture of Gaius and Lucius Caesar*, New York.

—— (1986) 'Review of Ganzert *Das Kenotaph für Gaius Caesar in Limyra*', *American Journal of Archeology*, 90: 134–6.

Price, S. F. R. (1980) 'Between Man and God: Sacrifice in the Imperial Cult', *Journal of Roman Studies*, 70: 28–43.

Purcell, N. (1986) 'Livia and the Womanhood of Rome', *Proceedings of the Cambridge Philological Society* 32: 78–105.

Raaflaub, K. and M. Toher (eds) (1990) *Between Republic and Empire: Interpretations of Augustus and his Principate*, Berkeley, Calif.

Raditsa, L. F. (1980) 'Augustus' Legislation concerning Marriage, Procreation, Love Affairs and Adultery', *Aufstieg und Niedergang der Römischen Welt*, 2 (13): 278–339.

Rawson, B. (ed.) (1991) *Marriage, Divorce and Children in Ancient Rome*, Oxford.

Reinhold, M. (1933) *Marcus Agrippa: A Biography*, New York.

Richardson, L. Jr. (1992) *New Topographical Dictionary of Ancient Rome*, Baltimore, Md.

Richlin, A. (1992) 'Julia's Jokes', in B. Garlick, S. Dixon, and P. Allen (eds) *Stereotypes of Women in Power: Historical Perspectives and Revisionist Views*, New York.

Roddaz, J.-M. (1984) *Marcus Agrippa, Bibliothèque de l'Ecole Francaise de Rome*, Rome.

Römer, F. E. (1978) 'Gaius Caesar's Military Diplomacy in the East', *Transactions of the American Philological Association*, 108: 199–214.

Rose, C. B. (1990) 'Princes and Barbarians on the *Ara Pacis*', *American Journal of Archeology*, 94: 453–67.

—— (1997a) *Dynastic Commemorations and Imperial Portraiture in the Julio-Claudian Period*, Cambridge.

—— (1997b) 'The Imperial Image in the Eastern Mediterranean', in S. E. Alcock (ed.) *The Early Roman Empire in the East*, Oxford, pp. 108–19.

Rowe, G. (2002) *Princes and Political Culture: The New Tiberian Senatorial Decrees*, Ann Arbor, Mich.

Saller, R. P. (1986) '*Patria Potestas* and the Stereotype of the Roman Family', *Continuity and Change*, 1: 7–22.

—— (1987) 'Men's Age at Marriage and its Consequences in the Roman Family', *Classical Philology*, 82: 21–34.

Sanzi di Mino, M.-R. (1998) *Museo Nazionale di Roma: Villa Farnesina in Palazzo Massimo alle Terme*, Rome.

Sasel, J. (1969) 'Julia und Tiberius; Beiträge zur römischen Innenpolitik zwischen den Jahren 12 vor und 2 nach Chr.' in W. Schmitthenner (ed.) *Augustus*, Darmstadt, pp. 486–530.

Scheid, J. (1975) 'Scribonia Caesaris et les Julio-Claudiens: Problèmes de vocabulaire de parenté', *Mémoires de l'École francaise de Rome et Athènes*, 87: 349–71.

—— (1976) 'Scribonia Caesaris et les Cornelii Lentuli', *Bulletin de Correspondence Hellénique* 100: 185–201.

Schmitthenner, W. (ed.) (1969) *Augustus*, Darmstadt.

Shaw, B. (1987) 'The Age of Roman Girls at Marriage: Some Reconsiderations', *Journal of Roman Studies*, 77: 30–46.

Simon, E. (1967) *Ara Pacis Augustae*, Tübingen, repr. New York.

Snyder, J. M. (1989) *The Woman and the Lyre: Women Writers in Classical Greece and Rome*, Carbondale, Ill.

Spargo, J. W. (1934) *Virgil the Necromancer*, Cambridge, Mass.

Swan, P. M. (1987) 'Cassius Dio and Augustus: A Poverty of Annalistic Sources', *Phoenix*, 41: 271–92.

—— (2004) *The Augustan Succession: Cassius Dio, Books 55–56*, Oxford.

Syme, R. (1939) *The Roman Revolution,* Oxford.

—— (1979) *History in Ovid*, Oxford.

—— (1984a) 'History or Biography: The Case of Tiberius Caesar', in A. R. Birley (ed.) *Roman Papers*, Vol. III, Oxford, pp. 937–52.

—— (1984b) 'The Crisis of 2 BC', in A. R. Birley (ed.) *Roman Papers*, Vol. III, Oxford, pp. 912–36.

—— (1985) *The Augustan Aristocracy*, Oxford.

Thibault, J. (1964) *The Mystery of Ovid's Exile*, Berkeley, Calif.

Treggiari, S. M. (1991a) *Roman Marriage: Iusti Coniuges from the Time of Cicero to the Time of Ulpian*, Oxford.

—— (1991b) 'Divorce, Roman Style: How Easy and How Frequent Was It?' in B. Rawson (ed.) *Marriage, Divorce and Children in Ancient Rome*, Oxford, pp. 31–46.

—— (1996) 'Social Status and Social Legislation', *Cambridge Ancient History*, Vol. X, Cambridge, pp. 673–904.

Von Blanckenhagen, P. H. and C. Alexander (1962) *The Paintings from Boscotrecase, DAI Römische Abteilung, Erganzungsheft*, 6.

Wallace-Hadrill, A. (1982) '*Civilis Princeps*: Between Citizen and King', *Journal of Roman Studies* 72: 32–48.

—— (1994) *Houses and Space in Roman Pompeii*, Princeton, NJ.

—— (1996) 'The Imperial Court', *Cambridge Ancient History*, Vol. X, Cambridge.

Weinstock, S. (1971) *Divus Iulius*, Oxford.

Wieland, C. M. (1796) *Zur Ehrenrettung drei berühmter Damen des Altertums*, reprinted in *Sämmtliche Werke* (1984), Vol. XXIV, Leipzig.

Winkes, R. (1995) *Livia, Octavia, Iulia: Porträts und Darstellungen*, Louvain and Providence, RI.

Wiseman, T. P. (1994) *Historiography and Imagination*, Exeter.

—— (2004) *The Myths of Rome*, Exeter.

Wood, S. (1999) *Imperial Women: A Study in Public Images, 40 BC–AD 68*, Leiden.

Woodman, A. J. (1983) *Velleius Paterculus: The Caesarian and Augustan Narrative*, Cambridge.

—— (1995) 'A Death in the First Act: Tac. *Ann.* 1.6', *Papers of the Leeds Latin Seminar*, 8, 257–73.

Zanker, P. (1988) *The Power of Images in the Age of Augustus*, trans. H. A. Shapiro, Ann Arbor, Mich.

Zetzel, J. G. E. 1970) 'New Light on Gaius Caesar's Eastern Expedition', *Greek, Roman and Byzantine Studies* 11: 259–66.

Index of persons and places

Subject index

adoption: of Gaius and Lucius Caesar by grandfather Augustus 59; of Germanicus by Tiberius 92; of Livia by Augustus' will 79; of C. Octavius by Caesar 19; of Tiberius and Agrippa Postumus by Augustus 92

adultery: accusations against women 42–3, 85, 86,111–15; adulteries of Augustus, 39 (*see under* legislation)

aedicula, imitation of shrine in two-dimensional wall-painting

betrothal: of Augustus and Livia 22; of Claudius to Aemilia 108, 161 n.1; of Julia to Antyllus 24, and to son of Cotison 149 n.19

births and problems of fertility 2

coinage: showing Agrippa 51, 66 (Pergamum), Agrippa and Julia 66 (Ephesus); Gaius as cavalry officer 98 (Lyons mint); Gaius and Lucius as *Principes Iuventutis* 102, 136–7; Julia with sons 67, 94

commemoration: acts of mourning for deaths of Gaius and Lucius Caesar 105

cubiculum, small room for private use 74, 75

daughters: their role in the family 2, 3–4; education of 2

divorce: 5, 6, 13 (*see under* Agrippa, Caesar, Augustus, Tiberius, etc. in *Index of Persons and Places*)

dowry: 2, 11, 12–13, 14

education of elite men: by *Grammaticus* 23, 27, 95–6; *with Rhetor* 27, 96

elegy and love poetry: 15, 30–5, 111–15

exile (strictly relegation to fixed place outside Rome or Italy): of Agrippa Postumus 116; of Julia 85; Julia the younger 111; of Ovid 112; of Silanus 110

family councils 11

funeral: state funeral of Caesar's daughter 8; of Marcellus 30; of Gaius and Lucius Caesar 105

houses: Boscotrecase 76–7; house of Antony (formerly Pompey's) given to Agrippa 51; house of Augustus on Palatine 69–70, 71–2, 156 n.6; 'house of Livia' 70; villa under Farnesina 74–6

inheritance: daughters' share 1; disinheritance of Julia, 89; of Agrippa Postumus 106

inscriptions: on bases of lost statues 59, 61, 63, 93–4, 134–6; of decrees of colony at Pisa 105; of provincial decrees: 62, 63, 66

marriage: age of marriage 1, 147 nn.1 and 5; good and bad marriages, 9–14 (*see also under* Agrippa, Augustus, Caesar, Cato, Pompey, Tiberius, etc. in *Index of Persons and Places*); sample political marriages from the late republic 1–9 (*see also* remarriage)

moral and social legislation of Augustus: 15–16, 38–43, 60; *Lex Iulia Theatralis* 40–1; *Lex Iulia De*